The History of
Magic in the Modern Age

Related titles by the same author

THE HISTORY OF
MAGIC
IN THE MODERN AGE

A QUEST FOR PERSONAL TRANSFORMATION

Nevill Drury

CARROLL & GRAF PUBLISHERS, INC.
New York

Carroll & Graf Publishers, Inc.
19 West 21st Street
New York
NY 10010–6805

First published in the UK by Robinson Publishing,
an imprint of Constable & Robinson Ltd 2000

First Carroll & Graf edition 2000

ISBN 0–7867–0782–8

Printed and bound in the EU

For Anna

Contents

Illustrations

Acknowledgements

Over the years many people have assisted me along the magical path and I would like to thank them for contributing either directly or indirectly to the creation of this book. They include Stephen Skinner, who first introduced me to the study of the Kabbalah, John Cooper, Jonn Mumford, Dolores Ashcroft-Nowicki, Moses Aaron and Michael Harner, who taught me the technique of shamanic drumming. I am also indebted to those who agreed at different times to be interviewed for my research – Rosaleen Norton, Alex Sanders, Lawrence and Olivia Robertson, Janet and Stewart Farrar, Z Budapest, Selena Fox, Margot Adler, Michael Aquino, H. R. Giger, Timothy Leary and Terence McKenna. I would also like to thank Sinclair Swain and Ashley Tattersall for lending me materials on role-play and Leon Wild for providing me with current information on the Setian philosophy.

Finally I would also like to acknowledge my general debt to a select group of visionary thinkers and artists whose work has substantially influenced my own perspective: Carl Jung, Mircea Eliade, Max Ernst, Arthur Machen, Jorge Luis Borges, Lord Dunsany, Wifredo Lam and Austin Osman Spare. For me they have all been inspirational.

Preface

For those unfamiliar with occult beliefs, the world of magic and the esoteric traditions produces a wide variety of responses. The magical realm can seem – to different people – frightening, potentially demonic, or irrational. To others it may simply be irrelevant. The subject has attracted much shallow and sensational media coverage, with its more superficial aspects such as fortune-telling, horoscopes and superstitions receiving the most public attention.

However, in recent times there has been an increasing interest in alternative religious and spiritual perspectives, and with the exception of the Kabbalah most of these alternatives have tended to lie outside the Judaeo-Christian tradition. While many have found a sense of spiritual fulfilment in exploring Eastern forms of mysticism and meditation, in the West these spiritual alternatives have included revivals of various forms of goddess worship, Celtic neopaganism and shamanism, and metaphysical frameworks like Gnosticism, alchemy and the Tarot. There has also been renewed interest in the mysteries of ancient Greece and Egypt and an ongoing focus on Jewish mysticism – since the Kabbalah and the Tree of Life provide a key spiritual framework for the expansion of magical consciousness.

There can be no doubt that in contemporary Western society the rise of rational and scientific thought has challenged the divine-authority base of mainstream Christianity to such an extent that church attendance is now rapidly declining. Indeed, it would seem that our society is at a spiritual crossroads. Our Western culture continues to perpetuate the enshrined belief systems of our formal religious institutions but for many people the prevailing religious orthodoxies have a hollow ring about them and do not reflect deeply felt personal experience.

So where does this leave the occult? How do practitioners of magic, witchcraft, neopaganism and goddess worship respond to the modern world?

Ironically, although they may be reviving archaic belief systems and practices, the majority of occultists today are supporters of the new technologies – especially if they are seen to be helpful to the community at large. A surprisingly high number of occult devotees and neopagans work in the computer industry or in other areas of communication and information technology. However, they tend to believe that the demands of urban existence should be complemented by a sense of spiritual attunement to the broader world outside. There is a general consensus that the cycles of Nature and the universe as a whole provide a broader scope for meaning than can be found in the daily urban routines that most of us endure.

The perspective that emerges within this broad-based metaphysical movement is a type of spiritual humanism – an approach based on the belief that all human beings have within them an intrinsic spiritual connection with the cosmos, an innate potential divinity which can be brought into conscious expression. The magical traditions recognise this potential and invite us to explore the visionary realms within our own being.

Another interesting aspect of the 'occult' is that, increasingly, its so-called magical secrets are no longer hidden. This is particularly a phenomenon of the latter half of the twentieth century. In the early years of the century esoteric groups were still obsessed with grades of hierarchy and the idea of ritually structured spiritual attainment – a hangover from the influence of Freemasonry and the idea of 'secret societies'. But this emphasis now seems less important. The really worthwhile aspects of occult belief and practice are now fully out in the open, as more and more people seek to explore the different potentials for visionary and spiritual expression.

This book is not an encyclopedia of magic and the occult, and does not claim to cover all the diverse metaphysical philosophies and organisations that currently present themselves as part of the modern esoteric spectrum – that would be beyond the scope of any book. My focus has been instead to describe in some detail the key activities and concepts of the most influential groups and individuals who have contributed to twentieth-century magical thought.

Contemporary magical consciousness owes a huge debt to the Hermetic Order of the Golden Dawn, and this magical organisation really provides the starting point for this overview, although the opening chapter of this book deals with metaphysical precursors to the modern era. Aleister Crowley, a member of the Golden Dawn, has also been extremely influential, and one could argue that he has even given rise to an alternative religion of his own. More recently, and partly as a consequence of the international feminist movement, we have seen a renewed interest in the archetypal feminine – expressed in various forms of goddess worship and neopaganism. This focus on the feminine is, I believe, the most significant single factor affecting the contemporary revival of magical thinking in Western culture. However, I have not neglected the so called 'left-hand path' of magic – the realm of 'black magic' – for this is also an occult phenomenon one must consider. In my chapter 'Dark Forces' I discuss both the Church of Satan and its successor, the Temple of Set. I do not endorse either of these organisations but I have endeavoured to describe their activities and philosophies in a fair and unbiased way. I feel it is important to distinguish between witchcraft, or Wicca as it is usually known, and the various forms of 'black magic' – for these are frequently confused in the popular imagination. As will become clear, though, witchcraft and neopaganism on the one hand, and black magic on the other, are actually very different from each other, both in terms of their spiritual orientation and their magical aspirations.

Finally I must admit to writing this book as one who is basically sympathetic to the Western esoteric tradition. On a personal level I have tended to gravitate more towards the visionary side of magic, rather than towards the theatre of ritual and ceremony, and have been involved with guided imagery pathworkings and shamanic visualisation groups for many years. So I am writing here as an 'insider', rather than as an outsider looking in and trying to make sense of it all. I think this point is worth making simply because in my view most academic attempts to 'explain' contemporary magical thinking – in either psychological or sociological terms – have been woefully inadequate.

I know that I myself have benefited enormously from my exploration of the Western esoteric tradition over the last thirty years or so, and I value my personal contact with people all over the world who share a similar interest. I also believe quite strongly that at this time in our history – a time when many people are expressing feelings of personal despair, despondency and aimlessness – we can all learn from each other's individual quest for sacred visionary experience. In fact, one of the most relevant tasks now, it seems to me, is to explore the various pathways that lead to the transformation of human consciousness. The revival of magic in modern times is a direct response to this need.

Nevill Drury
May 1999

I feel like I am the earth, I'm sea,
I'm everything feminine.
And the priest and priestesses before me –
as I look into their eyes, and they look into my eyes,
there is a most incredible openness that one doesn't find
in the mundane world.
We can only experience that within
the sacredness of a ritual . . .

LEVANAH

I also am a Star in Space, unique and self-existent,
an individual essence incorruptible;
I also am one Soul; I am identical with All and None.
I am in All and all in Me;
I am, apart from all and lord of all, and one with all.

ALEISTER CROWLEY

1

The Roots of the
Western Magical Tradition

Magical thought is commonly identified with superstition and regarded as a form of pre-science – an earlier and less sophisticated phase of human intellectual development. Indeed, elements of this perception have entered popular folklore. One thinks immediately of evil-eye amulets, of black cats or magic spells cast by wicked, toothless crones. However, the sort of magic described in this book has little to do with superstition. As we will see, the magic of twentieth-century occultism has an altogether different thrust. Here the concept of magical consciousness relates much more to the concept of will or intent – to the idea that one can bring about specific effects or changes within one's sphere of consciousness. This form of magic is basically about personal transformation – more specifically, about the transformation of one's perception or state of awareness. And this has distinct spiritual and psychological connotations. This form of magic invites us to find out more about who we really are as human beings.

Some have regarded occult exploration as inherently dangerous – as a foray into uncharted waters. To some extent this fear is warranted, for magic by definition is an esoteric tradition and involves the exploration of hidden or unknown human potentials. As the English artist and occultist Austin Osman Spare once observed, the aim of magic is 'to steal the fire from heaven'. However, one of my aims in this book is to show that magic can have a spiritual intent. It can take us into transcendental realms of consciousness where an encounter with the gods and goddesses becomes possible. It can help us experience, first-hand, the sacred archetypes of the Western psyche.

The Concept of Magical Will

It is in relation to the issue of will that magic differs from mysticism and the more mainstream forms of religion. The magician, unlike the mystic or religious devotee, draws not so much upon the concept of grace bestowed by God as on the idea that one may alter one's state of consciousness magically at will – that the gods will respond if one undertakes certain ritual or visualisation procedures. It may be that the magician dresses ceremonially to capture their likeness and in so doing invokes their sacred and symbolic energy. Perhaps sacred god names are uttered or intoned, like those found in the Kabbalah, in the pagan traditions of witchcraft and in certain Gnostic formulations. Here the core idea is that the name of the god or goddess embodies the very essence of the deity and that by invoking that sacred vibration one is not only tuning in to the archetypal level of awareness associated with these sacred beings but actually attaining mastery of them.

As will become evident in later chapters of this book, the idea of will is vital to the magical attitude. We find it in the magic of the Hermetic Order of the Golden Dawn, where focused intent enables the magician to rise through the planes of 'inner space' – through the symbolic and mythological realms of the Tree of Life. We find it in the quest for the higher self, anthropomorphised in Aleister Crowley's writings as the Holy Guardian Angel. And we find it in the shamanic accounts of Carlos Castaneda, where the magical apprentice has to whirl his spirit catcher near the sacred waterhole and concentrate on the 'spaces' within the conjured sounds, in order to will a magical 'ally' to appear. In all of these instances the idea of magical will is central to the activity in question. And often magic of this sort has a spiritual or metaphysical intent. Indeed, Gareth Knight, in his *History of White Magic*, has defined magic as a means of assisting the 'evolution of spiritual will'.[1]

All this is of course quite foreign to most established religious traditions. Prayer and supplication, offerings of thanks to a saviour god, and acts of worship in a church are in no way intended to capture the god. Quite the reverse, in fact. Western religious devotion is an attitude of mind where one humbly submits oneself before God in the hope that he will bestow grace and salvation. There is no implied act of control or mastery here – no stealing fire from heaven. One waits, passively, until grace is received.

The magical attitude, on the other hand, is clearly more active and often more assertive. The magician or witch is at the centre of their own particular universe. With their sacred formulae, ritual invocations and concentrated willpower, they believe they can bring certain forces to bear. The magician believes that he or she can *will* to effect.

In one sense the 'primitivism' of this approach has been legitimised by existential philosophy and the rise of the contemporary human-potential or 'personal growth' movement. It has become common for recent interpreters of the Western magical tradition to regard the gods of high magic as emanations of the creative imagination, as forces of the transcendent psyche.

A noted authority on Western magic, the late Dr Israel Regardie – who was also a practitioner of Reichian therapy – employed the Jungian model of the archetypes of the collective unconscious to explain to his contemporary audience what he meant by invoking a god. For him it was nothing other than a ritual means of channelling into conscious awareness a specific archetypal energy form from the universal or 'collective' psyche. Colin Wilson has similarly related his long involvement with the European existentialist tradition to a study of Western magic in order to show that such an approach offers both a transcendental and an optimistic goal – that human beings can overcome their feelings of isolation by engaging with universal aspects of consciousness and being.

It is only fair to point out, however, that many magicians, witches and occultists view their pantheon of gods and goddesses as existing in their own right – as beings beyond the human psyche, as entities belonging intrinsically to another plane of existence. For these devotees magic becomes a vital means of communication. The gods provide knowledge of these esoteric domains to the enquiring magician and thereby allow the devotee to grow in awareness. Several notable magicians, including Michael Aquino of the Temple of Set, Anton LaVey and the Australian witch Rosaleen Norton, have held this view.

Nevertheless, modern magicians – irrespective of the tradition they follow – do tend to share one feature in common and that is the notion of a hierarchy of supernatural beings or 'powers' with whom they can interrelate. These powers in turn provide sacred knowledge and wisdom – wisdom which allows the magical devotee special insights into the dynamics of the universe and the sacred potentials of humanity. In a sense, magic would make gods and goddesses of us all. Considered in this light, magic is essentially about growth and renewal on an archetypal level of being. In its most profound and spiritual expressions it is about transforming our perception of the world from one which is profane and devalued to one which is sacred. This type of magic is about vision and deep, insightful spiritual knowledge. This is high magic, or gnosis.

All this leads us now to consider the actual roots of the Western magical tradition – those vital forces and ideas that have shaped this body of thought over many centuries. I personally believe that contemporary magical consciousness has its origins in the Gnostic mystical formulations which first took root in the early centuries of the Christian era. However, there have been many twists and permutations since then, and we will consider some of these in turn.

The Gnostic Impulse

The origins of Gnosticism remain a matter of debate, but there is broad consensus that Gnosticism as a historical movement parallels the rise of early Christianity. Some scholars have seen in Gnosticism residues of pre-Christian Iranian dualism, while others believe that it developed in response to the failure of Jewish apocalyptic expectations and have dated its origins to around 70 CE – coinciding with the fall of the Jerusalem Temple.[2] Others regard Gnosticism as a response to the failure of Christian messianic expectations, when some early Christian devotees, feeling that the Messiah had not returned as soon as had been hoped, turned away from religious faith towards spiritual inner knowledge.

Whether or not any of these speculations provide the core basis for the development of Gnostic mysticism, we know that Gnostic thought was certainly well established by the second century of the Christian era, with Basilides acknowledged as an influential intellectual and spiritual force in Alexandria during the reigns of the emperors Hadrian and

Antoninus Pius. The Egyptian Gnostic Valentinus, author of *The Gospel of Truth*, was also active in the middle of the second century, and around the year 140 came to Rome from Alexandria as a candidate for election as the bishop of Rome. Had he been successful in this quest to succeed Bishop Pius – he was rebutted by Tertullian – Christianity would have had its first Gnostic pope and the movement which in due course would become heretical might have established itself as mainstream. In addition to figures like Basilides and Valentinus, other important Gnostic figures also established a following, including the libertine teacher Carpocrates, active during the reign of Hadrian, and Mani, founder of Manichaeism – a fascinating blend of Christianity and Mandean dualism – whose teachings subsequently spread into Syria, Palestine and North Africa and even as far as central Asia and China.[3]

In addition to the Gnostic groups which centered around these leading figures, there were also several major Gnostic sects, each with its own cosmology and points of emphasis – groups like the Cainites, the Sethians, the Ophites and the Ebionites. However, what is of most interest to us here is the central Gnostic attitude, which relates essentially to the nature of good and evil and to the quest for gnosis, or spiritual knowledge.

The unearthing of a major Gnostic library near the town of Nag Hammadi in Upper Egypt in 1945 provided a rich body of source material on the Gnostic philosophies. Until this time much of the existing Gnostic scholarship had been based on other surviving Gnostic commentaries written by Church Fathers like Irenaeus, Clement and Hippolytus, who were hostile to Gnostic tenets. What was so fascinating about the Nag Hammadi codices – an Ophite-Sethian collection of texts written in Coptic – was that they revealed the syncretistic nature of Gnosticism. As a movement Gnosticism seemed to incorporate elements from Christianity, Judaism, Neoplatonism and the Greek mystery religions as well as material from Egypt and Persia. But essentially Gnosticism was a call for transcendence – a movement seeking a return to the spirit, away from the constrictions of the material world. For the material world was a source of pervasive evil, a realm as far away from the spiritual realm as it was possible to be. James M. Robinson, editor of the English translation of the Nag Hammadi Library, explains the Gnostic philosophy in these terms:

In principle, though not in practice, the world is good. The evil that pervades history is a blight, ultimately alien to the world as such. But increasingly for some the outlook on life darkened; the very origin of the world was attributed to a terrible fault, and evil was given status as the ultimate ruler of the world, not just a usurpation of authority. Hence the only hope seemed to reside in escape . . . And for some a mystical inwardness undistracted by external factors came to be the only way to attain the repose, the overview, the merger into the All which is the destiny of one's spark of the divine.[4]

In the Gnostic conception there is a clear divide between the spiritual world, which is good, and the physical world, which is evil. Expressed another way, there is a clear demarcation between the cosmic and the divine on the one hand, and the physical, or material, on the other. The Gnostic texts portray humanity as being increasingly separated from the sustaining realm of divinity and spirit, and this in turn provides a rationale for spiritual transcendence – there is a vital need to liberate the 'divine spark' entombed in the physical world.

While Gnosticism emphasised the need to experience the supreme reality of the divine, its cosmological solutions soon took it in different directions from those pursued by the early Church Fathers. In some cases Gnostic perspectives differed only slightly in emphasis from the emerging Christian orthodoxy, but in other instances the differences were more extreme. Some early Christian devotees clearly had Gnostic leanings. Marcion of Sinope, born near the Black Sea at the end of the first century, considered himself to be a Christian but regarded Jesus as the son of the 'Good God' of the Spirit and not as the son of the Old Testament creator God (or demiurge). Marcion rejected the Old Testament completely, as well as most of the New Testament, but nevertheless considered Jesus Christ to be a saviour figure. Meanwhile the Ebionites were essentially a community of Greek-speaking Jewish Christians who rejected the apostle Paul but followed the Gospel according to Matthew.

Basilides, Valentinus, Carpocrates and Mani, for their part, emerge as major figures whose cosmologies and mystical perspectives provide a conceptual basis for what would later become the Western magical tradition. Basilides conceived of a universe with 365 heavens and proposed a hierarchy of 'divine emanations', a pattern of spiritual creation also associated with the Jewish Kabbalah – an important symbolic framework that has profoundly influenced modern magical thought. In the system of Basilides the supreme reality is that of the 'ungenerated' or 'nonexistent' God, sometimes conceived of as a seed or egg while nevertheless symbolising nothingness. This 'nonexistent' or nonmaterial God in turn emanated Mind (*nous*), Word (*logos*), Understanding (*phronesis*), Wisdom (*sophia*) and Power (*dynamis*). From Wisdom and Power emerged the archons and angels who formed the first heaven. Each heaven gave rise to another in turn, until there were 365 in all. The year was defined as consisting of 365 days because this mirrored the number of heavens. Meanwhile the angels of the final heaven created the world as we know it. The last of these creator beings was the God of the Jews and he decreed that his people would be the chosen race on Earth. However, according to Basilides, this All Father or demiurge was an archon who was ignorant of his comparatively lowly position in the heavenly hierarchy and as a consequence chaos reigned in the world. The Father was obliged to send his son Jesus to work miracles on Earth but according to Basilides Christ did not suffer on the cross because his spirit was liberated. The physical death of Christ was of no consequence. For Basilides, as one Gnostic scholar has written, 'salvation is for the soul alone'.[5]

The system of Valentinus similarly regards creation as a process which unfolds from a state of divine immateriality. The Gnostic tract entitled *The Valentinian System of Ptolemaeus*, written by Valentinus's leading disciple,[6] begins with these words: 'There is a perfect pre-existent Aeon, dwelling in the invisible and unnameable elevations; this is Pre-Beginning and Forefather and Depth. He is uncontainable and invisible, eternal and ungenerated, in quiet and deep solitude for infinite aeons.'[7] As in the system of Basilides, this 'ungenerated' realm of sacred formlessness then begins to emanate subsequent levels of being:

With him is Thought, which is also called Grace and Silence. Once upon a time, Depth thought of emitting from himself a Beginning of all, like a seed, and he deposited this projected emission, as in a womb, in that Silence who is with him. Silence received this seed and became pregnant and bore Mind, which resembled and was equal

7

to him who emitted him. Mind alone comprehends the magnitude of his Father, he is called Only-Begotten and Father and Beginning of All. Along with him, Truth was emitted; this makes the first Four, the root of all: Depth and Silence, then Mind and Truth.[8]

Here Mind is masculine (Greek *nous*) but Thought is feminine (*ennoia*). In Valentinian cosmology Thought is the creator mother who gives rise both to the primal man and to God the creator of Heaven and Earth. She is identified also with Sophia, goddess of wisdom, an important figure in Gnostic thought. In this cosmology Sophia gives rise to a demiurge (or creator god) who assumes he is the highest god. However, according to Valentinus, he is actually ignorant. He lacks the gnosis or spiritual knowledge required for his salvation.

Like Basilides and Valentinus, Carpocrates also challenged the emerging Christian orthodoxy. Not only did he argue that the universe had been created by comparatively lowly powers – as the Church Father Ireneus put it, 'by angels much inferior to the unbegotten Father' – but he also disputed Christ's divine origins. Carpocrates believed that Jesus was simply the son of Joseph – a man of the Earth – although Carpocrates does credit him with having a secret teaching which he passed on to his disciples in the form of a deeper and more symbolic body of esoteric instruction.

This too infuriated Ireneus, and Carpocrates attracted criticism for other reasons as well. Extending the central Gnostic tenet that the soul was much more important than the body, Carpocrates and his followers believed that indulgences of the flesh were completely acceptable. Carpocrates and his son Epiphanes condoned promiscuity and believed that human beings owed it to themselves to experience all aspects of life to their fullest, for only by doing so could one hope to transcend the limitations of physical existence. Carpocrates followed Plato in regarding the body as a prison from which the soul would have to escape, but his libertine philosophy was a radical departure from Platonic thought and made him an easy target for the early Church Fathers critical of Gnosticism. Indeed, one can see in Carpocrates a unique expression of hedonistic mysticism – an early precursor of the beliefs of a number of modern occult groups and reminiscent, too, of the more indulgent aspects of the American counter-culture and personal-growth movement. Carpocrates was a strong advocate of sexual licence – a libertine somewhat before his time.

Mani emerges from the Gnostic movement as a figure who might have been quite capable of challenging the eventual dominance of Christian thought. A sensitive and complex thinker, Mani – like Jesus – experienced profound archetypal visions of the spiritual realm and came to regard himself as an apostle of God. Manichaeism has provided us with a rich legacy of mystical literature and according to the religious scholar Kurt Rudolph it should be considered a major world religion, alongside Buddhism, Christianity and Islam.[9]

By his own account – recorded by the Arab scholar Al-Biruni – Mani was born in 216 CE in the village of Mardinu in northern Babylonia (now Iraq). He grew up in a Mandaean baptist community but when he was twelve years old received a spiritual revelation inspired by the 'King of the Paradise of Light'. From this time onwards he renounced the community of his birth and became a type of Gnostic apostle. According to the Manichaean text *Kephalaia*, after his revelation Mani became the 'twin' of the Holy Ghost. He is credited with saying:

> The Living Paraclete came down and spoke to me [for the first time]. He revealed to me the hidden mystery, hidden from the ages and the generations of Man: the mystery of the Deep and the High: the mystery of Light and of Darkness, the mystery of the Contest, the War, and the Great War, these he revealed unto me.[10]

Like Muhammad, whose revelations similarly came through angelic visions, Mani was appointed as a 'messenger', or prophet, of God. After converting his father and other members of his family to his new spiritual perspective, Mani set out to preach his doctrine, journeying to the Iranian provinces of Turan and Makran as well as visiting northwestern India. Later he travelled to Persia before returning to Babylonia. Mani seems to have been strongly impressed by Buddhism during his visit to India but his religion is primarily a Gnostic synthesis of Christianity and Iranian belief. As in classical Gnosticism, Mani distinguishes between God and Matter, but this becomes tinged with Iranian dualism and the eternal conflict between Ohrmazd/Ahura Mazda (symbolising good) and Ahriman/Ahra Mainyu (evil). In Manichaeism good is inherently superior to evil and eventually triumphs.

During Mani's time a particular form of Zoroastrianism prevailed in which Ohrmazd and Ahriman were said to have been begotten by a divine primordial being called Zervan, who was androgynous. Zervanism influenced Mithraism – a mystery religion which became popular in ancient Rome – and the figure of Zervan is also thought to have a connection with the cosmic entity Abraxas, who features in the cosmology of Basilides as the great archon who rules 365 heavens.

Mani rejected the Zervanite concept that the forces of good and evil could be regarded as 'brothers' within the same pantheon of archetypal beings. Instead he described a cosmology in which the highest spiritual reality was that of 'God the Father of the blessed light'. Mani conceived of God the Father sitting on a throne, embodying within his sacred form the divine principles of light, force and wisdom. In Manichaean cosmology God the Father then 'calls' the Mother of Life into being, and she in turn 'calls' the Primeval Man – who is then her son. These three figures constitute the Manichaean trinity.

In Manichaean cosmology Primeval Man engages in continuous conflicts with the forces of evil and darkness. In one Manichaean legend, Primeval Man is defeated by the Prince of Darkness and loses his armour. On another occasion the five sons of Primeval Man are devoured by demons. However, Manichaeism proclaims the eventual triumph of the forces of light, for Primeval Man will return in glory to the welcoming embrace of his mother in paradise. As Geo Widengren emphasises in his study of Mani, Primeval Man symbolises the redeemer who is himself in need of redemption, and this becomes a central Gnostic myth.[11] Primeval Man has to overcome the formidable obstacles within the darkness in order to retrieve his true 'self' or 'soul'. His return to his celestial home represents the liberation of the soul and its return to the world of light.

This is a message of gnosis, of the return of the 'divine spark' to the realm of spirit whence it came. It is a theme of 'eternal return' which we find also in the Hermetic tradition, in the medieval Kabbalah and in the esoteric tradition of Western high magic. And it is found similarly in the teachings of Plotinus, the third-century Neoplatonist philosopher who earned widespread recognition during the Renaissance.

Interestingly, Plotinus wrote tracts directed against the Gnostics. A pagan follower of Plato, he was a Hellenised Egyptian who spent most of his life in Rome. His writings (six books known collectively as the *Enneads*) influenced several early Christian theologians and in one sense his criticism of Gnosticism aligns him with Church Fathers like Ireneus, Hippolytus and Clement. Plotinus rejected the Gnostic idea that human beings are born into a hostile world created by an evil demiurge-creator. He was also personally opposed to the idea of invoking the gods through sacred incantations, although he accepted that the stars had a symbolic, esoteric meaning and were essentially divine. Plotinus was fundamentally optimistic, whereas the Gnostics felt an abiding sense of deep alienation in relation to the world around them. However, despite his opposition to the Gnostics on several major issues, when we consider his mystical cosmology Plotinus is quite close to the Gnostics and his concepts of spiritual reality seem much more closely attuned to Gnostic principles than to mainstream Christian thought.

Like the Gnostics, Plotinus considers the supreme spiritual reality to be a state of undifferentiated unity – this is the world of the One. This realm of the One transcends duality. In the ultimate sense there is nothing else – no distinction between subject and object. When the human soul returns finally to its spiritual home it is absorbed within the One, for this is the source of all being.

According to Plotinus, it is the One that causes the world to come into existence, but this act of creation does not give rise to something 'other', for there is no dualism in this process. Instead, the world is an emanation from the One. The first emanation from the One is intelligence (*nous*) and the second is soul. Soul in turn emanates matter, which is darkest because it is furthest from the spiritual sun. An advocate of spiritual visualisation, Plotinus instructed his followers to 'shut their eyes and wake to another way of seeing'. The soul acknowledges the presence of light and increasingly becomes one with it, removing the duality of good and evil until awareness of the One alone remains.

According to Plotinus, the mystical ascent to the Godhead is accompanied by different stages of perfection, and as for the Gnostics this is essentially an act of transcendence, 'a liberation from all earthly bonds, a life that takes no pleasure in earthly things, a flight of the alone to the Alone'.[12]

The Medieval Kabbalah

The medieval Kabbalah continues the emanationist cosmology developed by the Gnostics and, indeed, Gershom Scholem has referred to the esoteric tradition of the Kabbalah as a form of Jewish Gnosticism.[13] Traditionally the Kabbalah is regarded as a mystical commentary on the Pentateuch – the written Torah, or 'five books of Moses'. The word 'Kabbalah' itself refers to an oral or secret tradition (passed from mouth to ear), and has much earlier antecedents than its medieval context would suggest. Indeed, the *Zohar*, the central text of the Kabbalah – compiled in written form by the Spaniard Moses de Leon circa 1280 CE – has clear spiritual links with the earlier schools of Gnosticism and Neoplatonism. In all three we find the concept of sacred emanations from the Godhead, the idea of the pre-existence of the soul and its descent into matter, and allusions to the sacred names of God. In all three we find references to archetypal powers which have shaped creation – archons, angels, demiurges and various patriarchal deities – and there are references also to the female aspect of the divine – Sophia or the Mother of the World – from whose womb all forms emerge. The Manichaean Primeval Man has a Kabbalistic counterpart in the form of Adam Kadmon, who represents the archetypal human form and who also symbolises the body of God. And in all three traditions we find an interest in the cyclic journey of the soul through a succession of existences, as it ventures steadily towards union with the source of all being.

In the Kabbalah all aspects of manifested form, including the sacred archetypes of the Godhead, have their origin in Ain Soph Aur ('the limitless light') – a realm entirely beyond form and conception which 'has neither qualities nor attributes'. In Kabbalistic cosmology the subsequent emanations which emerge from this profound mystery, and which constitute the spheres upon the Tree of Life or *Otz Chiim*, reveal different aspects of the sacred universe, but are nevertheless considered as part of a divine totality. Ain Soph Aur, writes Gershom Scholem, 'manifests . . . to the Kabbalist under ten different aspects, which in turn comprise an endless variety of shades and gradations'.[14] As we have said, these emanations reflect a unity, and because the human form is said to have been created 'in the image of God', the spheres on the Tree of Life are also spheres within the body of Adam Kadmon. Mystical self-knowledge becomes a journey of regaining undifferentiated oneness with the divine.

According to the Kabbalah, the mystical universe is sustained by the utterance of the holy names, and the ten emanations represented upon the Tree of Life – the *sephiroth*, or 'spheres' – are none other than 'the creative names which God called into the world, the names which He gave to Himself'.[15]

In the *Zohar* we read:

> In the Beginning, when the will of the King began to take effect, he engraved signs into the divine aura. A dark flame sprang forth from the innermost recess of the mystery of the Infinite, *En-Sof* [Ain Soph] like a fog which forms out of the formless, enclosed in the ring of this aura, neither white nor black, neither red nor green, and of no colour whatever. But when this flame began to assume size and extension it produced radiant colours. For in the innermost centre of the flame a well sprang forth from which flames poured upon everything below, hidden in the mysterious secrets of *En-Sof*. The well broke through, and yet did not entirely break through, the ethereal aura which surrounded it. It was entirely unrecognisable until under the impact of its breakthrough a hidden supernal point shone forth. Beyond this point nothing may be known or understood, and therefore it is called *Reshith*, that is 'Beginning', the first word of Creation.[16]

Scholem writes that the 'Primordial Point' was thought of by the majority of Kabbalists not as Kether, the Crown – normally considered the first emanation upon the Tree of Life – but as the Great Father, Chokmah, or Wisdom. In Kabbalist cosmology the energy of the Great Father unites with that of Binah, the Great Mother (Understanding), and from her womb all archetypal forms come forth. And as Christian Ginsburg notes in his seminal book *The Kabbalah: Its Doctrines, Development and Literature*, 'It is not the *En-Sof* who created the world, but this Trinity . . . the world was born from the union of the crowned King and Queen . . . who, emanated from the *En-Sof*, produced the Universe in their own image.'[17] The seven subsequent emanations beneath the trinity of Kether, Chokmah and Binah constitute the seven days of Creation.

To this extent, as with the Gnostic cosmologies referred to earlier, the Tree of Life, with its ten *sephiroth* – or emanations of divine consciousness – describes a symbolic process by which the infinite becomes tangible. The ten levels are as follows:

Kether	The Crown, or first point of Creation
Chokmah	Wisdom (the Father)
Binah	Understanding (the Mother)
Chesed	Mercy
Geburah	Severity, or Strength
Tiphareth	Beauty, or Harmony (the Son)
Netzach	Victory
Hod	Splendour
Yesod	The Foundation
Malkuth	Kingdom, or Earth (the Daughter)

These emanations align themselves into three pillars, the outer two being the Pillar of Mercy headed by Chokmah, symbolising light and purity, and the Pillar of Severity headed by Binah, symbolising darkness and impurity. Beneath them lies the Garden of Eden, with its four rivers Chesed, Geburah, Netzach and Hod converging in Tiphareth, located at a central point on the Middle Pillar. A. E. Waite has suggested that perhaps this central pillar can be regarded as the perfect pillar, for it reaches to the Crown, Kether.[18] The other two pillars provide a duality of opposites and represent the 'Tree of Knowledge of Good and Evil'. As mentioned earlier, the Gnostics considered the world as evil because as the most material, or grossest, emanation it was the furthest removed from the Godhead – the realm of divine spirit. In the Kabbalah, however, there is a different emphasis because all the ten spheres are a mirror of the divine. In the Kabbalah the final emanation, the World, is represented by Malkuth, who is the Daughter – Shekinah – and a reflection of the Great Mother, Binah.

So if there is a major difference between Gnosticism and the Kabbalah, it is this: in Gnosticism there is a dualistic distinction between divinity and matter, whereas the Kabbalah is based on a concept of sacred unity. Judaism is strongly monotheistic and nothing exists beyond God. As Professor John Ferguson has observed in relation to the spiritual quest in the Kabbalah;

> We must see God as the First Cause, and the universe as an emanation from his Will or Wisdom. The finite has no existence except in the light of the Infinite, which contracted so that the finite might be . . . Man is the highest point of the created world, and his soul contains animal and moral elements, but also an element of pure spirit, which in the righteous ascends to God.[19]

In a subsequent section of this book we will consider in more detail how the symbolism of the Kabbalistic Tree of Life has assumed a central place in modern magical consciousness, and how its original monotheistic structure has been extended to encompass all the pantheons of gods and goddesses which feed the occult imagination.

The Hermetic Tradition

During the fifteenth and sixteenth centuries another body of mystical thought – now referred to as the Hermetica or Hermetic tradition – would also enjoy intellectual and philosophical influence in Europe. Hermetic philosophy has its roots in Hellenism and enters Western esoteric thought as an essentially Neoplatonic-Gnostic revival. During the Renaissance, Florence became the focus of the Hermetic tradition, for it was here, in the royal courts, that this metaphysical perspective would receive significant endorsement. In 1460 a monk named Leonardo da Pistoia brought with him to Florence the Greek manuscripts that would later become known collectively as the *Corpus Hermeticum*, or *Hermetica*. These texts had been found in Macedonia and were presented to Cosimo de Medici, who was a noted collector of Greek manuscripts. Two years later Cosimo passed the manuscripts to his young court scholar Marsilio Ficino, and requested that he translate them into Latin. This work was completed in 1463 – Cosimo was able to read the translation before his death the following year – and Ficino's texts are now held in the Medici Library in Florence.

The Hermetic material was essentially a body of Greek mystical and philosophical writings which drew on Platonism and Stoicism, and perhaps also Mithraism, and then developed within a Gnostic-Egyptian context. Most scholars agree that the Hermetic texts date from the latter half of the second century CE through to the end of the third century. In these writings the central figure, Hermes Trismegistus ('Thrice Greatest Hermes'), is presented as a wise spiritual teacher, a Gnostic master who in a sense is a composite of Hermes and Thoth. The *Corpus Hermeticum* itself takes the form of a series of philosophical exchanges between Hermes Trismegistus and his followers. The best-known text, the *Poimandres* 'Shepherd of Man', or *Pymander*, which is attributed to Hermes Trismegistus, describes Creation in the form of a dream. The master falls asleep and is visited by Poimandres, who explains how knowledge of God may be attained. Marsilio Ficino felt that much of the text was divinely inspired:

> They called Trismegistus thrice great because he was pre-eminent as the greatest philosopher, the greatest priest, and the greatest king. As Plato writes, it was a custom among the Egyptians to choose priests from among the philosophers, and kings the company of priests . . . Being thus the first among philosophers, he progressed from natural philosophy and mathematics to the contemplation of the gods and was first to discourse most learnedly concerning the majesty of God, the orders of daemons, and the transmigration of souls. He is therefore called the first inventor of theology . . .[20]

Although it is now acknowledged that the Hermetic texts date from the Christian era, Ficino seems to have believed that Hermes Trismegistus was a contemporary of Moses, and at times implies that Hermes and Moses may have been one and the same. While this may seem surprising, the Renaissance mind assumed that many of the ancient gods had actually lived on Earth at one time or another, and Moses, after all, had been born in Egypt. Ficino also accepted that Moses had been entrusted with the secret teachings of the Kabbalah on Mount Sinai – so, like Thoth-Hermes, he was a custodian of the ancient wisdom.

For Ficino the Hermetic texts – in particular the *Asclepius* and the *Pymander of Hermes Trismegistus* – offered profound inspirational instruction. As Ficino writes in his Introduction:

Mercury [i.e. Hermes Trismegistus] knows how to instruct . . . in divine matters. He cannot teach divine things who has not learned them, and we cannot discover by human skill what is above Nature. The work is therefore to be accomplished by a divine light, so that we may look upon the sun by the sun's light. For, in truth, the light of the divine mind is never poured into a soul unless the soul turns itself completely toward the mind of God, as the moon turns toward the sun . . .[21]

Ficino saw no contradiction in blending Neoplatonism with orthodox Catholic theology at the court in Florence. Interestingly, Hermes had already been endorsed by Christian figures like St Augustine and the fifth-century Christian poet Lactantius, so it would have seemed quite acceptable to Ficino to combine Greek mystical philosophy and Christianity. In this new syncretic cosmology the Christian concept of God the Father, enthroned and surrounded by choirs of angels, mirrored Plato's idea of an uncorrupted archetypal domain. Humanity, meanwhile, lived in a kind of shadow world which was but a pale reflection of its heavenly spiritual counterpart. In the Hermetic philosophy this idea was conveyed through the mystical axiom 'As above, so below'.

As mentioned earlier, Plotinus believed that the mystical realm could only be apprehended through *nous* – a blend of higher intellect and intuitive power – but innate to the Neoplatonic (and Gnostic) attitude was a belief that human beings have the potential to transcend the world of appearances through spiritual will and intent. The Hermetic devotees of the Renaissance similarly conceived of a universe in which human beings could earn their place in the celestial realms and become one with God. As Tobias Churton notes in his overview of the Gnostic tradition, in the Renaissance it was possible to blend Neoplatonic and Christian perspectives:

The wish was to return to the One, the source from which the power derived enabling the philosopher-magician to work the 'miracle of creation'. Christ had opened the way, the 'veil of the temple' had been rent and the true followers of Christ could ascend. 'Hermes', he of ancient wisdom, mediator between spirit and matter, with winged feet and winged mind, was both prophet and symbol of this possibility.[22]

In the Hermetic model of the universe all things came from God. God had made the world, the world had given rise to perceptions of time, and time in turn gave rise to the idea of 'becoming'. Eternity was the domain of God but the temporal world moved within eternity. In this way, and in a holistic sense, one could proclaim that 'All is One'. However, from the Hermetic perspective this single universe was divided into three worlds, or emanations. The lowest sphere was the world of Nature, which in turn received divine influences from the more sanctified realms above. At the next level one encountered the stars, as well as spirits and 'guardians'. Higher still was the supercelestial world of *nous* – the world of angelic spirits, or archons, who had a superior knowledge of reality because they were closer to the One, the Godhead or divine source of Creation, who lay beyond the three worlds. In the Hermetic concept, transcendence – achieving oneness with God – entailed liberating oneself from the constrictions of temporal life and entering the realm of pure and divine thought.

A dominant theme which pervades the Hermetic texts is that Hermes Trismegistus embodies the wisdom teachings because he understands the essential oneness of the universe. From the perspective of those who hoped to learn from Hermes Trismegistus – figures like Asclepius with whom he entered into dialogue – this was a wisdom which had to be earned, and a certain discrimination was required if one was to distinguish between the deceptive nature of physical appearances and the true world of sacred reality. And there is a clear suggestion here, too, of a secret or esoteric tradition:

> Hermes saw the totality of things. Having seen, he understood, he had the power to reveal and show. And indeed what he knew, he wrote down. What he wrote, he mostly hid away, keeping silence rather than speaking out, so that every generation on coming into the world had to seek out these things.[23]

Ficino's work with the *Corpus Hermeticum* was continued by Giovanni Pico, Count of Mirandola, who similarly held an emanationist view of the world. Pico combined Ficino's Hermetic Neoplatonism with an extensive knowledge of the Kabbalah, Christianity and 'high magic' (*mageia*). He also brought to the court of Cosimo's successor, Lorenzo de Medici, an extensive knowledge of astrology, geometry, medicine and astronomy. In his collection of 900 theses – a work known collectively as *Oratio*, or *The Oration* – Pico explored what he called 'the dignity of man' and maintained that one could come to know God as a 'friend', rather than as a 'fact'. 'Philosophy seeks the truth,' he wrote, 'theology finds it, religion possesses it . . . We may more easily love God than comprehend Him or speak of Him.'

Like Ficino, Pico conceived of a universe which emanates from the Godhead. At the highest level Mind is devoted to the contemplation of the divine Being, and below this realm are the celestial world and lower still the domain in which we live. However, Pico's conception was not simply that of the devotional mystic. According to Pico, man is unique in his capacity to transcend his worldly context. Not only can man come to know God but he can become a type of god himself:

> Exalted to the lofty height, we shall measure therefrom all things that are and shall be and have been in indivisible eternity; and, admiring their original beauty, full of divine power, we shall no longer be ourselves but shall become He Himself Who made us . . .
>
> For he who knows himself in himself knows all things, as Zoroaster first wrote. When we are finally lighted in this knowledge, we shall in bliss be addressing the true Apollo on intimate terms . . . And, restored to health, Gabriel 'the strength of God', shall abide in us, leading us through the miracles of Nature and showing us on every side the merit and the might of God.[24]

This was Pico's idea of *mageia* – a type of high magic which could provide humanity with access to the inner workings of Nature and the cosmos. In this magical conception of the universe, Nature is pervaded by spirit. Matter cannot enter spirit, but spirit can enter matter. To this end *mageia* can be employed 'in calling forth into the light, as if from their hiding places, the powers scattered and sown in the world by the loving-kindness of God'. The role of the sacred magician – the practitioner of high magic – is to raise Earth (matter) to the level of Heaven

(spirit). As Tobias Churton observes, this is essentially a gnostic under-
taking:

> The method, or secret of working, lies within the gnosis or know-
> ledge of Man as he is and can be – he knows he has access to the
> divine world. In a process of contemplation or alchemy he rises
> through an inner imagination of ascending principles until he feels
> he is full of 'light'. In such a condition the *magus* sets to work. That
> work might be artistic, turning paint into vision, stone into form;
> mechanical, turning wood and brass into machinery; religious, turn-
> ing ill thoughts and bitterness into love and brotherhood; landscaping,
> building, singing, travelling, loving, cooking, writing, capitalising
> – the possibilities are endless. In a holy mind the world may be
> transformed.[25]

In the opening paragraph of this book, I quoted from the writings of
the twentieth-century occultist Austin Osman Spare, who maintained
that the aim of magic is 'to steal the fire from heaven'. Inspirational
imagery of this kind may also be found within the Hermetic literature.
As Hermes Trismegistus says in the *Asclepius*, in a text which was also
quoted by Pico:

> He takes in the nature of a god as if he were himself a god . . . He
> is united to the gods because he has the divinity pertaining to gods
> . . . He takes the earth as his own, he blends himself with the elements
> by the speed of thought, by the sharpness of spirit he descends to
> the depths of the sea. Everything is accessible to him; heaven is not
> too high for him, for he measures it as if it were in his grasp by his
> ingenuity. What sight the spirit shows to him, no mist of the air can
> obscure; the earth is never so dense as to impede his work; the
> immensity of the sea's depths do not trouble his plunging view. He
> is at the same time everything as he is everywhere.[26]

Similarly we read in the *Corpus Hermeticum* (*Libellus XIII*):

> I see myself to be the All. I am in heaven and in earth, in water and
> in air; I am in beasts and plants; I am a babe in the womb, and one

that is not yet conceived, and one that has been born; I am present everywhere.

Here, it seems to me, we have a quintessential statement about the spiritual nature of the magical quest. At its most profound level, high magic embraces the entire cosmos and proposes an archetypal process of mythic renewal. The quest is to be 'reborn' from the limited and restricted world of material form into the realm of spirit. This is certainly implicit in Platonic and Neoplatonic concepts of the world and has also shaped the Gnostic-Hermetic tradition, as we have seen. I also believe that this core idea permeates several contemporary magical belief systems.

But there is the potential here, too, for a type of magical fundamentalism – a narcissistic attraction to the idea that we are all gods in the making. When we consider the ploys of human egotism combined with the pursuit of power – a less attractive element in the contemporary magical revival – we are forced to concede that this idea is also capable of producing unintended consequences. We will explore this theme in subsequent chapters of this book.

For the moment, though, I would prefer to focus on the mystical aspects of the Hermetic tradition and the holistic view of consciousness which underlies the Hermetic perspective – especially the idea that, in the most complete sense, everything is an aspect of the body of God. From this viewpoint, far from pursuing grandiose notions that we have acquired the status of gods, we acknowledge instead that as fellow human beings, we all participate in the sacred dynamism – or life force – of the universe. Indeed, from the Hermetic perspective this sacred ground of being is what bonds us together. The Gnostic quest – the journey of high magic – is essentially a return to the source of our being, a journey culminating in the realisation of divine unity which transcends the limitations of form and material appearances. As the well-known exponents of the Western magical tradition John and Caitlin Matthews have written:

Again and again this message is affirmed: there is a god within which gives life to the body and inspiration of all that we do: events in the sphere of incarnation reflect those in the heavenly sphere. It is this emphasis on unity rather than disharmony which marks out the Hermetic mysteries: unity of all things, of God with man, of higher and lower, of divine with mundane. It finds its clearest expression in the famous injunction 'As above, so below', so often quoted and so little understood by occultists throughout the ages.[27]

The Spiritual Dimension of Alchemy

Just as Gnosticism, Neoplatonism and the Hermetic tradition are con-cerned with the liberation of the human spirit, so too can alchemical transmutation be regarded as a metaphor of spiritual renewal. Many scholars, including Titus Burckhardt, Kurt Seligmann, Carl Jung, Mircea Eliade and Robert Segal, have considered it in this light, and it is in this capacity that alchemical symbolism has influenced modern magical beliefs.

Western alchemy dates from the beginning of the second century CE and flourished in Hellenistic Egypt, where there was a high level of proficiency in metalworking skills, especially in relation to silver and copper alloys which resembled gold. Two papyri found in a gravesite in Thebes (the so-called Leiden and Stockholm papyri which date from around 300 CE) include recipes for changing the colour of a metal so that it would resemble gold or silver – a fascinating precursor, perhaps, of the metaphysical concept of the transmutation of base metals into gold. The word 'alchemy' itself is thought to derive from an Egyptian word *chem* or *qem*, meaning 'black' – a reference to the black alluvial soils bordering the Nile. The fourth-century alchemical writer Zosimos of Panopolis (Akhmim) in Egypt maintained that a person named Chemes had given rise to the quest for gold and had authored a book of supernaturally inspired instruction called *Chema*, but proof of Chemes's historical existence has not been established. However, we know that in due course the Greek word *chyma*, meaning 'to fuse or cast metals', established itself in Arabic as *al kimia*, from which the more familiar term 'alchemy' is in turn derived.

As a pagan practice the study of alchemy thrived in Alexandria in buildings adjacent to the famous Temple of Serapis, but this temple – the Serapeum – together with numerous statues and works of art, was destroyed in 391 on the orders of the Christian archbishop of Alexandria,

Theophilus. The persecuted alchemical scholars then withdrew to Athens, where the Thracian Neoplatonist Proclus was teaching, and in this way a more comprehensive knowledge of Egyptian alchemy was introduced to Greece. Although pagan traditions were finally suppressed by Emperor Justinian in 529, interest in alchemy was rekindled in the seventh century when Stephanos of Alexandria dedicated his *Nine Lessons in Chemia* to the Byzantine emperor Heraclitus, and in the eleventh century when Psellus revived Platonism. According to Kurt Seligmann, the writings of Stephanos inspired a number of medieval alchemical poets and these writers also extolled the virtues of the Hermetic philosophy.[28] Not surprisingly, there are strong philosophical and mystical connections between alchemy, Neoplatonism and the Hermetic tradition.

Like their Neoplatonic and Hermetic counterparts, the medieval alchemists believed in the unity of the cosmos and maintained that there was a clear correspondence between the physical and spiritual realms, with comparable laws operating in each domain. As the sixteenth-century Moravian alchemist Michael Sendivogius writes in *The New Chemical Light*:

> the Sages have been taught of God that this natural world is only an image and material copy of a heavenly and spiritual pattern; that the very existence of this world is based upon the reality of its celestial archetype; and that God has created it in imitation of the spiritual and invisible universe, in order that men might be the better enabled to comprehend His heavenly teaching and the wonders of His absolute and ineffable power and wisdom. Thus the Sage sees heaven reflected in Nature as in a mirror; and he pursues this Art, not for the sake of gold or silver, but for the love of the knowledge which it reveals; he jealously conceals it from the sinner and the scornful, lest the mysteries of heaven should be laid bare to the vulgar gaze.[29]

The alchemists adopted the Hermetic concept that the universe and humanity reflect each other – in essence this is the core meaning behind the idea of the macrocosm and microcosm. It was assumed by the alchemists that whatever existed in the universe must also, to some degree, be latent or present in every human being. A Syriac Hermetic text makes this point very eloquently:

> What is the adage of the philosophers? Know thyself! This refers to the intellectual and cognitive mirror. And what is this mirror if not the Divine and original Intellect? When a man looks at himself and sees himself in this, he turns away from everything that bears the name of gods or demons, and, by uniting himself with the Holy Spirit, becomes a perfect man. He sees God within himself . . .[30]

In medieval alchemical thought, each individual person consisted of spirit, soul and body, and to this extent contained the very essence of the universe as a whole. Alchemy affirmed, as the Hermetic texts had similarly conveyed, that the universal mind is indivisible and unites all things in the material universe. The various metals – a specific alchemical concern – were similarly one in essence, and had sprung from the same seed in the womb of Nature. However, the alchemists did not regard all the metals as equally mature or 'perfect'. Gold was seen as the highest development in Nature and as an element came to stand for human renewal or regeneration. A 'golden' human being was one who was resplendent with spiritual beauty and who had triumphed over temptations and the lurking power of evil. By way of contrast, the most base of all the metals, lead, represented the sinful and unrepentant individual who continued to wallow in sin and was readily overcome by the forces of darkness. As H. Stanley Redgrove has written, 'alchemy was an attempted application of the principles of mysticism to the things of the physical world'.[31]

Gold was known to resist the action of fire and corrosive liquids (with the exception of *aqua regia*) whereas lead was readily affected by chemical agents. The philosopher's stone, said to be capable of bringing about a state of alchemical transmutation, was associated by some Christian alchemists with the figure of Jesus himself. Here alchemical transmutation was considered to be a type of spiritual redemption and the imagery of base and precious metals provided a metaphor for personal transfiguration.

According to the alchemists, all aspects of matter were a reflection of God and matter itself consisted of four elements: earth, fire, air and water – which in turn proceeded from the *quinta essentia*, or 'quintess-ence'. Sometimes this symbolic division was represented by a cross within a circle, the four quadrants representing the four elements and the central point the *quinta essentia*. On other occasions the elements were designated by triangles; a triangle pointing upwards represented fire, because fire 'rises', and a triangle pointing downwards represented water. An upturned triangle with a line through it symbolised air, and its downward-facing counterpart, earth. The alchemists also associated certain metals with the astrological 'planets':

Sun	gold
Moon	silver
Mercury	quicksilver
Venus	copper
Mars	iron
Jupiter	tin
Saturn	lead

However, the alchemists believed that the process of transmutation from a base metal into silver or gold was not possible without the metal first being reduced to its *materia prima*, or 'fundamental substance'. This was analagous to reducing each metal initially to a state of 'soul' or 'essence':

> According to the alchemists, the soul, in its original state of pure receptivity, is fundamentally one with the *materia prima* of the whole world. In one way this is but a restatement of the theoretical premise of all alchemy, namely that macrocosm and microcosm corespond to one another. At the same time it is also an expression of the goal of the alchemical work.[32]

The idea of the *materia prima* itself referred to the potential of 'soul' to take a material form. At this level one could consider a metal to be latent, or 'unrealised'. The alchemists themselves described a metal in this condition as 'uncongealed' – free of specific qualities. On the other hand specific metals were normally, and by definition, rigid, restricted, or 'coagulated'. Alchemical transformation therefore involved a shift from the initial coagulation through such processes as burning, dissolving and purification, in order to produce a new outcome – a quite different 'coagulation' or reformulation from the original substance.

On one level alchemy was a physical attempt to produce gold from base metals, and some practitioners – precursors of modern laboratory scientists – understood it on this level. If we consider alchemy as a symbolic expression of the potential for human renewal, however, this is more meaningfully seen as an essentially spiritual process. Just as the alchemists believed that amorphous *materia* could be burned, dissolved and purified and then subsequently 'coagulated' into the form of a perfect metal like gold – a symbol of wholeness – this process could also be applied to the mystical quest for oneness with God. Titus Burckhardt has written:

> The form of the soul thus 'born again' is nevertheless distinguishable from the all-embracing Spirit, as it still belongs to conditioned existence. But at the same time it is transparent to the undifferentiated Light of the Spirit and its vital union with the primordial *materia* of all souls, for the 'material' or 'substantial' ground of the soul, just like its essential or active ground, has a unitary nature. We are all like waves within the same sea . . .
>
> The highest meaning of alchemy is the knowledge that all is contained in all, and its *magisterium* is none other than the realisation of this truth on the plane of the soul. This realisation is effected by means of the creation of the 'elixir', which unites in itself all the powers of the soul, and thus acts as a transmuting 'ferment' on the psychic world and in an indirect fashion on the outward world also.[33]

Freemasonry, Rosicrucianism and Symbolic Rebirth

Allied to the alchemists within the Western esoteric tradition are two other mystical fraternities – the Freemasons and the Rosicrucians. Both have continued to the present day in various permutations – in some instances more as social organisations than as advocates of a mystical tradition – and have contributed strongly to modern magical consciousness, especially through the structure and formation of the Hermetic

Order of the Golden Dawn, which will be discussed in the next chapter. Freemasonry and Rosicrucianism both build on mystical metaphors and themes of spiritual transformation which continue to underpin contemporary occult perspectives.

Modern Freemasonry has eighteenth-century origins. The Masonic Grand Lodge of England was established in London in 1717 when members of four London lodges met in a tavern in Covent Garden and constituted themselves 'A Grand Lodge pro Tempore (for the time being) in Due Form and . . . resolved to hold the Annual Assembly and Feast, and then to choose a Grand Master from among themselves, till they should have the Honour of a Noble Brother at their Head'. All forms of Freemasonry today can be traced to this meeting, and since 1721, when the Duke of Montague was appointed to the position, the so-called Grand Master has been a person of noble or royal birth. The present incumbent is the Duke of Kent.

As a tradition however, Freemasonry extends back much further than the eighteenth century and derives from the practices of the highly skilled European stone masons who built magnificent cathedrals and worked on other large-scale constructions during the Middle Ages. These masons formed lodges and recognised 'degrees' in order to maintain their professional skills and standards. An itinerant builder, for example, would be required to answer veiled questions and respond to special signs and passwords in order to establish his credentials as a master mason. In due course an elaborate system of Masonic rituals developed, sheathed in secrecy and maintained by oaths of fidelity and fraternity.

Despite its secret rituals it is important to emphasise that Freemasonry is not itself a religion so much as a symbolic response to the universe. Joseph Fort Newton, a leading authority on Freemasonry, has emphasised that Freemasonry has its spiritual roots in a mystical appreciation of architecture, and that architecture in turn encompasses both physical necessity and spiritual aspiration:

Of course, the first great impulse of all architecture was need, honest response to the demand for shelter; but this demand included a Home for the Soul, not less than a roof over the head . . .

The story of the Tower of Babel is more than a myth. Man has ever been trying to build to heaven, embodying his prayer and his dream in brick and stone. Freemasonry is built on the idea of uniting material and spiritual realities.[34]

Indeed, in terms of spiritual origins, there are resonances of the philosophy of Freemasonry even in the Bible. For example, in Hebrews iii:4 we read 'For every house is builded by some man; but the builder of all things is God . . . whose house we are.' I Peter ii; 5 expresses a similar idea: 'Ye also, as living stones, are built into a spiritual house'; and similarly in 2 Corinthians v:1 it is written: 'For we know that when our earthly house of this tabernacle is dissolved, we have a building of God, an house not made with hands, eternal in the heavens.'

According to some sources, the medieval stonemasons derived their secret signs and passwords from the builders of the Temple of Solomon. Traditionally Masonic lodges include figures representing the steps that led to Solomon's Temple as well as symbolic motifs derived from ancient Egypt. All lodges have a vaulted ceiling, painted blue and covered with golden stars to represent the heavens. The floor is traditionally mosaic, its variegated colours representing the earth covered with flowers after the withdrawal of the waters of the Nile. In the modern lodge two bronze pillars are located in the west, inscribed J and B (representing Jachin and Boaz and, symbolically, the summer and winter solstices), and there are ten other pillars connected to them by an architrave. Masonic initiatory ritual also focuses on the figure of Hiram, the architect who was slain during the building of the Temple of Solomon. In a ritual context Hiram represents Osiris, the ancient Egyptian deity associated with vegetation and fertility who was slain by Set and restored to life by Isis. In a masonic context the figure of Hiram is therefore symbolic of death and spiritual rebirth.[35]

Despite its symbolic references to the Temple of Solomon and the mythology of ancient Egypt, Freemasonry does not limit its conception of the divine. Adherents are now asked simply to confess their faith in 'God the Father Almighty, the Architect and Master-builder of the Universe'. Indeed one could readily discern in Freemasonry a pantheistic element, for according to the masonic outlook, 'behind the pageant of Nature, in it and over it, there is a Supreme Mind which initiates, impels and controls all . . . In short the first and last thing in the universe is mind, the highest and deepest thing is conscience, and the final reality is the absoluteness of love.'[36]

Traditionally, although Freemasonry has itself been a secret organisation, it has championed the freedom of body, mind and spirit – a sentiment it shares with certain forms of Gnosticism. Here the human soul is seen as 'akin to God', the edifice on which all of creation is built. Modern Freemasonry seeks to combine science, logic and faith so that these elements become the basis for living spiritually in the world. Freemasonry is strongly opposed to sectarian differences, and recognises a diversity of spiritual expression which in turn acknowledges that love should provide the basis for tolerance. This acknowledgement of spiritual diversity has made it a traditional enemy of the Roman Catholic Church in some countries – it is still banned in Spain and Portugal, though not in Italy – but for Joseph Fort Newton the essence of Masonry is friendship combined with an attitude of tolerance and understanding. The so-called 'great secret' of Freemasonry is that 'it makes a man aware of that divinity within him, wherefrom his whole life takes its beauty and meaning, and inspires him to follow and obey it.'[37] Winwood Reade in his *The Veil of Isis* similarly emphasises the innate tolerance and universality of Freemasonry as a mystical tradition:

> Love is the key-stone which supports the entire edifice of this mystic science. Love one another, teach one another, help one another. That is all our doctrine, all our science, all our law. We have no narrow-minded prejudices; we do not debar from our society this sect or that sect; it is sufficient for us that a man worships God, no matter under what name or in what manner.[38]

The Rosicrucians, meanwhile, have had a quite different, and more obscure, history. Virtually unknown until the second decade of the seventeenth century, the Rosicrucian fraternity announced their existence with the release of four pamphlets in 1614–16. The first of these documents was the *Fama Fraternitatis Rosae Crucis* issued in Cassel in 1614, together with a satirical work by the Italian writer Boccalini called *The General Reformation of the World*. In 1615 an anti-papal document entitled *Confessio* appeared, and this in turn was followed by the allegorical *Chemical Marriage of Christian Rosencreutz* (Rosycross). The last of these is especially important in the context of contemporary occult thought because of its alchemical themes and spiritual rebirth symbolism, and its later influence on the Hermetic Order of the Golden Dawn. Both the *Fama* and the *Confessio* contain brief information on the life of the mythical figure Christian Rosencreutz and the formation of his order.

The *Fama* begins by declaring that God has now revealed a more profound understanding of Jesus Christ and Nature. There are now men of wisdom who understand the nature of the microcosmos. The reader is then introduced to Brother Rosencreutz, 'an illuminated man' who has travelled extensively and received the wisdom of the East. The text presents the view that in Germany today there are many learned magicians, Kabbalists, physicians and philosophers who should collaborate with each other. The writer explains how the Church can be reformed through this new sacred knowledge and goes on to explain how the Rosicrucian fraternity came into existence, initially with four members and later through a much expanded following. Members met annually in the House of the Holy Spirit. The text also mentions that a vault has been discovered where the original Brother Rosencreutz is buried.

The vault had seven sides and was said to have been illuminated by an inner sun. In the vault there was also a round altar, covered with a plate of brass on which was engraved these words: 'I have made this Tomb a compendium of the Universe.' Around the brim were the words 'Jesus is all things to me.' There were geometrical figures on the walls, lamps, magical mirrors and bells, and writings by the alchemist Paracelsus (who is not claimed as a member of the fraternity). Most significant of all, when the altar was moved aside by the Rosicrucian brethren and the brass plate lifted, they found a 'fair and worthy body, whole and unconsumed . . . In his hand he held the book T . . . which next to our Bible is our greatest treasure.'

Clearly Christian Rosencreutz had strong spiritual associations with the figure of the seventeenth century perfect Christ. It is especially significant that the seventeenth century Rosicrucian apologist Robert Fludd should have interpreted the story of the vault of Christian Rosencreutz as symbolic of mystical rebirth and the quest for spiritual perfection:

Some writers have dealt with this mystery in dark sayings and methinks the great Rosarius hath described it shrouded in sacred symbols. For here we see a corpse, buried, wherefrom the soul hath gone and seemeth to soar heavenward. The body duly prepared for burial, or even now decaying; yet we see the soul that belongeth thereto, clothed with greater powers, descending to its body. We see a light, as if it were the Sun, yet winged and exceeding the Sun of our heaven, arising from the tomb. We see displayed with wondrous courage, a picture of the making of the perfect man.[39]

The discovery of the vault – supposedly in 1604 – was also proclaimed as the symbolic beginning of a new era of spiritual reformation: 'We know . . . that there will now be a general reformation, both of divine and human things, according to our desire and the expectations of others . . .' The followers of Christian Rosencreutz would bring about this spiritual transformation.

The *Fama* was published in German but the first edition of the *Confessio* was in Latin, implying that it was aimed at a more learned audience.[40] The *Confessio* boldly declared that the pope of Rome was the Antichrist and, like the *Fama*, it urged readers of the tract to cooperate with the order in bringing about a new spiritual orientation, equivalent to the state of Adam in Paradise. God would allow light and truth to flood the land and the pope would be overthrown. It was said that new stars had appeared in the constellations of Serpentarius and Cygnus as omens of what was to come.

Many readers tried to contact the fraternity when these pamphlets were issued, but there were no replies. As one might expect, this intensified great interest in the Rosicrucian mystery, especially since the identity of the Brothers remained unknown. According to the Renaissance scholar Frances A. Yates, it now seems certain that the *Monas Hieroglyphica* by the Elizabethan philosopher and ceremonial magician Dr John Dee may have influenced the Rosicrucian writers – his text representing the 'secret philosophy' behind them – and it is also evident that the Lutheran pastor Johann Valentin Andrae (1586–1654) played a central role in issuing the tracts. Andrae is generally regarded as the author of *The Chemical Marriage*, and in Kurt Seligmann's view Rosencreutz and Andrae were 'one and the same person'.[41] It is also possible that the physician Oswald Croll – a follower of Paracelsus – was involved in the movement.[42]

Of all the Rosicrucian documents, though, *The Chemical Marriage* is undoubtedly the most fascinating. It describes how, just before Easter, Christian Rosencreutz is summoned by a female angelic being to attend a royal wedding. The summons shows a cross with a solar disc and lunar crescent. The next day Christian Rosencreutz wakes early and prepares for his journey. He is wearing four red roses in his hat and carrying with him bread, salt and water.

When he finally departs on his journey and ventures through a forest, he discovers that four different roads lead to the Palace of the King. Only one of these is the Royal Road but whichever he chooses he must persist with, because to turn back will result in his death. Initially Christian Rosencreutz cannot decide which road to take but after offering bread to a snow-white dove who is being tormented by a black raven, he finds himself before a large gate inscribed with various 'noble figures' and devices. Christian Rosencreutz is asked to give his name and replies that he is a brother of the Rosy Cross. In exchange for water he is given a gold token and now comes to a second gate which is similarly inscribed with mystical symbols and is guarded by a lion. He is allowed through after giving the gift of salt. Christian Rosencreutz ventures through a third gate and is just in time for the wedding feast. In the wedding hall he discovers a 'great multitude of guests', including emperors, kings, princes and lords and also poor and 'ignoble' people. After the feast the guests are told that the following day they will be weighed in the Scales of Judgement.

Most of the guests fail this test and are given a potion which dissolves their memory of the event. They are then turned away from the palace. However, Christian Rosencreutz and a few others continue. Each member of this group is presented with a Golden Fleece and Medal of Gold surmounted with the Sun and Moon, before being summoned to a banquet and shown various mysteries of the Palace, including the Great Phoenix (a resurrection symbol associated with Christ). The next day the candidates attend the banquet but after they have removed their white garments and replaced them with black ones, a black man appears, beheads the King and Queen and places them in coffins.

Christian Rosencreutz and his colleagues now journey with a guide called the Virgin to a seven-storeyed Tower of the Gods where they prepare material for the Great Work – the supreme achievement of the alchemists. Employing the blood of the Phoenix, they bring the King and Queen back to life and in turn are proclaimed by the Virgin to be Knights of the Golden Stone.

Here, as in the Masonic myth of Hiram, the theme of death and spiritual rebirth plays a central role. It is an enduring theme in the Western esoteric tradition and re-emerges, as we will see, in the defining initiatory ritual of the Hermetic Order of the Golden Dawn.

A point that should be emphasised here, though, is that the Western esoteric tradition has many strands which are nevertheless united by some central themes. We have seen how the mystical universe has been variously interpreted by the Gnostics, Neoplatonists and Hermeticists as emanationist – revealing successive layers of mystery in the creation of different levels of being, each emanating in turn from a divine and transcendent source. The medieval alchemists and their later counter-parts, the Freemasons and Rosicrucians, have been shown to share a common interest in spiritual rebirth and the idea of the archetypal figure of the perfected human. It seems to me that these elements are all central to the ever-mutating but nevertheless essentially Gnostic idea that has evolved finally into the stratum of twentieth-century magical consciousness, culminating in our own time in the individual transpersonal quest to incarnate the god and goddess. High magic, or gnosis, is essentially about embodying deity – about becoming like gods and goddesses on the path to transcendence.

From the perspective of conventional Western religion, gnosis of this type remains a potent heresy, and it is not hard to see why the mystical and neopagan traditions should have been so strongly persecuted by the Roman Catholic Inquisition during the Middle Ages. The magical traditions consistently advocate the view that direct contact with the divine – archetypal sacred consciousness – is not only possible but desirable. This heresy persists to this day, albeit in less confrontational terms, and it comes as no surprise that Pope John Paul II has vociferously denounced 'New Age' philosophies, both in his publications and in an encyclical.

But it remains true, too, that until very recent times the fragments of the esoteric tradition that have been described here have remained truly hidden – occult in the literal meaning of the word. I believe that this inclination towards secrecy is changing, and that more magically inclined individuals are sharing their knowledge and their wisdom openly. However, this is a very recent phenomenon. At the turn of the century, occultists were still occult. As in the traditions of Freemasonry and Rosicrucianism, secrets had to be preserved and enlightenment earned gradually – literally by degrees.

The Masonic author Joseph Fort Newton has made some fascinating, and still relevant, observations about the 'occult myth' in his book *The Builders*, first published in 1918:

God ever shields us from premature idea, said the gracious and wise Emerson; and so does Nature. She holds back her secrets until man is fit to be entrusted with them, lest by rashness he destroy himself. Those who seek find, not because the truth is far off, but because the discipline of the quest makes them ready for the truth and worthy to receive it. By a certain sure instinct the great teachers of our race have regarded the highest truth less as a gift bestowed than as a trophy to be won. Everything must not be told to everybody. Truth is power, and when held by untrue hands it may become a plague.

Newton says that the 'more withdrawn teaching' has become known as the Secret Doctrine or Hidden Wisdom:

A persistent tradition affirms that throughout the ages, and in every land, behind the system of faith accepted by the masses an inner and deeper doctrine has been held and taught by those able to grasp it . . . those who have eyes to see have no difficulty in penetrating the varying veils of expression and identifying the underlying truths; thus confirming in the arcana of faith what we found to be true in its earliest forms – the oneness of the human mind and the unity of truth.[43]

This is the 'occult myth':

We are told that behind the age-long struggle of man to know the truth there exists a hidden fraternity of initiates, adepts in esoteric

34

lore, known to themselves but not to the world, who have had in their keeping, through the centuries which they permit to be dimly adumbrated in the popular faiths, but which the rest of the race are too obtuse, even yet, to grasp save in an imperfect and limited degree. These hidden sages, it would seem, look upon our eager aspiring humanity much like the patient masters of an idiot school, watching it go on forever seeking without finding, while they sit in seclusion, keeping the keys of the occult.[44]

Significantly, Newton himself does not subscribe to this view. 'It is,' he says, 'only one more of those fascinating fictions with which mystery-mongers entertain themselves and deceive others.' Newton acknowledges that there are sages in all lands and times but denies that it is a 'continuous fellowship of superior souls holding . . . secret truths denied to their fellow men'.

Nevertheless, Newton does subscribe to the idea of society and culture being shaped by visionaries guided by the grace of God and by 'the divine right of genius'. These people embody what he calls the Open Secret of the world. Essentially the truth is always there for those who persist on the spiritual quest and who prove themselves capable of receiving it. 'What kept it hidden,' he say, 'was no arbitrary restriction, but only a lack of insight and fineness of mind to appreciate and assimilate it.'

Newton finally distinguishes between faith and spiritual knowledge in true Gnostic style:

What then, is the Secret Doctrine but . . . the kinship of the soul with God . . . Now to accept this faith as mere philosophy is one thing, but to realise it as an experience of the innermost heart is another and a deeper thing. *No man knows the Secret Doctrine until it has become the secret of his soul, the reigning reality of his thought, the inspiration of his acts, the form and colour and glory of his life.*[45]

In a contemporary context, Newton's remarks seem quaintly expressed, and even unwittingly chauvinistic. Yet it seems to me that philosophically they are very much to the point. The occult is only as hidden as one makes it, and mystical enlightenment is finally an individual act of transcendence.

At the turn of the century the magical traditions were still undergoing a period of consolidation. The 'secret society' which would later help stimulate the revival of contemporary magical consciousness – and bring 'the occult' out into the open – had only just been born. This was the Hermetic Order of the Golden Dawn.

2

The Hermetic Order
of the Golden Dawn

In 1887 Dr Wynn Westcott, a London-based coroner and Freemason, acquired a manuscript in cipher form which had been discovered among the papers of a deceased member of an English esoteric society. This society was the Societas Rosicruciana in Anglia (SRIA) and its principal activities were the exploration of alchemical symbolism and ceremonial ritual. Westcott was its secretary-general.

By means of an alchemical code, Westcott was able to transcribe the manuscript, which yielded five Masonic rituals. Westcott then invited a friend, Samuel Liddell Mathers, to expand the material so that it could perhaps form the basis of a 'complete scheme of initiation'.[1] Westcott also claimed to have found among the leaves of the cipher manuscript the name and address of a certain Fräulein Anna Sprengel, said to be an eminent Rosicrucian adept. On her authority, and following a lengthy correspondence, Westcott announced in Masonic and Theosophical circles that he had been instructed to found an English branch of her German occult group, calling it the Hermetic Order of the Golden Dawn.

Research into the history of the order suggests that both the correspondence and the identity of Fräulein Sprengel were fictitious.[2] Westcott seems to have concocted them in an effort to compete with the esoteric school which Madame Helena Blavatsky had established within the Theosophical Society after bringing her organisation to

London in 1884. Blavatsky claimed to be inspired by mahatmas, or spiritual masters, living in Tibet, with whom she had psychic rapport, and this had widespread appeal to devotees seeking some sense of mystical 'authority'. While Westcott was not at this stage claiming such exalted metaphysical inspiration for his new Hermetic Order, he was nevertheless appealing, through the persona of Fräulein Sprengel, to a sense of authentic occult lineage. And he would soon develop the notion of 'Secret Chiefs' to rival Madame Blavatsky's mahatmas.

In contrast to the Hermetic Order of the Golden Dawn, which focused specifically on fusing different elements of the Western esoteric tradition, the Theosophical Society sought to introduce the concept of a universal wisdom tradition which encompassed both Western and Eastern esoteric thought. Founded in New York in 1875 by Madame Blavatsky, Colonel H. S. Olcott and William Q. Judge, the Theosophical Society soon included the chemist and psychic researcher Sir William Crookes, the inventor Thomas Alva Edison, the astronomer Lord Crawford and the German mystic Rudolf Steiner – who later broke away to establish the Anthroposophical Society. The Irish poet William Butler Yeats was a member of both the Theosophical Society and the Hermetic Order of the Golden Dawn.

The Dawn of the Order

In the same way that Theosophy attracted a diverse and interesting coterie of mystical seekers, the Hermetic Order of the Golden Dawn would in turn attract a range of fascinating, and often very talented, individuals. These included the distinguished homeopath Dr Edward Berridge; the Scottish Astronomer Royal, William Peck; Arthur Edward Waite, an authority on the Kabbalah, Rosicrucianism and the Holy Grail legends; Yeats, who would later win the Nobel Prize; a well known physician and pioneer of tropical medicine, Dr R. W. Felkin; the lawyer Dr John Brodie-Innes; the fantasy novelists Arthur Machen and Algernon Blackwood; and the controversial ritual magician and adventurer Aleister Crowley. And despite its patriarchal connections with Freemasonry, the order would also include within its membership several notable women, among them Annie Horniman, later a leading patron of Irish theatre; the artist and scholar Moina Bergson, sister of the influential French philosopher Henri Bergson; the Celtic revivalist Maude Gonne; the actress Florence Farr; and in later years Violet Firth – better known as the magical novelist Dion Fortune.[3]

As a Freemason Westcott was very attracted to the concept of ritual degrees, and he designed the grades of the Hermetic Order of the Golden Dawn to correlate with the *sephiroth*, the levels of mystical consciousness upon the Kabbalistic Tree of Life. The five rituals contained within the cipher manuscript were grades in the Societas Rosicruciana in Anglia. Four of these ritual grades were referred to by imposing Latin names; Zelator, Theoricus, Practicus and Philosophus. There was also a 'Neophyte' grade which, in a symbolic sense, was located below the Tree of Life because here the mystical seeker had not yet really embarked on the magical journey of the higher spheres. Westcott, however, wanted to expand the grade system so that it covered all the stages of consciousness potentially attainable upon the Tree of Life. Having designated the first series of grades from Neophyte to Philosophus the First Order, he developed a Second Order of grades. These were known as Adeptus Minor, Adeptus Major and Adeptus Exemptus, and they corresponded to the sixth, fifth and fourth spheres upon the Tree respectively.

The grades were numbered in this way because the spiritual journey that the occult devotee would undertake was one of mystical ascent from the lowest levels of the Tree of Life to the highest – an essentially Gnostic process of transcending Creation and returning to the One Source of All Being. The fourth sphere of consciousness lies just below the Trinity on the Kabbalistic Tree and in Jewish cosmology represents the first of the seven days of Creation. The three higher *sephiroth* on the other hand constitute the Trinity – levels of sacred being untarnished by the so-called 'Fall' of the Spirit into successive levels of manifest reality. Between the seven lower and three higher *sephiroth* upon the Tree is the Abyss, which symbolically distinguishes the domain of Creation *below* from the sacred purity of the transcendent Godhead *above*. In the Jewish mystical tradition symbolic forms are rarely ascribed to levels of mystical reality above the Abyss because, essentially, they lie beyond the realm of Creation.

Nevertheless, Westcott conceived of a mystical Third Order which corresponded to the exalted and transcendent levels of awareness above the fourth *sephirah*. For Westcott this sacred domain could be regarded as the home of beings known as 'Secret Chiefs', whose inspiration could then be said to be guiding the vision of the Golden Dawn as a whole. In claiming exclusive access to these Secret Chiefs, Westcott was acting in a way which would have enormous significance for the history of the order, because he was really appointing himself and his selected colleagues as members of a visionary elite who claimed privileged access to a unique source of divine power. Westcott maintained that contact with this transcendental realm above the Abyss would be possible only through 'astral consciousness', through a mystical process known as 'rising on the planes', or through the performance of specific esoteric rituals designed to inflame the sacred imagination. It was a challenge of truly cosmic proportions.

Westcott established the Isis-Urania Temple of the Hermetic Order of the Golden Dawn in London in 1888, inviting Mathers and his Masonic friend Dr William Woodman to join him as 'Chiefs' in the new Temple. By implication they were the Secret Chiefs incarnate. All three assumed the grade of $7° = 4°$, which meant that they had risen through seven sephiroth; but since these are numbered in descending order, the grade $7° = 4°$ refers to the ritual attainment of Chesed, the fourth emanation on the Tree of Life, and the sphere symbolically associated with the ruler of the universe (represented by Jehovah/Yahweh in Judaism, Zeus in ancient Greece and Jupiter in ancient Rome). In this capacity the Secret Chiefs functioned by using secret magical names, for as a matter of principle Golden Dawn members could only be allowed to know the magical names of their peers and those with grades beneath them. Westcott became *Sapere Aude*, Woodman *Magna est Veritas*, and Mathers *Deo Duce Comite Ferro*.

According to Kabbalistic tradition, in addition to the Abyss which divides the Trinity and Creation, there is also said to be a 'veil' named Paroketh between the sixth and seventh emanations upon the Tree of Life. This represents the transition between old and new being. The sixth emanation, Tiphareth, is located in the very heart of the Tree of Life and represents the visionary state of consciousness where spiritual transformation, or 'rebirth', occurs. Westcott, Mathers and Woodman used different mottoes associated with this grade in order to interact with those lower-ranking members of the order who had not yet been fully initiated – that is, those with ritual grades below the Veil of Paroketh.

The three supreme grades upon the Tree of Life were those of the Third Order: $8° = 3°$ (Magister Templi), $9° = 2°$ (Magus) and $10° = 1°$ (Ipsissimus). In Westcott's mind this sacred domain approximated the inspirational levels of Madame Blavatsky's mahatmas. In appointing themselves Chiefs with exclusive access to these transcendent levels of being, Westcott, Mathers and Woodman clearly considered themselves as spiritual leaders who could bring the other order members through into the Light.

Westcott's system, like Freemasonry, was hierarchical and he was able to appeal to Fräulein Sprengel's illuminating and guiding authority in addition to that of the Secret Chiefs. Shortly after Sprengel's alleged death in 1891, Westcott claimed that 'all the knowledge was safe with him'. Indeed, in all probability it had never resided anywhere else. However, his own dominance failed to endure. Following Dr Woodman's death in the same year as Anna Sprengel's, and Mathers's increasing importance as author of the recently elaborated rituals of the Golden Dawn, Westcott was forced into an administrative role of secondary importance.

In 1892 Mathers claimed to have established a special spiritual connection with the Secret Chiefs which enabled him to write rituals for the Second Order which encompassed the sixth, fifth and fourth *sephiroth* – Tiphareth/Adeptus Minor ($5° = 6°$) Geburah/Adeptus Major ($6° = 5°$) and Chesed/Adeptus Exemptus ($7° = 4°$), which he and Westcott already held in an honorary capacity. This situation gave Mathers the spiritual edge as a 'communicant' of the higher ritual grades. He gave these grades of the Second Order the illustrious composite name of the Rosae Rubae et Aurea Crucis: the Red Rose and the Cross of Gold (often abbreviated to RR et AC).

Meanwhile the Golden Dawn temples continued to grow in number. In 1896, in addition to the Temple of Isis-Urania in London, there were Temples of Osiris in Weston-Super-Mare, Horus in Bradford, Amen-Ra in Edinburgh and Ahathoor in Paris. It was while Mathers was in absentia in Paris that the first power struggle within the order occurred.

Mathers had moved to Paris with his wife Moina Bergson – they had married in 1890 after meeting in the British Museum some three years earlier – and he was now engaged in translating from French a lengthy and important occult manuscript entitled *The Sacred Magic of Abramelin the Mage*. Although only a clerk and infantryman by profession, Mathers had certain social pretensions and was now referring to himself as MacGregor Mathers, MacGregor of Glenstrae and Count of Glenstrae to feign rank and importance. Supported financially by the wealthy Golden Dawn member Annie Horniman, a tea heiress and key member of the London Isis-Urania Temple, Mathers was presiding over the Ahathoor Temple while simultaneously attempting to maintain dominance over the English temples across the Channel. Annie Horniman would later query aspects of the funding of Mathers's stay in Paris, and Mathers's reply to her reveals aspects of his potentially authoritarian 'magical' personality and his appeal to 'occult authority':

> Prior to the establishment of the Vaults of the Adepts in Britannia (the First of the Golden Dawn in the Outer being therein actively working) . . . it was found absolutely and imperatively necessary that there should be some eminent Member especially chosen to act as the link between the Secret Chiefs and the more external forms of the Order. It was requisite that such Member should be me, who, while having the necessary and peculiar educational basis of critical and profound occult archaeological knowledge should at the same time not only be ready and willing to devote himself in every sense to a blind and unreasoning obedience to those Secret Chiefs – to pledge himself to the fidelity of those to whom this Wisdom was to be communicated: to be one who would shrink neither from danger physical, astral or spiritual, from privation or hardship, nor from terrible personal and psychic responsibility . . . he must further pledge himself to obey in everything the commands of the aforesaid Secret Chiefs *'perinde ac cadaver'*, body and soul, without question and without argument whether their commands related to: Magical Action in the External World; or to Psychic Action in Other Worlds, or Planes, whether Angelic, Spiritual or Demonic, or to the Inner Administration of the Order to which so tremendous a knowledge was to be communicated.[4]

It is clear that belief in the Secret Chiefs was a central doctrine which helped maintain Mathers' position as head of the hierarchy of graded Golden Dawn members – indeed, this hierarchical structure was something of an occult equivalent to the feudal concept of the divine right of kings. Nevertheless, while endeavouring to consolidate his own position within the occult hierarchy of the Golden Dawn, Mathers was unable to supply his followers with any detailed information about these essentially mysterious spiritual entities:

> I do not even know their earthly names. I know them only by certain secret mottoes. I have *but very rarely* seen them in the physical body; and on such rare occasions *the rendezvous was made astrally by them* at the time and place which had been astrally appointed beforehand. For my part I believe them to be human and living upon this earth but possessing terrible superhuman powers.[5]

The concept of magical beings whose mystical inspiration emanated from a source beyond the Abyss on the Tree of Life was an intriguing one, for it suggested that there were 'living gods' who could be contacted once one reached the highest initiatory grades. And Mathers was not alone in subscribing to the idea of visionary guidance from higher spheres of spiritual reality.

Florence Farr, who conducted a splinter offshoot within the Golden Dawn known as the Sphere Group, believed her coterie to be controlled by a 'certain Egyptian astral form'. And Dr R. W. Felkin, who founded the Order of the Stella Matutina (Morning Star) after several members of the London Temple deserted Mathers in 1900, continued to strive for contact with the Secret Chiefs even though the members of Felkin's order had broken their allegiance to their former leader. In May 1902 Felkin wrote to his colleagues: 'We beg to assure you that we are in entire sympathy with the view that if in fact the Order is without the guidance and inspiration of higher intelligences its rationale is gone.'

It occurred to certain members of the Golden Dawn, however, that it might be possible, by reverting to the original constitution, to re-establish a link with the Third Order.[6] Meanwhile Felkin opted instead for certain 'Sun Masters' and then for a mysterious being named Ara Ben Shemesh, whom he described as a 'discarnate Arab [with a]

Temple in the Desert where the Sons of Fire live [who] are in personal communication with the Divine and are no longer bound in the flesh so that their material life is a matter of will.' There is also evidence that William Butler Yeats believed in the existence of transcendental guides. In his essay 'Is the Order of the RR & AC to remain a Magical Order?', written in 1901, Yeats refers to 'the stream of lightning awakened in the Order, and the *Adepts of the Third Order* and of the Higher Degrees of the Second Order summoned to our help'.[7]

Such issues were of course primarily of interest to those who had actually entered the Inner Order of the Rosae Rubae et Aurea Crucis, and who had taken the following pledge:

> I will from this day forward apply myself to the Great Work which is to purify and exalt my Spiritual nature, that within the Divine aid I may at length attain to be more than human, and thus gradually raise and unite myself to my Higher and Divine Genius and that in this event I will not abuse the Great Power entrusted to me.[8]

The majority of Golden Dawn members, however, remained in the Outer Order and their spiritual endeavours focused ritually and meditatively on the four *sephiroth* Malkuth, Yesod, Hod and Netzach located at the lower levels of the Tree of Life.

The Grades

The starting point on the magical journey was the Neophyte degree. This was not assigned a position on the Tree of Life as such, but was nevertheless a vital milestone. Francis King has described this degree as 'unquestionably the most important, since it gave [the individual] not only a glimpse of the Light to be experienced in the future but a key (albeit in an embryonic and undeveloped form) to the inner and hidden significance of the entire Order'.[9] This view is also endorsed by Dr Israel Regardie, who was himself a member of the Stella Matutina:

> If one idea more than any other is persistently stressed from the beginning that idea is the word *Light*. From the candidate's first reception in the Hall of the Neophytes when the Hierophant adjures

him with these words – ' Child of Earth, long hast thou dwelt in darkness. Quit the night and seek the day' – to the transfiguration in the [Second Order] Vault Ceremony, the whole system has as its objective the bringing down of the Light.[10]

As a Neophyte the aspirant was instructed in the First Knowledge Lecture which provided details of the four elements of the ancients (fire, earth, air and water) and the twelve signs of the zodiac. The correlations between these signs and the elements were explained, so that Aries, Leo and Sagittarius were said to be fire signs; Taurus, Virgo and Capricorn earth signs; and so on. Some elementary Hebrew was also included in a table which provided the letter of the alphabet, its English equivalent, its name and its meaning. Finally the elementary symbolism of the *sephiroth* upon the Tree of Life was also explained. Meanwhile, on the practical side, the Neophyte was expected to know how to perform the Lesser Ritual of the Pentagram, an occult exercise designed to 'clear the air' of minor malevolent forces surrounding the magician during ritual invocations.

In the Zelator grade (1° = 10°) members were taught aspects of alchemical symbolism and provided with details of the Order of Elemental Spirits (gnomes: earth; sylphs: air; undines: water; and salamanders: fire) and also instructed in the links between the *sephiroth* and the planets. In the latter case, each *sephirah* was said to be associated with specific gods which could be drawn from any of the great pantheons and charted as 'Correspondences'. (This idea will be discussed in more detail in the following chapter.)

The candidate for Theoricus (2° = 9°) was taught the Kabbalistic division of the soul: Neschamah ('answering to the Three Supernals'); Ruach ('answering to the six *sephiroth* from Chesed to Yesod, inclusive') and Nephesch ('the lowest, answering to Malkuth'). It was emphasised, too, that Neschamah was associated with 'the higher aspirations of the soul', Ruach with 'the mind and reasoning powers' and Nephesch with 'the animal instincts'. In this way the Golden Dawn provided a structure for the spiritual evolution of humanity from its lowly uninitiated and secular status to that of the spiritual god-man and goddess-woman.

In the Practicus grade (3° = 8°) members were instructed in the symbolism of the Major Arcana of the Tarot – the twenty-two mythological or 'court' cards – and their association with the twenty-two paths linking the ten *sephiroth* upon the Tree of Life. (This correlation did not derive from the Jewish mystical tradition but was proposed by the nineteenth-century French occultist Alphonse Louis Constant, better known as Eliphas Levi.)

Finally, the Philosophus (4° = 7°) grade completed the Outer Order of the Golden Dawn. An important theme here was the concept of 'god names' – attributions of the archetypal Great Father and Great Mother – as well as links between alchemy and astrology. Details were also provided of the so-called qlippoth upon the Tree of Life: the negative cosmic energy centres which were the reverse counterparts of the ten *sephiroth*. Lilith was one such example, for, as the 'Queen of the Night and of Demons', she was correlated with Malkuth – the Divine Daughter – and was thus the dark equivalent of Persephone, daughter of Demeter, queen of the underworld and embodiment of the harvest.

Earth, Moon and Sun

The practical rituals of the Golden Dawn were extensive – published for the first time, in four volumes, by Dr Israel Regardie.[11] However, in order to represent the mythological impact of the ceremonial grades, it is possible to summarise the rituals associated with the spheres upon the Middle Pillar of the Tree of Life. These provide the very essence of the spiritual rebirth process and correlate with the archetypal sequence of Earth, Moon and Sun – the symbolic act of coming forth into the light. In the Golden Dawn different members assumed mythological roles and wore appropriate symbolic regalia during the carefully structured ritual procedures, enabling the ceremonial events to make a profound impact upon the imagination of the candidate engaging in the ritual process.

We begin with the grade of Neophyte, which introduces the candidate to the Outer Order of the Golden Dawn.

Neophyte

On the dais of the east, quarter of the rising sun, sit three Chiefs, representing Thoth, Isis and Nephthys, gods who assisted in the resurrection of Osiris. The Hierophant, Osiris himself, the god who is reborn, is enthroned in their midst upon the mystical path Samekh, which leads to harmony.

In the west is Hiereus, representing Horus the Avenger, and in the north and south, Stolistes and Dadouchos, bearers of water and fire. In the south west, Kerux and the Sentinel, forms of Anubis, guard the sacred hall to keep away intruders. Hegemon, personifying the goddess of truth, Maat, presides over the weighing of the scales of truth between the black and white pillars near the centre. Here also is the altar of the elements showing its white upper face, symbolic of light issuing forth from the darkness.

The Hierophant says:

> *My station is on the Throne of the East in the place where the Sun rises and I am the Master of the Hall, governing it according to the Laws of the Order, as He whose Image I am, is the Master of all who work for the Hidden Knowledge. My robe is red because of Uncreated Fire and Created Fire and I hold the Banner of the Morning Light which is the Banner of the East. I am called Power and Mercy and Light and Abundance, and I am the Expounder of the Mysteries.*

The Hall is purified with water and with fire. Kerux opens the Hall of the Neophytes in the northeast, facing west, and declares:

> *In the Name of the Lord of the Universe, who works in Silence and whom naught but Silence can express, I declare that the Sun has arisen and the Shadows flee away . . .*

Robed and hooded so that he cannot see, the Neophyte – 'Child of the Earth' – enters and is purified symbolically with water and fire. He is questioned with regard to his purpose of entry and presents himself like Ani in the Hall of Maat, hopeful of spiritual rebirth: '*My soul wanders in darkness and seeks the Light of the Hidden Knowledge.*' He then pledges secrecy, undergoes ritual oaths and passes to the northern quarter – home of forgetfulness and darkness. From this domain, he seeks to come forth from the darkness as light from the Abyss.

After ritual purification, the Neophyte now enters the gates of the west and the east, headed by Kerux and protected by magical words of entry, *hekau* – the ineffable formulae of magical power uttered by Hegemon, goddess of truth.

The Hierophant allows them to pass onwards to the Cubical Altar of the Universe and, standing to the east of the altar between the mystical pillars, pronounces these words:

> *I come in the Power of Light*
> *I come in the Light of Wisdom*
> *I come in the Mercy of the Light*
> *The Light hath healing in its Wings*

An invocation to the Lord of the Universe is now made, and the light of inspiration sought upon the Neophyte. The Neophyte is now brought between the pillars and taught the sign of the Enterer and the sign of Silence, both ascribed to Horus (the latter in his symbolic form as Harpocrates). Further purifications of fire and water are made and the Mystic Circumambulation of Light performed – a ritual enactment of the passage of the ancient Egyptian Sun god through the different domains of the Underworld. This circumambulation is then reversed as an expression of fading light, and the ceremonial comes to a close.

Zelator (Earth)

An earth tablet and cup, symbolic of the receptive maiden, are placed in the north. Hiereus and Hegemon flank the altar and in the west stand Stolistes, Kerux and Dadouchos. The Hierophant resides at the entrance to the thirty-second path (the sphere of Malkuth).[12]

The Temple is purified with water and fire and an adoration made by the Hierophant to Adonai ha Aretz, Lord of the Earth. Here the magician is about to become a master of the elements:

And the Elohim said: 'Let us make Adam in our image, after our likeness, and let him have dominion over the fish of the sea and over the fowl of the air and over the cattle, and over all the Earth . . .'

In the Name of Uriel, the Great Archangel of Earth, and by the sign of the Head of the Ox – Spirits of Earth, adore Adonai!

In the names of God: EMOR DIAL HECTAGA

In the name of the Great King of the North: IC ZOD HE CHAL

In the name of ADONAI HA ARETZ

At this point in the ceremony the Neophyte is holding the Fylfot Cross, a symbol of the Sun, the elements and the zodiac. He is now asked to state his personal quest upon the path of spiritual knowledge, and, having demonstrated the ritual signs of his grade, is then led to the west and positioned between the Pillars of Extremity. Here he is facing towards the east, the quarter of the mystical dawn. He casts forth the salt of the Earth, and is purified by fire and water. The Hierophant then instructs him in the mysteries of his grade:

And Tetragrammaton [JHVH] Elohim planted a Garden Eastward in Eden, and out of the ground made Jehovah Elohim to grow every tree that is pleasant to the sight and good for food; the Tree of Life also, in the midst of the Garden, and the Tree of Knowledge of Good and Evil. This is the Tree that has two Paths, and it is the Tenth Sephirah Malkuth, and it has about it Seven Columns, and the Four Splendours whirl around it as in the Vision of the Merkabah of Ezekiel; and from Gedulah [also known as Chesed on the Tree of Life] *it derives an influx of Mercy, and from Geburah an influx of Severity, and the Tree of Knowledge of Good and Evil shall it be until it is united with the Supernals in Daath.*[13]

But the Good which is under it is called the Archangel Metatron and the Evil is called the Archangel Samael, and between them lies the straight and narrow way where the Archangel Sandalphon keeps watch. The Souls and the Angels are above its branches and the Qlippoth or Demons dwell under its roots.

The Neophyte now passes to the region of Samael, where he is instructed by the Prince of Darkness, and to the region of Metatron, where he learns of the Ineffable Light of the Creator God. Passing along the way of mediation between them he encounters Sandalphon, 'reconciler for Earth', who 'prepares the way to the Celestial Light'. He is told that emerging from Malkuth on the Tree of Life are three paths, each of these allocated a letter of the Jewish alphabet – Tau, Qoph and Shin. Together these form Qesheth, the Bow of Promise.

The Neophyte is led out and the Temple transforms to represent the Holy Court of the Tabernacle, the place of Burnt Sacrifice. On his return, the Neophyte is purified with fire and water and passes to the entrance between the pillars where he demonstrates the ritual signs of the Neophyte and the Zelator of Malkuth. The Neophyte is told the secrets of the Bread of Life, the Rose of Creation, the Lamp of the Sun and the Signs of the Zodiac. He learns the symbolic basis of the Jewish alphabet and the connotations of the altar of the elements. He is then awarded the grade of the *sephirah* Malkuth, which is also known as 'the Gate of the Daughter of the Mighty Ones' and represents the entrance to the mystical Garden of Eden.

Theoricus (Moon)

The Temple remains as before. Kerux resides in the north, Hegemon is in the south, Hiereus in the west and the Hierophant in the east. An adoration is made to the Lord of the Air, Shaddai El Chai:

> *And the Elohim said: 'Let us make Adam in our image, after our likeness, and let him have dominion over the fowl of the Air.'*
> *In the names* YOD HE VAU HE *and* SHADDAI EL CHAI
> *In the name of the Great Archangel* RAPHAEL
> *In the names of* ORO IBAH AOZPI *and* BATAIVAH, *Spirits of Air . . .*

Zelator enters the Temple and provides the signs of his ritual grade. Embodying the profound paradox in which death leads to rebirth, he takes as his guide the Egyptian deity Anubis, the master embalmer whose knowledge assisted Osiris in the resurrection:

> *I am the synthesis of the Elemental Forces. I am also the symbol of Man. I am Life and I am Death. I am the Child of the Night of Time.*

Kerux and Zelator approach the Gate of the East, which opens on the utterance of the names of Nu, the Air, and Hormaku, the Lord of the Eastern Sun. Zelator is now purified by the fourfold symbols of the resurrection – man, lion, eagle and ox – and comes between the pillars. The Hierophant provides instruction regarding the twenty-two sacred letters upon the cubical cross, for these constitute the Vault of Heaven. Zelator also learns the symbolism of the maiden of the twenty-first Tarot key, the goddess Persephone, the queen of the Underworld who dwells in the mythic space between Earth and Moon. Zelator is also taught the sacred seventy-two-fold name of God and the names of the elemental orders, and he is encouraged to perceive them in a state of visionary consciousness.

Zelator is then led out. When he returns to the Temple it represents the Path of Tau. Before him on the altar are the symbols of the Tree of Life – the twenty-two letters and the ten *sephiroth* constituting the thirty-two fold Path of Wisdom, and the Cross within the Triangle, representing the four rivers of Eden and the conjunction of male and female (Adam and Eve).

Zelator receives the symbol of the Ruach and the grade of Theoricus and an adoration is made to the sacred god-name associated with the sphere of Yesod: SHADDAI EL CHAI.

Adeptus Minor (Sun)

After also attaining the grades associated with Hod and Netzach on the Tree of Life, the Golden Dawn candidate is now ready to approach the Inner Sanctum. He is already a Philosophus (the grade associated with the preceding *sephirah* Netzach) and he prepares for the Ritual of the Portal of the Vault of the Adepti.

Symbolically he stands in the primordial darkness – 'the Realm of Chaos and of Ancient Night'. The Dragon of the Qlippoth rages triumphant in the deep until Thoth utters the word of Creation which allows light to come forth.

In the Rite of the Pentagram and the Fire Paths, Philosophus is accorded mastery over the paths of light which come forth from the dark: Mem, Ayin, Samekh, Nun and Kaph, symbolising the pentagram of man as the microcosm. Philosophus is also reminded of Qesheth, the Bow of Promise, and the Arrow Samekh, 'soaring upward to cleave open the Veil unto the Sun in Tiphareth'. The bowman is Sagittarius the Archer:

> *There is a vision of the fire-flashing courser of Light, or also a child borne aloft upon the shoulders of the Celestial Steed, fiery or clothed with gold, or naked and shooting from the bow shafts of light, and standing on the shoulders of a horse. But if thy meditation prolongeth itself thou shalt unite all of these symbols in the form of a Lion, reconciler in Teth, of Mercy and Severity, beneath whose centre hangs the glorious Sun of Tiphareth.*

Philosophus must now sacrifice his lower self upon the cross of the four elements, in the name of Paroketh, the veil whose name also incorporates Peh (water), Resh (air), Kaph (fire) and Tau (earth):

> *It is the Word of the Veil, the Veil of the Tabernacle, of the Temple, before the Holy of Holies, the Veil which was rent asunder. It is the Veil of the Four Elements of the Body of Man which was offered upon the Cross for the Service of Man. This is the sign of the rending of the Veil . . .*

Philosophus has now become the Lord of the Paths of the Portal of the Vault of the Adepti. And in the Ceremony of the Grade of Adeptus Minor he becomes Hodos Chamelionis, Lord of the Lights upon the Path of the Chameleon. He undergoes a symbolic burial and emergence in the Tomb of the Adepti identifying with Christian Rosencreutz, the Rose and Cross of the Immortal Christ, and the risen Osiris. The tomb has seven sides representing the seven lower *sephiroth* beneath the Supernal triad (the seven days of Creation) and is situated symbolically in the centre of the Earth, just as Tiphareth resides in the centre of the Tree of Life. The spiritual rebirth occurs after 'one hundred and twenty years', symbolic of the ten *sephiroth* multiplied by the twelve signs of the zodiac, and follows ritually the form of the myth of Osiris whereby the body of the slain king of Egypt is magically revitalised. The five earlier rites, and his symbolic death upon the elemental cross, have prepared the candidate for his entry into the Tomb of the Sacred Mountain.[14]

Philosophus lies clothed with the symbols of the embalmed Osiris, and the symbol of the Rosy Cross also rests upon his breast:

Eternal One . . . let the influence of thy Divine Ones descend upon his head, and teach him the value of self-sacrifice so that he shrink not in the hour of trial, but that thus his name may be written on high and that his Genius may stand in the presence of the Holy Ones, in that hour when the Son of Man is invoked before the Lord of Spirits and His Name in the presence of the Ancient of Days. It is written: 'If any man will come after Me, let him take up his cross, and deny himself, and follow Me.'

Philosophus extends his arms so that his body forms a cross, the ritual expression of spiritual rebirth:

Buried with that Light in a mystical death, rising again in a mystical resurrection . . . Quit then this Tomb, O Aspirant, [whose arms have been earlier] crossed upon thy breast, bearing in thy right hand the Crook of Mercy and in thy left the Scourge of Severity, the emblems of those Eternal Forces betwixt which the equilibrium of the universe dependeth; those forces whose reconciliation is the Key of Life, whose separation is evil and death.

The sacred magician, renewed and enriched with mystical light, now comes forth as Christ–Osiris, the reborn Christian Rosencreutz:

And being turned, I saw Seven Golden Lightbearers, and in the midst of the Lightbearers, One like unto the Ben Adam, clothed with a garment down to the feet, and girt with a Golden Girdle. His head and his hair were white as snow and His eyes as flaming fire; His feet like unto fine brass, as if they burned in a furnace. And His voice was as the sound of many waters. And He had in His right hand Seven Stars, and out of His mouth went the Sword of Flame, and His countenance was as the Sun in His Strength. I am the First and I am the Last. I am He that liveth and was dead, and behold! I am alive for evermore, and hold the Keys of Death and Hell . . . I am the purified. I have passed through the Gates of Darkness into Light . . .

I am the Sun in his rising. I have passed through the hour of cloud and of night.

I am Amoun, the Concealed One, the Opener of the Day. I am Osiris Onnophris, the Justified One.

I am the Lord of Life, triumphant over Death.

There is no part of me which is not of the Gods.

3

The Mythology
and Symbols of Magic

For the Golden Dawn magician, the ultimate mythic attainment was to come forth ritually into the light, for this was the very essence of spiritual rebirth. The act of ascending the Kabbalistic Tree of Life through sacred ceremonial involved a powerful act of creative imagination – the magician had to feel that he was fully engaging with each sphere of consciousness in turn.

Judaism and the Kabbalah are monotheistic: each *sephirah* is an aspect of the Godhead, a face of the Divine, not an individual deity in itself; and in the Jewish mystical tradition there is finally only the unity consciousness of Ain Soph Aur. This presented the Golden Dawn occultists with a paradox, for while they acknowledged the sacred unity of the Tree of Life in all its emanations, they also believed that they had to focus their creative awareness upon specific archetypal images if they were to ascend to the light. The solution to this was to regard the Kabbalistic Tree of Life as a type of unifying matrix upon which the archetypes of the great Western mythologies could be charted. It then became possible to correlate the major deities from the pantheons of ancient Egypt, Greece, Rome and Celtic Europe in what amounted to a cumulative approach to the Western mythological imagination. In due course other aspects of magical symbolism would also be charted upon the Tree so that various precious stones, perfumes, minerals and sacred plants could be assigned to specific gods and goddesses in a ceremonial context. These charted mythological images were known to the Golden Dawn magicians as 'magical correspondences'.

Guided in this particular task by MacGregor Mathers, the members of the Golden Dawn made sure that their cosmology became a very elaborate one indeed. Despite his modest social origins, Mathers was a self-taught scholar with a sound knowledge of French, Latin and Greek, as well as some Coptic and Hebrew. He had translated Knorr von Rosenroth's Latin text of *Kabbala Denudata* (*The Kabbalah Unveiled*) into English – the specialist esoteric publisher George Redway issued it in 1887 – and one of his main interests was to translate key magical documents which might otherwise have been doomed to obscurity in museum archives. It was primarily through Mathers's initiative that the magical rituals of the Golden Dawn, in whose shaping and formation he had assumed a major role, would come to draw on every significant mythology in Western culture.

As we have seen, the Tree of Life can be regarded as a cosmological metaphor which describes the hierarchy of energy levels in the manifested universe. Mathers's vision for the Golden Dawn was that the magicians in his order could follow the mythic pathways on the Tree of Life and grow in spiritual awareness as they ascended through each level. Several methods were open to them. They could simulate each of the levels imaginatively through ritual, they could meditate upon each sphere of consciousness, or they could 'rise on the inner planes' in a state of magical trance. The essence of Mathers's approach was to list the deities from the different pantheons and cross-correlate them as important magical archetypes.

In due course this work was published in 1909 under the title *777* – not by Mathers himself but by his friend and fellow Golden Dawn occultist Aleister Crowley, who appears to have added a number of Oriental listings to Mathers's original table of magical correspondences as well as including some individual elements of his own.[1]

The listings in *777* are complex and extend beyond classical Graeco-Roman and Egyptian mythology to include Scandinavian gods, Western astrology, Buddhist meditations, magical weapons and the letters of the Greek, Arabic and Coptic alphabets. When we sample some of the core data included in *777* we find listings like the following:

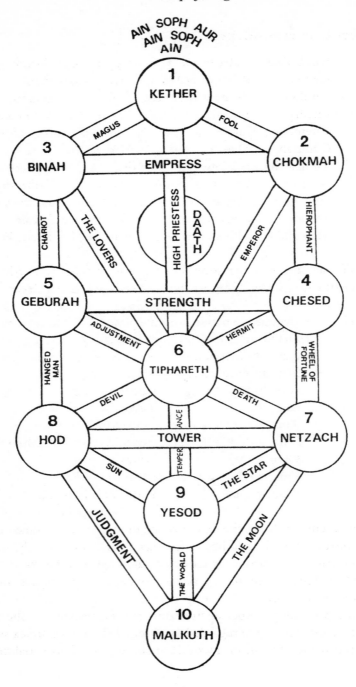

Magical Correspondences

Level	Kabbalah	Astrology	Egyptian	Greek
1	Kether	Primum Mobile	Harpocrates	Zeus
2	Chokmah	Zodiac/fixed stars	Ptah	Uranus
3	Binah	Saturn	Isis	Demeter
4	Chesed	Jupiter	Amoun	Poseidon
5	Geburah	Mars	Horus	Ares
6	Tiphareth	Sol (Sun)	Ra	Apollo
7	Netzach	Venus	Hathor	Aphrodite
8	Hod	Mercury	Anubis	Hermes
9	Yesod	Luna	Shu	Diana
10	Malkuth	The elements	Seb	Persephone

The perfumes and precious stones listed below were considered appropriate in rituals corresponding to the invoked god or goddess:

Level	Precious stones	Perfumes
1	Diamond	Ambergris
2	Star ruby, turquoise	Musk
3	Star sapphire, pearl	Myrrh, civet
4	Amethyst	Cedar
5	Ruby	Tobacco
6	Topaz	Olibanum
7	Emerald	Benzoin, rose, sandalwood
8	Opal	Storax
9	Quartz	Jasmine
10	Rock crystal	Dittany of Crete

As a document 777 shows the extent of the modern magical imagination, and its historic significance lies in the fact that it was an early attempt to systematise the various images associated with different levels of spiritual awareness – predating Jung's concept of archetypes and the collective unconscious.

From a psychological perspective one can see clearly that the magicians of the Golden Dawn regarded the Tree of Life as a complex symbol of the spiritual world within, a world containing sacred potentialities. To simulate the gods and goddesses was to become like them. The challenge was to engage oneself in the mythological processes of the psyche through methods of direct encounter.

The magicians in the Golden Dawn had therefore to imagine that they were partaking of the nature of each of the gods in turn, embodying within themselves the very essence of the deity. The rituals were designed to control all the circumstances that might assist them in their journey through the subconscious mind and mythic imagination. They included all the symbols and colours of the god, the utterance of magical names of power, and the burning of incense or perfume appropriate to the deity concerned.

In the Golden Dawn tradition – an approach to archetypal magic which remains influential a century later – the ritual magician imagines that he has become the deity whose forms he imitates in ritual. The process of the gods ruling humanity is thus reversed so that the magician now controls the gods – he has seized the fire from heaven. It is now the magician himself and not the gods of Creation who utters the sacred names which sustain the universe. In the approach employed by the Golden Dawn magicians, one entered the underworld of the subconscious mind through Malkuth at the base of the Tree, and then proceeded along various pathways culminating in the solar vision of Tiphareth, at the very heart of the Tree of Life.

The most direct route along the Tree was the vertical path from Malkuth through Yesod to Tiphareth, on the Middle Pillar. The Golden Dawn grades, however, also encompassed the other *sephiroth* Hod and Netzach on the outer extremities of the Tree and the process here was one of following the 'zig-zag lightning flash' of sacred manifestation – retracing the path of the divine energy of Creation through each of the *sephiroth* in turn.

Mythological Levels on the Tree of Life

When one considers the Tree of Life as a composite matrix of archetypes, the ten *sephiroth* acquire a richly mythological character.

Malkuth

Associated with the Earth, crops, the immediate environment, living things. This sphere of consciousness represents the beginning of the inner journey. In Roman mythology the entrance to the underworld was through a cave near Naples, and symbolically Malkuth is the entrance through the Earth – the totality of the four elements – leading to what in psychological terms is the subconscious mind. Malkuth in itself represents familiar everyday consciousness.

Yesod

Associated with the Moon, Yesod – like Malkuth – is a predominantly female sphere. It is both the recipient of impulses and fluxes from the higher realms upon the Tree of Life and the transmitter of these energies into a more tangible physical form in Malkuth. Consequently it abounds in an ocean of astral imagery, and is appropriately associated with water. Yesod is also the seat of the sexual instinct, corresponding to the genital area when mapped upon the figure of Adam Kadmon, the archetypal human being. Yesod is the sphere of subconscious activity immediately entered through sexual magic and is the level of awareness activated through basic forms of witchcraft. The ancient rites of Wicca were primarily a form of lunar worship; the traditional dance around the maypole derived from the worship of an enlarged artificial phallus worn by the coven leader who assumed the role of the goat-headed god. Yesod is thus regarded as a transitional *sephirah* in which the individual's animal nature is resolved.

Hod

Associated with the planet Mercury – representing intellect and rational thinking – Hod is a lower aspect of the Great Father (Chokmah: Wisdom) for Mercury is the messenger of the gods. As the next stage beyond Yesod, Hod represents in some measure the conquest of the animal instincts, albeit at an intellectual rather than an emotional level. Hod symbolises the structuring principle in the universe and is considered a levelling and balancing *sephirah* which embodies a sense of order. It is in this capacity that we perceive 'God the architect' manifested in a world of myriad forms and structures.

Netzach

Associated with the planet Venus, Netzach complements Hod, for whereas Hod is to some extent clinical and rational, this *sephirah* represents the arts, creativity, subjectivity and the emotions. In the same way that Hod lies on the Pillar of Form (the left-hand pillar) on the Tree of Life, Netzach resides on the Pillar of Force (the right-hand pillar). It is outward-going in its emphasis, with an element of instinctual drive as opposed to intellect, and is the sphere of love and spiritual passion. A fine balance exists between Hod and Netzach upon the Tree of Life as the process of Creation weaves a fine web of love energy between the polarities of force and form. These potencies flow through the uniting *sephirah* of the Moon, lower on the Tree, and in turn are channelled through to the Earth, where they are perceived as the beauty innate within living forms.

Tiphareth

Just as Hod and Netzach are opposites, so too are Yesod and Tiphareth, for they are embodiments of the Moon (feminine) and Sun (masculine) respectively. If Yesod represents the animal instincts, Tiphareth is the mediating stage between humanity and the Godhead on the journey of mystical ascent. It is here that the individual experiences spiritual rebirth. The personality has acquired a sense of true and authentic balance and one's aspirations are now oriented towards higher states of being. Tiphareth is associated with deities of rebirth and resurrection and in a planetary sense with the Sun as a giver of life and light. Tiphareth is also the sphere of sacrifice, for the old limited and restricted persona is now offered in place of new understanding and insight. The individual now begins to function in a spiritual way.

Geburah

Associated with Mars, traditionally a god of war, Geburah represents severity and justice. The energies of Geburah are absolutely impartial, since there can be no flaw of self-pity or sentiment in the eye of a wise ruler. The destructive forces of this sphere are intended as a purging, cleansing force and are positive in their application. Geburah thus embodies a spiritual vision of power operating in the universe to destroy unwanted and unnecessary elements after their usefulness has passed. As an aspect of the ruler, demiurge, or 'Father of the gods' below the Abyss, Geburah shows discipline and precision in his destructiveness. His mission in the battlefield of the cosmos is to inculcate a rational economy of form which at a lower level upon the Tree is reflected in Hod.

Chesed

Associated with Jupiter, Chesed is the other face of the destructive ruler, and represents divine mercy and majesty. Geburah breaks down forms; Chesed is protective and tends to reinforce and consolidate. Whereas Mars rides in his chariot, Chesed is seated upon his throne, where he overviews his kingdom – the entire manifested universe. Through his stabilising influence the sacred potencies which originate in the transcendent spheres above the Abyss (i.e. at the level of the Trinity) are channelled down the Tree into various forms of being. Within Chesed are all archetypal ideas for he is mythologically located at the highest level of the collective unconscious.

Binah

At the first of the three levels known collectively as the Trinity we find the Great Mother in all her mythological aspects. She is the Womb of Forthcoming, the source of all the great images and forms which will enter the manifested universe as archetypes. She is also the supreme female principle in the process of Creation, and as such is invariably the mother of the god–man or messiah who in turn provides the bridge between humanity and the gods (or God). Binah is thus associated with the Virgin Mary, mother of Christ in Tiphareth, but she is also associated with Rhea and Isis. Because she is also so intimately connected with the archetypal world as the mother of Creation, she is often the wife of the ruler of the manifested universe. In this way Demeter, mother of Persephone, is the wife of Zeus.

Chokmah

The next of the Trinitarian god images is the Great Father. He provides the seminal spark of life which is potency only, until it enters the womb of the Great Mother. From the union of the Great Father and the Great Mother come forth all the images of Creation. Associated with those transcendent male gods whose realm lies beyond time and the manifested universe, Chokmah is associated with deities who sustain existence itself.

Kether

This stage of consciousness represents the first spark of Creation which emanates from beyond the veils of non existence (Ain Soph Aur – 'the Limitless Light'). Kether is located on the Middle Pillar of the Tree of Life and thus transcends the duality of male and female polarities. Sometimes represented as the heavenly androgyne for this reason, Kether represents a level of sublime spiritual transcendence.

Magic and the Senses

Although most of the Golden Dawn magicians focused their attention on mythic levels associated with the lower *sephiroth* of the Tree of Life, they nevertheless developed specific techniques for the expansion of spiritual awareness. These included a rich application of magical symbols and mythic imagery in their ritual adornments, ceremonial procedures and invocations, all of which were intended to focus the imagination during the the performance of a given magical ritual. In one of his most important books, Israel Regardie described magical ritual as 'a deliberate exhilaration of the Will and the exaltation of the Imagination, the end being the purification of the personality and the attainment of a spiritual state of consciousness, in which the ego enters into a union with either its own Higher Self or a God'.[2] MacGregor Mathers would surely have agreed with this definition.

Because the consciousness of the ceremonial magician is to be transformed in its entirety, any given ritual must enhance each of the senses in fine degree and with a specific purpose in mind. The way in which this is done can be summarised as follows:

Sight   The ritual robes, actions and implements are a visual representation relevant to the specific end which is sought (e.g. the invoking of a particular deity). In this drama carefully chosen colours and symbols play a paramount role. The ritual magician's vestments, and also the motifs mounted upon the wall of the Temple, are intended to stimulate the mythic imagination and help consolidate the spiritual connection with the gods and goddesses to whom the ritual is addressed.

Sound   This involves the vibration of sacred god names, chants or invocations (predominantly derived from the Kabbalah) whose auditory rhythms have a profound impact on one's consciousness.

Taste   This may take the form of a sacrament which relates symbolically to the nature of the god or goddess in the ritual.

Smell   Incense and perfumes may be used to increase the sense of rapport with a specific deity or being from the magical cosmology.

Touch   The magician endeavours to develop a sense of tactile aware-
         ness beyond the normal functions of the organism since
         assimilation with 'god-forms' takes place in a trance state. The
         magician's imaginal 'soul body' performs functions parallel to
         those undertaken in a physical context although here they
         are in a sacred ritual setting.

The Power of the Sacred Word

In the Western esoteric tradition, sound – and more particularly the
power of the magical utterance – has been traditionally emphasised as
being of central importance. According to the Kabbalistic *Zohar*, the
world was formed by the utterance of the sacred name of God, a
forty-two letter extension of the Tetragrammaton JHVH (*yod, he, vau,
he,* usually transposed as Jehovah or Yahweh). The word, or Logos,
therefore permeates the entire mystical act of Creation. Ritual magicians
both within the Golden Dawn and also in other magical orders have
held a similar view. According to the late Franz Bardon, 'the divine
names are symbolic designations of divine qualities and powers'[3] and
the nineteenth-century occultist Eliphas Levi stated in his seminal text
The Key of the Mysteries that 'all magic is in a word, and that word
pronounced Kabbalistically is stronger than all the powers of Heaven,
Earth and Hell. With the name of *Yod, He, Vau, He,* one commands
Nature . . .'[4]

In many ancient traditions the name was regarded as the very essence
of *being.* The Ethiopian Gnostics, in their sacred book *Lefefa Sedek,*
argued that God had created himself and the universe through the
utterance of his own name and therefore 'the Name of God was the
essence of God [and] was not only the source of His power but also
the seat of His very Life, and was to all intents and purposes His Soul'.[5]
In the apocryphal Gnostic-Christian literature we find the Virgin Mary
beseeching Jesus for his secret names since, as a source of power, they
were regarded as a protection for the deceased against all manner of
harmful devils. Similarly in the *Egyptian Book of the Dead* the deceased
newcomer to the Hall of Maat (Hall of Judgement) says to the deity
Osiris: 'I know thee. I know thy name. I know the names of the

two-and-forty gods who are with thee.'[6] For it follows that he who knows the secret name strikes home to the very heart of the matter, and has the ability to liberate his soul: he is in control, for the essence of the god is within his very grasp. According to the distinguished Egyptologist Sir Wallis Budge, in ancient Egypt 'the knowledge of the name of a god enabled a man not only to free himself from the power of that god, but to use that name as a means of obtaining what he himself wanted without considering the god's will'.[7]

In the Golden Dawn and elsewhere, magical ritual has invariably involved the invocation of beings or archetypal forces through the potency of the spoken word, and this also relates strongly to the idea of *will*, which distinguishes magic from passive forms of mysticism. As an initiated member of the Golden Dawn, Aleister Crowley took the magical name Perdurabo – 'I will endure to the end' – and he himself noted: 'Words should express will; hence the Mystic Name of the Probationer is the expression of his highest Will.'[8]

The Golden Dawn magicians believed that one of their most important goals was to communicate through the magical will with their higher self – often referred to as the Holy Guardian Angel – and this required a level of mystical awareness associated with the most transcendent levels of the Tree of Life.[9] Sometimes, too, it involved techniques of magical trance and 'rising in the planes' – which we will discuss subsequently. However, it is of interest here that Dion Fortune, who was a member of the Alpha and Omega Temple of the Golden Dawn, found it easier to project her 'body of light' when she uttered her magical name. In her book *Applied Magic* she writes:

In my own experience of the operation, the utterance to myself of my Magical name led to the picturing of myself in an idealised form, not differing in type, but upon an altogether grander scale, superhuman in fact, but recognisable as myself, as a statue more than life-size may yet be a good likeness. Once perceived, I could re-picture this idealised version of my body and personality at will, but I could not identify myself with it unless I uttered my Magical name. Upon my affirming it as my own, identification was immediate.[10]

The Symbols of Ritual Magic

We turn now to the actual symbols of ritual magic as it was practised in the Golden Dawn and also as it is found within derivative magical orders following the Golden Dawn tradition. The first of these is the place of the sacred working itself – the temple.

The temple contains all magical activities; it therefore represents the entire universe and, by inference, the magician himself, because of the relationship of the microcosm to the macrocosm. Upon the walls are mounted banners emblazoned with sacred symbols and colours appropriate to the mythic imagery of the ritual, and on the floor of the temple are certain inscriptions, the most important of which is the circle.

The circle incorporates many symbolic meanings but most significantly it represents the infinite Godhead – the alpha and omega – the divine self-knowledge which the magician aspires to. By standing in the centre of the circle, the magician is able to identify with the sacred source of Creation and consequently his magical will ensures that the 'ego-devils' of his lower self remain outside this sphere of higher aspiration.

The magician now takes on a role of authority in the sense that he intends to subject the invoked deity to his will. The god names, which have already been mentioned, are of vital importance in this respect. Inscribed around the periphery of the circle, these holy names stipulate the exact nature of the symbolic working. In addition, the circle may be circumscribed by an equal-sided geometric figure whose number of sides corresponds to the pertinent *sephirah* upon the Tree of Life. For example, a hexagram would be employed to invoke Osiris because as a god of rebirth Osiris is symbolically associated with Tiphareth, the sixth emanation upon the Tree.

The circle also contains a tau cross which, as an assertive masculine symbol, balances the receptive role of the circle itself – the two together producing an appropriate balance of opposites. The tau is made up of ten squares, one for each *sephirah*, and is vermilion in colour, as are the inscribed god names. The circle area is a complementary green. Nine equidistant pentagrams, each containing a small glowing lamp, surround the circle, and a tenth – the most important – hangs above the centre as a symbol of mystical aspiration. The circle must of course be large enough for the ritual magician to move around in. He must not leave it during the invocation, for to do so would destory its power as a focus for the magical will.

In terms of construction, where the circle is not a permanent fixture of the temple floor, it may be chalked in colour, or alternatively sewn or printed on cloth. Whenever the circle is already in existence, its sacred nature must be ritually reaffirmed in the mind of the magician, for otherwise the circle remains a profane symbol. The magician thus traces over its inscribed form with his ritual sword or outstretched hand, at the same time carefully reflecting upon the symbolic meaning of his action. If conditions for a temple working do not exist, the circle may be inscribed upon the ground – as in the case of working outdoors – or held within the imagination. The effectiveness of this latter type of circle naturally depends upon the magician's powers of visualisation.

Some magical rituals utilise the triangle, but this symbol has an essentially opposite role. Unlike the circle, which symbolises the infinite, the triangle represents finite manifestation, a focus for that which already exists. Symbolic of the triadic nature of Creation and the union of spiritual, mental and physical levels, the triangle represents evocation – a magical term for calling forth specific spirit-beings by means of spells or words of power.[11]

Like the circle, the triangle must be carefully constructed or mentally reinforced to impress the mind of the magician. In like fashion, the triangle must restrain the evoked entity, for otherwise the magician could lose control of the manifestation and might even find himself mentally conquered by it – that is to say, possessed. The magical talisman placed in the centre of the Triangle incorporates the seal, or sign, of the spirit and provides the focus of the ritual. Some ritual magicians have regarded evoked spirits as their 'spirit familiars' or 'astral guardians'. Evocation is more often than not associated with low magic rather than with the high magic of spiritual transformation, and it was not a central feature of the magic of the Golden Dawn temples. However, Mac-Gregor Mathers was fascinated by medieval tracts on the evocation of spirits and several such documents gained currency through his translations.[12] Aleister Crowley was also an enthusiastic practitioner of magical evocation.

Certain magical implements are also employed by the magician within the circle. Most of these objects are placed upon the central altar, which symbolises the foundation of the ritual itself. Consisting of a double cube of wood – usually made of acacia or oak – the altar has ten exposed faces, corresponding with the ten *sephiroth* upon the Tree of Life. The lowest face is Malkuth – the World – which represents things as they are in the manifested universe. The upper face represents Kether, the Crown – the First-Manifest – and Aleister Crowley recommended it be plated with gold, the metal of perfection. Upon the sides of the altar, Crowley wrote, one could inscribe 'the sigils of the holy Elemental Kings'.[13]

Placed upon the altar are certain symbolic implements designed to channel the imagination of the ritual magician towards transcendence:

The Holy Oil

This golden fluid is ideally contained in a vessel of rock crystal. In using it, the magician anoints the Four Points of the Microcosm (Kether, Chesed, Geburah and Malkuth) upon his forehead, left and right shoulders and solar plexus respectively, at the same time reflecting on the sacred task ahead. The holy ointment consists of the oils of olive, myrrh, cinnamon and galangual, these corresponding in turn to Chokmah (Wisdom), Binah (Understanding), Tiphareth (Harmony/Spiritual Awakening) and Kether-Malkuth (the so-called Greater and Lesser Countenance, the Union of Being and Creation upon the Tree of Life).

The Wand

This implement symbolises the pursuit of higher wisdom (Chokmah), achieved through the will. Symbolically the tip of the wand is in Kether, the first *sephirah* of the Tree of Life which contains the union of opposites and represents the transcendence of duality in all its forms. In the Golden Dawn a lotus wand was used which was multicoloured, with its upper end white and its lower, black. In between were twelve bands of colour corresponding to the different signs of the zodiac:

White	
Red	Aries
Red–orange	Taurus
Orange	Gemini
Amber	Cancer
Lemon–yellow	Leo
Yellow–green	Virgo
Emerald	Libra
Green–blue	Scorpio
Blue	Sagittarius
Indigo	Capricorn
Violet	Aquarius
Purple	Pisces
Black	

A lotus flower, with three whorls of petals, was placed upon the tip of the wand, the white end used for magical invocation, the black end for 'banishing', or removing malevolent forces.

The wand represents the first letter, *yod*, of the Tetragrammaton JHVH and also the element fire. The other ritual magical implements described here – the cup, sword and disc (also known as the pentacle) complete the sacred name of God and represent the elements water, air and earth respectively.

The Cup

As a feminine, receptive symbol, the cup aligns with Binah, the Mother of Understanding. The magician believes he must fill his cup of consciousness with an understanding and knowledge of his higher self. As a symbol of containment rather than of becoming, the cup is not used in rituals of invocation, but in ceremonies related to acts of manifestation.

The Sword

Indicative of the magician's mastery over evoked and invoked powers, the sword – which symbolises human force – parallels the wand, which represents divine power. Suggestive of control and order, the sword is the 'offspring' of wisdom and Understanding (Chokmah and Binah) and is therefore attributed to Tiphareth, the sphere of harmony. The symmetry of the sword is correspondingly appropriate. According to Aleister Crowley, the guard should consist of two moons waxing and waning, affixed to the back (Yesod) and the blade should be made of steel (corresponding to Mars). The hilt should be constructed of copper (the metal symbolically associated with Venus), indicating that ultimately the sword is subject to the rule of love. When the sword is placed symbolically upon the Tree of Life, the pommel rests in Daath – the 'sphere' associated with the Abyss beneath the Trinity – and the points of the guard lie in Chesed and Geburah. The tip rests in Malkuth. Crowley makes the observation that 'the Magician cannot wield the Sword unless the Crown is on his head'. That is to say, force and aspiration without inspiration are of no avail.

The Disc (Pentacle)

In the same way that the sword is paired with the wand – both being symbolically masculine – the disc is paired with the cup as a feminine symbol. Symbolic of Malkuth, the Heavenly Daughter and goddess of the manifest universe, the disc is said traditionally to 'induce awe' in the consciousness of the magician. Malkuth represents the first step upon the mystical journey back to the source of all being. It is also representative of the body of the magician which he would wish to be filled with the Holy Ghost, and symbolises the state of his personal being prior to spiritual transformation.

The ceremonial magician wears upon his head the crown, or headband, representative of Kether. Golden in colour, it is a symbol of aspiration towards the divine. Over his body falls the robe, whose function is to protect the magician from adverse 'astral' influences. Hooded, and normally black in colour, the robe symbolises anonymity and silence and is the dark vessel into which light will be poured. Attached to it or sewn across the chest is the lamen, or breastplate, which protects the heart (Tiphareth). And in the same way that Tiphareth is the focal point of all the *sephiroth* because of its central position upon the Tree of Life, the lamen has inscribed upon it symbols which relate to all aspects of the magical purpose. Considered an 'active' form of the passive disc, the lamen indicates strength. So too does the magical book, which the magician holds in his hands. This book contains all the details of one's ritual aims and practice and in a sense represents the unfolding 'history' of the effects of the magical will. As such, the magical book constitutes a steadfast symbol of power and resolve.

In addition, the ceremonial magician sometimes employs the use of a bell, worn on a chain around the neck. Representative of a state of alertness, it is said to be the bell that sounds 'at the elevation of the Host' and thus alludes to the sublime music of the higher spheres. In this respect the symbolism of the bell parallels that of the sacred lamp, which as 'the light of the pure soul' is positioned above the ritual implements on the altar and represents the descent of spirit into form, light into darkness, God into man. It stands for all that is eternal and unchanging and also represents the first swirlings of the primal energy in the universe ('Let there be light . . .'). 'Without this Light,' notes Aleister Crowley, 'the magicians could not work at all; yet few indeed are the magicians that have known of it, and far fewer they that have beheld its brilliance.'[14]

Magical Trance

Magicians working in the Golden Dawn tradition have often described the inner journeys of the psyche by referring to such terms as 'astral projection', 'pathworkings' and the 'body of light'. Essentially the trance meditation technique involves a transfer of focused awareness to the visionary world of symbols, through an act of willed imagination.

The Golden Dawn technique of magical trance combines bodily relaxation with a state of mental acuity, in which the magician focuses increasingly on his inner psychic processes. He may conjure specific images to mind, or endeavour to activate 'energy centres' within his spiritual body – equivalent to the chakras of yoga – while at the same time relaxing his body and restricting his outer vision.[15] Usually magical meditation of this type takes place in the dark: this enables the meditator to shift attention away from external visual stimuli to an inner perspective. The trance magician then attempts to reinforce the sense of the 'alternative reality' provided by the mythological images or visionary landscapes which arise as a result of willed imagination.

Personal accounts of magical trance are contained in a series of papers prepared by leading members of the Golden Dawn. These papers were known as 'Flying Rolls' and they include the magical records of Frater Sub Spe – Dr John W. Brodie-Innes – who was a prominent figure in the Golden Dawn's Amen-Ra temple in Edinburgh. Frater Sub Spe provides us with a graphic account of the switch in consciousness which takes place as one shifts one's field of awareness from the outer to the inner world:

> Gradually the attention is withdrawn from all surrounding sights and sounds, a grey mist seems to swathe everything, on which, as though thrown from a magic lantern on steam, the form of the symbol is projected. The Consciousness then seems to pass through the symbol to realms beyond . . . the sensation is as if one looked at a series of moving pictures . . . When this sensitiveness of brain and power of perception is once established there seems to grow out of it a power of actually going to the scenes so visionary and seeing them as solid, indeed of actually doing things and producing effects there.[16]

The Golden Dawn magicians also used the Tattva symbols of the five elements as an entry point for their magical visions. The Tattvas derive from Hindu mythology and are one of the few Eastern components directly incorporated within the Western esoteric tradition. In their basic form they are as follows:

Tejas, a red equilateral triangle	Fire
Apas, a silver crescent	Water
Vayu, a blue circle	Air
Prithivi, a yellow square	Earth
Akasha, an indigo or violet egg	Spirit

Golden Dawn Flying Roll XI describes a Tattva vision by Mrs Moina Mathers (Soror Vestigia) as she sat meditating in her ceremonial robes, contemplating a Tattva card combining Tejas and Akasha – a violet egg within a red triangle (spirit within fire). The symbol seemed to grow before her gaze, enabling her to pass into a 'vast triangle of flame'. She felt herself to be in a harsh desert of sand. Intoning the god name Elohim, she perceived a small pyramid in the distance and, drawing closer, she then noticed a small door on each face. She then vibrated the magical formula Sephariel and a warrior appeared, leading a procession of guards. After a series of tests involving ritual grade signs, the guards knelt before her and she passed inside:

> . . . dazzling light, as in a Temple. An altar in the midst – kneeling figures surround it, there is a dais beyond, and many figures upon it – they seem to be Elementals of a fiery nature . . . She sees a pentagram, puts a Leo in it [i.e. a fire sign], thanks the figure who conducts her – wills to pass through the pyramid, finds herself out amid the sand. Wills her return – returns – perceiving her body in robes.[17]

In this account and others like it, it is clear that the visionary landscape derives specifically from the focusing symbol. The intangible aspect of the vision – spirit – seems to be reflected in the mysterious and sanctified nature of the inner temple, which in this case the magician was privileged to enter. The beings which Moina Mathers perceived, however, were fire elementals, which, within the order of the occult hierarchy, are considered far beneath the level of gods. From a magical viewpoint we can see that this experience, while interesting, provided no profound insights of a self-transforming nature.

On another occasion, however, Moina Mathers was able to conjure beings of a more archetypal nature. Here she made use of the Tattva combinations water and spirit. Her account shows not only the link between the magical symbol and the visionary beings which appear, but also indicates the role of focused imagination:

> A wide expanse of water with many reflections of bright light, and occasionally glimpses of rainbow colours appearing. When divine and other names were pronounced, elementals of the mermaid and merman type [would] appear, but few of the other elemental forms. These water forms were extremely changeable, one moment appearing as solid mermaids and mermen, the next melting into foam.
>
> Raising myself by means of the highest symbols I had been taught,

and vibrating the names of Water, I rose until the Water vanished, and instead I beheld a mighty world or globe, with its dimensions and divisions of Gods, Angels, elementals and demons – the whole Universe of Water. I called on HCOMA and there appeared standing before me a mighty Archangel, with four wings, robed in glistening white and crowned. In one hand, the right, he held a species of trident, and in the left a Cup filled to the brim with an essence which he poured down below on either side.[18]

In this example, the perception of a hierarchy of magical beings and symbols actually produced a shift in consciousness. Moina Mathers was able to use a range of magical names to invoke beyond the level of the initial elemental symbols, causing an archangel to appear in her visions. She was also employing a technique known within the Golden Dawn as 'rising in the planes'.

Since occultists stress the role of the magical will and regard trance as a domain where the willed imagination actually produces perceptual effects, the technique of willing oneself to 'rise' meditatively from one level to another on the Tree of Life is crucial. In Flying Roll XI, MacGregor Mathers provides specific instructions on how this is achieved:

Rising in the Planes is a spiritual process after spiritual conceptions and higher aims; by concentration and contemplation of the Divine, you formulate a Tree of Life passing from you to the spiritual realms above and beyond you. Picture to yourself that you stand in Malkuth – then by use of the Divine Names and aspirations you strive upward by the Path of Tau towards Yesod, neglecting the crossing rays which attract you as you pass up. Look upwards to the Divine Light shining down from Kether upon you. From Yesod leads up the Path of Temperance, Samekh, the arrow cleaving upwards leads the way to Tiphareth, the Great Central Sun of Sacred Power.[19]

This practical magical advice points to the very heart of the visionary approach within the Golden Dawn. Mathers was showing his colleagues that a clear transcendental direction could be perceived, and the ecstasy of union with Tiphareth brought about, by visualising oneself coursing like an arrow to the higher realms. Here Mathers describes a twofold path from Malkuth through Yesod to Tiphareth: the mystical ascension of the Middle Pillar of the Tree of Life. However, there were other meditative paths upon the Tree of Life, and the Golden Dawn magicians utilised these as well. These were the paths connecting each of the ten *sephiroth* with each other – twenty-two paths in all – and they were symbolised by the Major Arcana of the Tarot.

The Mythic Doorways of the Tarot

Although Tattva meditations could clearly induce specific visionary states, the Golden Dawn magicians soon discovered that a more complete transformational process was possible by using the Major Arcana of the Tarot in conjunction with the Tree of Life. The Major Arcana are the twenty-two mythological cards of the Tarot deck as distinct from the 56 standard cards of the four suits, and their ascriptions upon the Tree of Life are as follows:

The World	Malkuth–Yesod
Judgement	Malkuth–Hod
The Moon	Malkuth–Netzach
The Sun	Yesod–Hod
The Star	Yesod–Netzach
The Tower	Hod–Netzach
The Devil	Hod–Tiphareth
Death	Netzach–Tiphareth
Temperance	Yesod–Tiphareth
The Hermit	Tiphareth–Chesed
Justice	Tiphareth–Geburah
The Hanged Man	Hod–Geburah
The Wheel of Fortune	Netzach–Chesed
Strength	Geburah–Chesed
The Chariot	Geburah–Binah
The Lovers	Tiphareth–Binah
The Hierophant	Chesed–Chokmah
The Emperor	Tiphareth–Chokmah
The Empress	Binah–Chokmah

The High Priestess	Tiphareth-Kether
The Magus	Binah-Kether
The Fool	Chokmah-Kether

We can now consider each of these mythological cards in turn.

The World

The World represents the descent into the underworld of the subconscious mind. In Greek mythology this theme is personified by the descent of Persephone into the land of the dead. However, symbolically, death is the obverse side of life and Persephone symbolises the wheat grain which grows and dies and undergoes a perpetual cycle of harvests. She dies to live again: her existence is manifest both in the realm of the living and of the dead. In the World she is androgynous, representing both male and female polarities despite her more obvious femininity. She dances within a wreath of wheat grains and around her are the man eagle, ox and lion, symbolic of spiritual resurrection. Her path is the first on the journey back to unity consciousness and she is a reflection of the highest *sephirah*, Kether, which is similarly androgynous – transcending duality.

Judgement

Judgement is similarly associated with a rebirth theme. Here we see figures rising from coffins, with their hands in the air. They are gesturing with their arms to form the word LVX – 'light' – as they rise in triumph from the grave of ignorance. One of the 'magical correspondences' for this path is Hephaestos, the blacksmith of Greek mythology, and the implication here is that the figures in the coffin are being reborn – their bodies fashioned anew – for the spiritual journey which lies ahead.

The Moon

The Moon typically mirrors the symbolism of the lunar sphere Yesod, and a lunar crescent dominates the imagery of the card. Two dogs are shown barking at the sky, one of them domesticated and the other untamed. The dog is sacred to the lunar goddess Hecate, who is also associated with Persephone in her deathlike aspect. Water is the predominant element here and it is interesting to note that Aphrodite, a goddess ascribed to the sphere of Netzach, is said to have been born in the foam. The Moon depicts the ebb and flow of the tides and is symbolic of spiritual evolution: a lobster is shown emerging from the sea to reinforce this effect.

The Sun

The Sun reflects the light of Tiphareth which is positioned above it on the Tree of Life. Young naked twins — a boy and a girl — are shown dancing in a magical ring beneath the Sun. They represent both a type of innocence and also the synthesis of opposite polarities — a common theme in the Tarot. They are clearly ruled by the Sun, representing unity and vitality and the path of enlightenment. However, here they are separated from the cosmic mountain by a wall. In an occult sense, the children are still young and inexperienced in their mystical quest and barriers still exist barring access to the more sacred regions of the Tree of Life.

The Star

The Star is associated with intuition, meditation and the hidden qualities of Nature, represented by Netzach. The beautiful naked White Isis — a lunar deity — kneels by a pool pouring water from flasks held in both hands. One of these flasks is made of gold (equating with the Sun) and the other is silver (equating with the the Moon). Reaching up towards a golden star in the sky, the goddess transmits its life energy down to the world below. She is a less transcendent aspect of the Great Mother archetype associated with Binah, a mediator between different worlds. The essential message of this card is that the magician, in his quest for the grail of enlightenment, will have to purify his vessel of perception if he is to be filled with the pure and abundant waters of spiritual insight and intuition.

The Tower

The Tower acts as a consolidation to the preceding experiences. Linking Hod and Netzach upon the Tree, it unites the intellect and rational thought identified with Hod and the intuitive, subjective qualities of Netzach. The symbolism of the card itself is instructive. Potentially the Tower reaches right up to Kether – that is to say, it embraces the entire universe. A lightning flash strikes its upper turrets causing it to crumble, and figures are shown falling to their death. The Tower serves as a reminder that humility is required on the inner journey, and that the influx of divine energy from the higher realms of the Tree will produce a devastating effect upon the magician unless his personality is well balanced and has a solid foundation. The Tower is ruled by Mars, who ruthlessly destroys ignorance and vain conceptions.

The Devil

Here we are shown a 'demonic' man and woman bound by chains to a pedestal upon which sits a gloating, torch-bearing Devil. Capricorn the goat represents darkness and bestiality. He has the legs of eagles, parodying the union of the symbolic opposites, air and earth, and upon his brow rests an inverted pentagram indicating that his spiritual aspirations are directed more towards earth than to the transcendent realms above. In this context the Devil reflects the plight of all unenlightened human beings, with their limited knowledge and understanding. Nevertheless, the light of Tiphareth lies beyond – so all is not lost.

Death

Like the Devil, Death indicates humanity's shortcomings and the limited, temporal nature of the ego-bound personality. But death is also symbolically the herald of new life, and beyond the scythe-wielding skeleton figure in the foreground we see new light appearing on the horizon. The scythe is associated with Kronos, the ancient Greek creator-god who transcended time, and the path of Death itself is also called Nun, meaning a fish. Christ was often symbolised by a fish ('I am a fisher of men') and Nun leads into Tiphareth, the sphere of spiritual awakening. Despite its confronting imagery, the path through Death takes us to rebirth.

Temperance

This card represents the line of direct mystical ascent to a state of spiritual illumination. The archangel of air, Raphael, stands in the desert, representing the arid toil of the dark night of the soul prior to spiritual fulfilment, and pours the waters of life from a Sun vessel into a Moon vessel. This constitutes a tempering, or union of opposites – a blending of solar and lunar energies. All aspects of the lower subconscious find their unity or resolution on this path for the elements are synchronised. Raphael has one foot on earth and the other in water and he is also shown reconciling an eagle (air) and a lion (fire). Above him arches a beautiful rainbow symbolising God's covenant with humanity, and new light is dawning over a distant mountain peak. One of the visions associated with Temperance is that of Sagittarius, the archer who fires his arrow aloft and who therefore symbolises spiritual aspiration. Tiphareth marks the halfway point between humanity and divinity: at this point the level of the god–man has been reached.

The Hermit

Like the venerable figure in Jewish mysticism – the Ancient of Days – a bearded patriarchal figure can be seen holding his lantern aloft as he scales the magical mountain. Having reached Tiphareth, the magician must find his way now to the mystical source of life in Kether. The path between Tiphareth and Chesed is ruled by Mercury who, in a higher symbolic form, equates with Chokmah and Thoth – the Great Father archetypes of the Kabbalah and the Egyptian mysteries. This path is also called Yod, and is ascribed to Virgo, showing that in some measure a union of sexual polarities has been achieved. The Hermit wends his way upwards, towards the hazards and loneliness of the Abyss on the Tree of Life. But his final goal is firmly in his mind, and the lamp held aloft illumines his pathway.

Justice

In Eastern mysticism Justice would be considered a path of karma – a path where one encounters the consequences of one's actions. Justice demands balance, adjustment and total impartiality. Ruled by Venus, it leads to the sphere of her lover Mars, and is appropriately designated by the figure of Venus holding scales and the sword of justice. She resembles Maat, the Egyptian goddess of truth, who resided in the Osirian Hall of Judgement and weighed the heart of the deceased against a feather. There Thoth, the Great Scribe, would record the verdict.

Since in the Hall of Judgement only truth can be admitted, the magician will not be able to proceed higher until he has made retribution for his karmic imperfections. This path therefore calls for a full identification with one's spiritual self. The magician must overcome the more wordly qualitities of the finite, earthbound personality which have always provided his security. He now finds himself having to obliterate pretence and the illusory aspects of outer appearances in the act of rediscovering the true inner person. Mars, god of war, characterises the assault upon, and destruction of, human imperfections as a barrier to true spiritual realisation.

The Hanged Man

This path, like that of Justice, leads to Geburah, the sphere of action. The Hanged Man swings by his foot, symbolising sacrifice, but because of his position he also seems like a reflection in water, the element ascribed to the path. His head is aglow and like a beacon he seems to be reflecting light through to lower levels of manifestation upon the Tree of Life. The waters themselves flow from Binah, the Great Mother, and the female symbol associated with this element is the cup. The magician must become a vessel for the influx of higher spiritual energies, and allow them to fill his being. If this is done he will begin to reflect the transcendental purity beyond the Abyss.

The Wheel of Fortune

Appropriately, this card symbolises the forces of fate and destiny. In the Kabbalah words composed of similar letters have related meanings and TARO or ROTA – the word inscribed upon the Wheel of Fortune – reads ATOR in reverse. This is a variant spelling of the white goddess Hathor, showing her influence on this path. As the American Golden Dawn magician Paul Foster Case has observed, 'The Wheel of Tarot speaks the Law of Hathor.'[20] However, the path leads to Chesed and understandably comes under the jurisdiction of Jupiter. Chesed lies in the region of pure archetypes – a realm of sacred being just below the Abyss which reflects the higher energies of the Trinity in their most pristine form. Since Kether is androgynous we would expect both female and male polarities to feature on this path, for the magical quest involves a fusion of opposites – mastery over duality.

Strength

This card is positioned horizontally across the Tree of Life and occupies an equivalent position to the Tower, but higher up. Whereas the Tower lies just below the Veil of Paroketh and separates the ego–based personality from the true spiritual self, Strength lies just below the Abyss – the gulf between individuality and universality. On this card we are shown a woman prising open the jaws of a lion – a clear indication of the triumph of spiritual intuition over brute strength. This symbolises complete mastery over any vestiges of the animal soul (Nephesch) that may have remained, and also represents the need for the magician to endure the karmic impact of earlier lessons arising from the spiritual quest.

The Chariot

The Chariot represents motion and is a direct reference to the Merkabah (= 'chariot') tradition in Jewish mysticism. Here the Chariot carries the king in his active aspect through the furthest reaches of his realm, while on the opposite side of the Tree, in Chesed, he views his kingdom from the stationary vantage point of his heavenly throne. On this path the king is empowered to bring down the watery potencies of Binah into archetypal manifestation. He is a mediator in the same way that the magician seeks to become a receptor or carrier of light. This is indicated by the central symbolism of the card, which is of the king bearing the Holy Grail. Aleister Crowley writes: 'It is of pure amethyst, of the colour of Jupiter, but its shape suggests the full moon and the Great Sea of Binah . . . spiritual life is inferred; light in the darkness.'[21]

The Lovers

On this path the Twins (Gemini) stand naked in the innocence of Eden regained, the Holy Guardian Angel towering above them and bestowing grace. As male and female representations of Tiphareth and Binah, they remind us of the love of the Great Mother (Mary: Binah) for her son (Christ: Tiphareth). Greek mythology records a legend showing a similar bond in the form of the half-brothers Castor and Polydeuces (Pollux) – one mortal and the other immortal. In love and compassion, Zeus allowed both of them a common destiny, placing them in the sky as the constellation known as Gemini. The path of the Lovers flows upwards from Tiphareth (Harmony) and shows the happy and enduring union of opposites.

The Hierophant

This path is that of 'triumphant intelligence'. The paternal, merciful qualities of the Great Father (Chokmah-Chesed) are enhanced by the love and grace of Venus, who rules this card. We find here an enduring bond of wisdom and mercy. The inspiration of the spirit manifests in the Hierophant as an archetypal expression of enlightened intuition. Divine authority owes its inspirational origin to this realm of the Tree of Life.

The Emperor

The Emperor faces towards Chokmah, the unmanifested Great Father above the Abyss, and draws upon his spiritual energy as a basis for his authority in governing the universe below. The Emperor transforms the lightning bolt by giving it archetypal potential. He is paternal, wise and vigilant – the 'Ancient of Days' as the Kabbalists have traditionally described him. In the Emperor we find the qualities of divine mercy, for although he is capable of aggression in his Geburah aspect, he extends compassion to his subjects. And the universe itself has come into being through his union with the Empress, the Womb of All Becoming.

The Empress

On this path the magician enters the realm of pure illumination. The Empress links Binah and Chokmah and thus encompasses the great archetypal opposites, the Great Mother and the Great Father. The Empress is warm and beneficent. Laden with child, she is symbolically the Mother of All, since from her womb will flow all the potential images and forms capable of existence in the entire cosmos. Mythologically she is Hathor and Demeter, a greater form of Aphrodite-Venus, and she epitomises love and nature on a universal scale. She sits in a field of wheat amid luxuriant trees, with the River of Life flowing forth from her domain.

The Empress is the feminine embodiment of the sacred life energy which emanates from a still higher source upon the Tree of Life.

The High Priestess

This path, unlike the Empress, reaches to the very peak of Creation – the first *sephirah*: Kether, the Crown. And the High Priestess herself has an element of untaintedness about her. She is of Kether, she reaches up beyond the Abyss, she is unsullied and virginal. As Paul Foster Case has said, if the Empress is a mother-goddess aspect of Venus, then the High Priestess is a transcendental aspect of Diana, the virgin lunar goddess.[22] In her aloof, transcendent condition she has the potential for motherhood but has not yet brought to fruition the possibility of giving birth – of bringing essence into form. To this extent she is a deity who belongs above the Abyss. Those who follow her path undergo a dramatic transformation. They begin to rise above form itself, returning to a virginal, undifferentiated state of being. They approach the crowning glory of Kether and begin to transcend duality.

The Magus

Linked mythologically to Mercury – the cosmic intelligence – the path of the Magus represents the masculine aspect of transcendental spirituality which has not yet found union with its feminine counterpart. Located above the Abyss, this path reflects a type of masculine purity which equates with the virginity of the High Priestess. The Magus stands above Creation in an archetypal sense. He raises one of his hands to Kether so that he may draw its energy down and transmit it to the lower reaches of the Tree of Life. Around him is the garden of Paradise, indicating that he has within his being a dimension which seeks further manifestation within the world of Nature. But he also has access to the divine mysteries, since his knowledge encompasses the sphere of Kether. One of his mythological forms is Thoth, the *logos* of the universe. He embodies the divine will of the Godhead: 'In the Beginning was the Word . . .'

It is interesting to note that Thoth was a presiding deity at the court of Osiris in the Egyptian underworld and it was he whose word was believed to sustain the universe. Thoth, as the Magus, represents the divine utterance – the sacred name – which makes accessible, and transmits, the light of Kether downwards into form.

The Fool

The Fool is a symbol for 'he who knows nothing', and this can be interpreted esoterically as well as in an everyday sense. On this path the magician draws near to the veil of nonexistence – No–Thing – that which is unmanifest, or beyond the tangibility of Creation. This is truly a realm of mystery and of this dimension of reality nothing can meaningfully be said, nor attributes ascribed. On the card itself we are shown the Fool about to plunge into the Abyss of formlessness, embracing the infinite and sacred transcendence of Ain Soph Aur, the limitless light. This equates with the Gnostic and Neoplatonic Pleroma, the Oneness which encompasses all that is or could ever be. It is the ultimate spiritual reality within the Western esoteric tradition.

The Tarot as a Meditative Journey

The Tarot card of the Fool completes the mythic journey upon the Tree of Life, and as we have seen this journey leads finally beyond form itself, yielding to sacred infinity. We are dealing here with transcendent realms of consciousness which extend far beyond intellectual understanding.

Nevertheless it was meaningful to the trance magicians of the Golden Dawn to explore the different Tarot paths upon the Tree of Life as a way of directly encountering the sacred archetypes of Western mythology.

When MacGregor Mathers devised the visualisation of 'rising in the planes' upon the Tree, he also ascribed Kabbalistic 'names of power' to each of the ten *sephiroth* and noted that different letters of the Hebrew alphabet could be visualised upon each of the Tarot paths, thereby intensifying and authenticating the trance visions as they arose:

> There are three special tendencies to error and illusion which assail the Adept in these studies. They are Memory, Imagination and actual Sight. These elements of doubt are to be avoided by the Vibration of Divine Names, and by the Letters and Titles of the 'Lords Who Wander' – the Planetary Forces, represented by the Seven double letters of the Hebrew alphabet.
>
> If the Memory entice thee astray, apply for help to Saturn, whose Tarot Title is the 'Great One of the Night of Time'. Formulate the Hebrew letter Tau in whiteness.
>
> If the Vision change or disappear, your memory has falsified your efforts. If Imagination cheat thee, use the Hebrew letter Kaph for the Forces of Jupiter, named 'Lord of the Forces of Life'. If the Deception be of Lying – intellectual untruth – appeal to the Force of Mercury by the Hebrew letter Beth. If the trouble be of Wavering of Mind, use the Hebrew letter Gimel for the Moon. If the enticement of pleasure be the error, then use the Hebrew letter Daleth as an aid.[23]

A trance vision recorded in November 1892 by Soror Sapientia Sapienti Dona Data (Florence Farr) and Soror Fidelis (Elaine Simpson) survives in Flying Roll IV. It is particularly interesting because it indicates the trance magician's direct sense of encounter with the deities upon the Tree of Life. A blend of Christian and Egyptian elements is apparent – the Grail Mother is regarded here as an aspect of Isis – and a ritual gesture appropriate to the Roman goddess Venus is also included, reflecting the eclectic blend of cosmologies found in modern magical visualisation:

> The Tarot Trump *The Empress* was taken; placed before the persons and contemplated upon, spiritualised, heightened in colouring, purified in design and idealised.
>
> In vibratory manner, pronounced Daleth. Then, in spirit, saw a greenish blue distant landscape, suggestive of medieval tapestry. Effort to ascend was then made; rising on the planes; seemed to pass up through clouds and then appeared a pale green landscape and in its midst a Gothic Temple of ghostly outlines marked with light.
>
> Approached it and found the temple gained in definiteness and was concrete, and seemed a solid structure. Giving the signs of the Netzach Grade (because of Venus) was able to enter; giving also Portal signs and 5° = 6° signs in thought form.[24] Opposite the entrance perceived a Cross with three bars and a dove upon it; and beside this were steps leading downwards into the dark, by a dark passage. Here was met a beautiful green dragon, who moved aside, meaning no harm, and the spirit vision passed on. Turning a corner and still passing on in the dark emerged from the darkness onto a marble terrace brilliantly white, and a garden beyond, with flowers, whose foliage was of a delicate green kind and the leaves seemed to have a white velvety surface beneath. Here there appeared a woman of heroic proportions, clothed in green with a jewelled girdle, a crown of stars on her head, in her hand a sceptre of gold, having at one apex a lustrously white closed lotus flower; in her left hand an orb bearing a cross.
>
> She smiled proudly, and as the human spirit sought her name, replied:
>
> *I am the mighty Mother Isis; the most powerful of all the world, I am she who fights not, but is always victorious, I am that Sleeping Beauty who men have sought, for all time; and the paths which lead to my castle are beset with dangers and illusions. Such as fail to find me sleep – or may ever*

rush after the Fata Morgana leading astray all who feel that illusory influence – I am lifted up on high and do draw men unto me. I am the world's desire, but few there be who find me. When my secret is told, it is the secret of the Holy Grail.

Asking to learn it, [she] replied:

Come with me, but first clothe in white garments, put on your insignia, and with bared feet follow where I shall lead.

Arriving at length at a Marble Wall, pressed a secret spring and entered a small compartment where the spirit seemed to ascend through a dense vapour, and emerged upon a turret of a building. Perceived some object in the midst of the place, but was forbidden to look at it until permission was accorded. Stretched out the arms and bowed the head to the Sun which was rising a golden orb in the East. Then turning, knelt with the face towards the centre, and being permitted to raise the eyes beheld a cup with a heart and the sun shining upon these; there seemed a clear ruby coloured fluid in the cup. Then 'Lady Venus' said:

This is love, I have plucked out my heart and have given it to the world; that is my strength. Love is the mother of the Man-God, giving the Quintessence of her life to save mankind from destruction, and show forth the path to life eternal. Love is the mother of Christ . . .

Spirit, and this Christ is the highest love – Christ is the heart of love, the heart of the Great Mother Isis – the Isis of Nature. He is the expression of her power – she is the Holy Grail, and He is the life blood of spirit, that is found in this cup.

After this, being told that man's hope lay in following her example, we solemnly gave our hearts to the keeping of the Grail; then, instead of feeling death, as our human imagination led us to expect, we felt an influx of the highest courage and power, for our own hearts were to be henceforth in touch with hers – the strongest force in all the world.

So then we went away, feeling glad that we had learned that 'He who gives away his life, will gain it.' For *that* love which is power, is given unto him – who hath given away his all for the good of others.[25]

As we can see from this fascinating trance account, the blend of magical archetypes employed within the Golden Dawn resulted in an eclectic visionary mix. This particular episode contained ancient Egyptian, Christian and Celtic elements, all of them seen as interrelated, and all of them regarded as part of an essentially integrated spiritual revelation.

However, not all of the Golden Dawn magicians were content with Tattva and Tarot meditations and visionary encounters upon the Tree of Life. It would fall to one of their number to produce an entirely new cosmology. This magician was Aleister Crowley, and he would come to regard himself as the Lord of the New Aeon.

4

Aleister Crowley and the Magick of the New Aeon

Widely regarded as the most controversial and infamous member of the Golden Dawn, Aleister Crowley would come to be known as the Great Beast 666 or, as London's *John Bull* magazine would have it, 'the wickedest man in the world'. He was nevertheless a ceremonial magician of considerable style and originality and his legacy continues in occult circles to the present day.

Born at Leamington Spa, Warwickshire, on 12 October 1875, Crowley was raised in a fundamentalist Plymouth Brethren home. His father was a prosperous brewer who had retired to Leamington to study the Christian scriptures. Crowley came to despise the Plymouth Brethren primarily on the basis of his unfortunate experiences at the special sect school in Cambridge which he was obliged to attend, run by an especially cruel headmaster. Much of his subsequent school education was also unhappy – marked by poor health and a vulnerability to bullying attacks – but after he went up to Trinity College, Cambridge, in 1895 he was able to spend much of his time reading poetry and classical literature as well as confirming his well-earned reputation as a champion chess player. Crowley had an adventurous spirit and would later become an enthusiastic mountaineer, joining an expedition in 1902 to scale K2 (also known as Chogo Ri or Mount Godwin-Austin) – at the time the highest peak in the world open to European climbers. But Crowley's direct association with the Western esoteric tradition really began in

London in 1898 with his introduction to George Cecil Jones, a member of the Golden Dawn. By the following year Crowley had also become a close friend of the magical initiate Allan Bennett, who for a time rivalled MacGregor Mathers as a dominant figure among the English occultists of the period. Within the Golden Dawn, Bennett took the magical name Frater Iehi Aour ('Let there be light') and he became something of a guru figure for the young Aleister Crowley. Bennett tutored Crowley in the diverse paths of magic, teaching him applied Kabbalah and the techniques of magical invocation and evocation, as well as showing him how to create magical talismans.

Crowley quickly grasped the fundamentals of magic – or magick, as he would later spell it in his own writings on the subject. In one of his most influential books, *Magick in Theory and Practice*, privately published in 1929 and frequently reprinted since, Crowley outlined the basic philosophy of magic as he had come to see it: essentially as a process of making man godlike, both in vision and in power. Crowley's magical dictums are instructive because they reveal the particular appeal that magic had for him:

A man who is doing his True Will has the inertia of the Universe to assist him.[1]

Man is ignorant of the nature of his own being and powers. Even his idea of his limitations is based on an experience of the past and every step in his progress extends his empire. There is therefore no reason to assign theoretical limits to what he may be or what he may do.[2]

Man is capable of being and using anything which he perceives, for everything that he perceives is in a certain sense a part of his being. He may thus subjugate the whole Universe of which he is conscious to his individual will.[3]

The Microcosm is an exact image of the Macrocosm; the Great Work is the raising of the whole man in perfect balance to the power of Infinity.[4]

There is a single main definition of the object of all magical Ritual. It is the uniting of the Microcosm with the Macrocosm. The Supreme and Complete Ritual is therefore the Invocation of the Holy Guardian Angel, or, in the language of Mysticism, Union with God.[5]

Crowley was initiated as a Neophyte in the Golden Dawn on 18 November 1898. He soon came to appreciate that those with the loftiest ritual grades were able to wield profound spiritual influence over their followers while also claiming rapport with the Secret Chiefs whose authority emanated from higher planes of existence. Keen to ascend to as high a rank as possible, Crowley took the grade of Zelator and then those of Theoricus and Practicus in the following two months. Initiation into the grade of Philosophus followed in May 1899, and he also became the first of the Golden Dawn magicians to attempt the fifteenth-century rituals of Abramelin the Mage, described in the grimoire (manual) which had been translated by MacGregor Mathers. During these rituals, which he performed in a house called Boleskine near Loch Ness in Scotland, Crowley had visions of Christ and then saw himself crucified. As his principal biographer, John Symonds, writes:

> He stood within the Divine Light with a crown of twelve stars upon his head; the earth opened for him to enter to its very centre, where he climbed the peak of a high mountain. Many dragons sprang upon him as he approached the Secret Sanctuary, but he overcame all with a word. This was an alchemical vision of his success in the Great Work. Crowley realised that he was born with all the talents required for a great magician.[6]

Apart from allegedly providing the magician with the services of 316 spirit advisers, the Abramelin system of magic was said to grant the practitioner communion with the Holy Guardian Angel, an embodiment in visionary form of one's higher spiritual self. But there was another potential benefit as well: such an experience would enable Crowley to claim spiritual parity with Mathers in the Golden Dawn. However, for the time being Crowley was content to consider Mathers an ally on the path to magical power.

Accordingly, having attained the grade of Philosophus within the Golden Dawn, Crowley contacted Mathers in Paris and asked for ritual entry into the Second Order – the Red Rose and the Cross of Gold.

In January 1900, under Mathers's supervision, Crowley was admitted 'to the Glory of Tiphareth' – the archetype of spiritual rebirth – and then returned to England, where he challenged the authority of William Butler Yeats, who was now the leader of the Golden Dawn in England. Yeats was unimpressed by this affrontery, regarding Crowley as an 'unspeakable mad person', and Crowley was unsuccessful in his bid for ritual supremacy. The dispute caused a rift in loyalties among the Golden Dawn membership, since Crowley had been sent by Mathers – and Mathers, in a letter to Annie Horniman, had claimed a spiritual autocracy and infallibility over the order as his right.

Having failed to dislodge Yeats as the head of the Golden Dawn, Crowley now suddenly switched course. Unpredictably and apparently acting on pure impulse, he withdrew from the dispute altogether. Instead, in June 1900, he embarked upon a series of travels through Mexico, the United States, Ceylon and India before finally arriving in Cairo – a location which would facilitate the announcement of a new magical universe.

A Revelation in Egypt

On 17 March 1904, in his apartment in Cairo, Crowley performed a magical ceremony invoking the Egyptian deity Thoth, god of wisdom. Crowley's wife Rose appeared to be in a dazed, mediumistic state of mind and the following day, in a similar state of drowsiness, announced that Horus was waiting for her husband. Crowley was not expecting such a statement from his wife but according to his diary she later led him to the nearby Boulak Museum, which he had not previously visited. There Rose pointed to a statue of Horus (in one of its several forms – this one being Ra-Hoor-Khuit) and Crowley was amazed to find that the exhibit was numbered 666, the number of the Great Beast in the Book of Revelation. Crowley regarded this as a portent and returned to his hotel, where he invoked Horus:

> *Strike, strike the master chord!*
> *Draw, draw the Flaming Sword!*
> *Crowning Child and Conquering Lord,*
> *Horus, avenger!*

On 20 March Crowley received a mediumistic communication through Rose that 'the Equinox of the Gods had come' and in the ensuing days he arranged for an assistant curator at the Boulak Museum to make notes on the inscriptions from stele 666. Rose meanwhile continued in a passive, introspective state of mind and advised her husband that precisely at noon on 8, 9 and 10 April he should enter the room where the transcriptions had been made and for exactly an hour on each of these three days he should write down any impressions received. The resulting communications, allegedly dictated by a semi-invisible Egyptian entity named Aiwaz (or Aiwass) – a messenger of Horus – resulted in a document which Crowley later titled *Liber Al vel Legis* (*The Book of the Law*), and this became a turning point in his magical career.[7] In this communication Crowley was instructed to drop the ceremonial magic he had learned in the Golden Dawn (*Behold! the rituals of the old time are black. Let the evil ones be cast away; let the good ones be purged by the prophet!*). Now he was being advised to pursue the magic of sexual partnership instead:

> *Now ye shall know that the chosen priest and apostle of infinite space is the prince-priest The Beast, and in his woman called The Scarlet Woman is all power given. They shall gather my children into their fold: they shall bring the glory of the stars into the hearts of men. For he is ever a sun and she a moon . . .*

Crowley now increasingly identified with the Horus figure Ra-Hoor-Khuit whose statue he had seen in the museum. He came to realise that Aiwaz equated with Hoor-paar-Kraat (or Harpocrates, the god of silence), an entity whose sacred origins lay above the Abyss. It was clear that he had contacted a Secret Chief without the assistance of Mac-Gregor Mathers.

In Egyptian mythology the deities Nuit (female-the circle-passive) and Hadit (male-the point-active) were said to have produced through their union a divine child, Ra-Hoor-Khuit. According to Crowley, this combination of the principles of love and will brought into incarnation the 'magical equation known as the Law of Thelema'.[8] *Thelema* is the Greek word for 'will' – Crowley was eclectic in both his linguistic applications and his use of mythic imagery – and the main dictum in his *Book of the Law* was 'Do what thou Wilt, Love is the Law, Love under Will'. By this he meant that one should live according to the dictates of one's true will, or spiritual purpose. Crowley believed his own destiny had been clearly indicated by the communication from Aiwaz. As Kenneth Grant has written:

> According to Crowley the true magical revival occurred in 1904, when an occult current of cosmic magnitude was initiated on the inner planes. Its focus was Aiwaz and it was transmitted through Crowley to the human plane . . . The initiation of this occult current created a vortex, the birth-pangs of a New Aeon, technically called an Equinox of the Gods. Such an event recurs at intervals of approximately 2000 years. Each such revival of magical power establishes a further link in the chain of humanity's evolution, which is but one phase only of the evolution of Consciousness.[9]

In terms of this new cosmological perspective, Crowley was the 'divine child' who had been chosen by transcendent forces to bring through to humanity a consciousness of the union of Nuit and Hadit. Previously, according to Crowley, there had been two other aeons – one associated with the Moon and the other with the Sun. The first of these, the Aeon of Isis, was a matriarchal age characterised by the worship of lunar deities: 'The Virgin,' said Crowley, 'contains in herself the Principle of Growth . . .' The second epoch, the Aeon of Osiris, was a patriarchal age: 'the formula of incarnating demi-gods or divine Kings, these must be slain and raised from the dead in one way or another.' Osiris and the resurrected Christ both belonged to this aeon and both had now been superseded by the Aeon of Horus.

'With my Hawk's head,' Ra-Hoor-Khuit (Horus) proclaims in *The Book of the Law*, 'I peck at the eyes of Jesus as he hangs upon the Cross. I flap my wings in the face of Mohammed and blind him.' Other religions would fall too: 'With my claws I tear out the flesh of the Indian and the Buddhist, Mongol and Din. Bahlasti! Ompedha! I spit on your crapulous creeds.'

The Age of Horus would be based on the union of male and female polarities. In one sense this meant that the legendary symbol of the androgyne – a sacred figure in spiritual alchemy – assumed special importance. According to Crowley, in this new aeon every man would have to learn to cultivate his female polarity – and, although Crowley doesn't specifically say so, presumably a woman would similarly have to explore her innate masculine potential. In *Magick in Theory and Practice*, Crowley writes:

> God is above sex, and so therefore neither man nor woman as such can be said fully to understand, much less to represent, God. It is therefore incumbent on the male magician to cultivate those female virtues in which he is deficient, and this task he must of course accomplish without in any way impairing his virility.[10]

However, since Crowley had received his revelation through a deity designated 666 in the Boulak Museum, it was clear to him now that he must also be the Great Beast 666 – the Anti-Christ referred to in the Book of Revelation. Crowley quickly came to believe that he was a new magical messiah – the Lord of the New Aeon – whose doctrine would supersede Christianity and all the other outmoded religions which had constructed barriers to spiritual freedom. For him the basis of this freedom was sexuality. In *The Book of the Law*, the lunar principle was rendered as Babalon, the Scarlet Woman. (He spelled it Babalon rather than Babylon for numerological reasons.) And the so-called Great Work – sacred union, or the attainment of absolute consciousness – would be achieved through the sexual union of the Great Beast with the Whore of Babalon: 'The Beast, as the embodiment of the Logos (which is Thelema, Will) symbolically and actually incarnates his Word each time a sacramental act of sexual congress occurs, i.e. each time love is made under Will.'[11]

According to Kenneth Grant, who knew Crowley towards the end of his life, Crowley maintained that in the Aeon of Horus, 'physical life is recognised as a sacrament. The sexual act of union for Crowley involved possession by the Highest Consciousness (namely Aiwaz).'[12] Crowley would spend much of his life from this time onwards seeking lovers and concubines who could act as his 'Divine Whore'. And while he would be frustrated in his numerous attempts to find a suitable and enduring partner, there were many who filled the role temporarily.[13]

Crowley was thus proposing a very different form of magic from that advocated within the Golden Dawn. Mathers had considered Osiris a supreme symbol of spiritual rebirth and had included references to this deity in the Tiphareth ritual of the Second Order. Crowley, on the other hand, was proclaiming something much more controversial. As the new avatar, he could offer his followers transcendental consciousness through the sacrament of sex:

> In sexual congress each coition is a sacrament of peculiar virtue since it effects a transformation of consciousness through annihilation of apparent duality. To be radically effective the transformation must be also an initiation. Because of the sacramental nature of the act, each union must be magically directed . . . the ritual must be directed to the transfinite and non-individualised consciousness represented by Egyptian Nuit . . . The earthly Nuit is Isis, the Scarlet Woman.'[14]

Crowley believed he was now able to supplant Mathers, not merely in terms of magical technique, but also by virtue of his own cosmological significance as Lord of the New Aeon. Crowley provides an interesting commentary on this issue in his *Confessions*:

> I was told that 'The Equinox of the Gods had come', that is, a new epoch had begun. I was to formulate a link between the solar-spiritual force and mankind. Various considerations showed me that the Secret Chiefs of the Third Order (that is of the A . ˙ . A . ˙ . whose First and Second Orders were known as the G. D. and R. R. et A. C. respectively) had sent a messenger to confer upon me the position which Mathers had forfeited.[15]

Having received the communication from Aiwaz, Crowley now believed he could speak 'with absolute authority'.[16] Thelema, he noted,

> implies not merely a new religion, but a new cosmology, a new philosophy, a new ethics. It co-ordinates the disconnected discoveries of science. Its scope is so vast that it is impossible even to hint at the universality of its application . . . [The Aeon of Horus, that of the Crowned and Conquering Child] is not merely a symbol of growth, but of complete moral independence and innocence. We may then

expect the New Aeon to release mankind from its pretence of altruism, its obsession of fear and its consciousness of sin.[17]

In a sense Crowley was echoing the thoughts of Freud, whom he greatly admired. Freud held that there were three essential stages of personal growth in an individual: narcissism (self-centredness), dependence on one's parents, and maturity. Freud correlated these psychological stages with magical, religious and scientific perspectives respectively. But Crowley's magic was no mere magic; it was an application of solar-spiritual energy which could now embrace science by opening up 'an entirely new avenue to knowledge' as a result of 'a direct communication from some intelligence superior in kind to that of any incarnate human being'.[18] As such the Law of Thelema would provide a true liberation from the maternal and paternal forms of magic and religion which had existed in earlier periods of human history.

Crowley now felt obliged to let Mathers know that the Golden Dawn approach to magic had been well and truly superseded. As he notes in his *Confessions*:

> I wrote a formal note to Mathers informing him that the Secret Chiefs had appointed me visible head of the Order, and declared a new Magical Formula. I did not expect or receive an answer. I declared war on Mathers accordingly . . .[19]

Nevertheless, the next three years proved to be something of a magical hiatus for Aleister Crowley. For some time after the Cairo revelation he did not fully engage with the implications of *The Book of the Law* – perhaps he felt daunted by the cosmic role to which he had been appointed. It was, after all, a substantial task to take on the mantle of Lord of the New Aeon and sweep away centuries of earlier religious history – even if he had a deep personal conviction that these religions were completely misguided. Ironically, the manuscript of *The Book of the Law* was temporaily mislaid until Crowley discovered it again in an attic, in 1909.

After the extraordinary events in Cairo Crowley returned to Boleskine with Rose, who was now pregnant and would soon give birth to their daughter Nuit Ma Ahathoor Hecate Sappho Jezebel Lilith. Crowley also founded a publishing company called the Society for the Propagation of Religious Truth as an outlet for his erotic poetry. And soon he was planning a mountain trip to Kangchenjunga, the world's third highest mountain – but this would end in tragedy, with the deaths of several porters in an avalanche. Devastated by this outcome, Crowley wrote an impassioned letter to his brother-in-law Gerald Kelly:

> I say today: to hell with Christianity, Rationalism, Buddhism, all the lumber of the centuries. I bring you a positive and primaeval fact, Magic by name: and with this I will build me a new Heaven and a new Earth. I want none of your faint approval or faint dispraise; I want blasphemy, murder, rape, revolution, anything, bad or good, but strong.[20]

From Abramelin to Algeria – and Beyond

Despite the communications from Aiwaz, Crowley was still seeking a full spiritual experience of his Holy Guardian Angel and after a period of travel through China and North America in 1905–06 he once again turned his attention to the potent evocations of Abramelin the Mage. However, though his letter to Gerald Kelly had called for strength, the initial result of these new ritual magical workings was quite different – inducing a state of reverie which enabled Crowley to commence work on a series of mystical tracts he called the *Holy Books*. Spanning a period of four years between 1907 and 1911, these works were not the result of dictation like *The Book of the Law* but had come to Crowley almost like automatic writing: 'I can only say that I was not wholly conscious at the time of what I was writing . . .' The *Holy Books* are among Crowley's most sublime mystical writings and reveal an aspect of the man which stands in marked contrast to his more assertive and wilful persona:

> Into my loneliness comes
> The sound of a flute in dim groves that haunt the uttermost hills
>   Even from the brave river they reach to the edge of the
>   wilderness
> And I behold Pan . . .

But despite the inspirational quality of his *Holy Books*, the year 1907 was also a turning point for Crowley. He would later reflect on it as the year he 'went wrong', a time when he could, perhaps, have 'turned back'.[21] That year marked the establishment of Crowley's new magical order, the Argenteum Astrum, or Silver Star. Crowley mentions in a letter to John Symonds that at this time he took an oath to devote himself 'wholly to the uplifting of the human race',[22] and initially the Argenteum Astrum seems to have been quite innocuous, drawing as it did on conventional borrowed sources. Crowley had begun rewriting Mathers's rituals, employing an amended form of the Golden Dawn grades as well as including some yogic and Oriental material of his own. He also published the secret rituals of Mathers's Second Order, the Red Rose and Cross of Gold, in his occult journal *The Equinox*. Interestingly, although Crowley had made a commitment to the sex magic proclaimed in *The Book of the Law*, he did not initially include it within the grades of his new magical order. But the A ∴ A ∴ would nevertheless gradually develop as a vehicle for Crowley's increasingly explicit bisexuality, and this would eventually bring Crowley's sex-magic activities into public disrepute.

One of the early members of the A ∴ A ∴ was Victor Neuburg, a young poet who, like Crowley, had studied at Trinity College, Cambridge. Crowley heard about Neuburg from another A ∴ A ∴ member, Captain J. F. C. Fuller, and was interested to learn that Neuburg had experimented with mediumship. Crowley invited Neuburg to Boleskine and there he demonstrated a remarkable facility for 'rising in the planes', at one stage having a vision of the archangel Gabriel, clad in white, with green spots on his wings and a Maltese cross on his head.[23] Crowley recognised in Neuburg a kindred spirit, and they would soon enter into a homosexual magic liaison tinged with sado-masochistic tendencies, which would last until 1914.[24]

After a painful divorce from his wife Rose in 1909, Crowley went with Neuburg to Algeria, where they intended exploring the Enochian magic of the sixteenth-century occultists Dr John Dee and Edward Kelley. This involved conjuring thirty so-called 'Aethyrs' or 'Aires' – magical entities from another dimension of time and space. Deep in the Algerian desert, at such locations as Aumale, Ain El Hajel, Bou-Saada, Benshrur, Tolga and Biskra, Crowley summoned the different Aethyrs in turn. Crowley was carrying with him a large golden topaz set in a wooden rose-cross decorated with ritual symbols. Choosing a place of solitude, Crowley would recite the required Enochian conjuration and then use his topaz as a focusing glass to concentrate his attention on the visionary landscape as it unfolded before his gaze. As a result of his Enochian 'calls' Crowley had a number of visionary experiences which were then transcribed by Neuburg as they occurred.

Crowley's visions included 'spirit-journeys' to magical mountains and sacred shrines, as well as mystical encounters with archetypal beings, temple guardians and other mythological entities. Indeed, his visions are reminiscent of Gnostic apocalypses. Here is an extract from Crowley's conjuration of Aethyr 24, *Nia*, which provides something of the flavour of the enterprise:

An angel comes forward into the stone like a warrior clad in chain-armour. Upon his head are plumes of grey, spread out like the fan of a peacock. About his feet a great army of scorpions and dogs, lions, elephants, and many other wild beasts. He stretches forth his arms to heaven and cries: In the crackling of the lightning, in the rolling of the thunder, in the clashing of the swords and the hurling of the arrows: be thy name exalted!

Streams of fire come out of the heavens, a pale brilliant blue, like plumes. And they gather themselves and settle upon his lips. His lips are redder than roses, and the blue plumes gather themselves into a blue rose, and from beneath the petals of the rose come brightly coloured humming-birds, and dew falls from the rose – honey-coloured dew. I stand in the shower of it.

And a voice proceeds from the rose: Come away! Our chariot is drawn by doves. Of mother-of-pearl and ivory is our chariot, and the reins thereof are the heart-strings of men. Every moment that we fly shall cover an aeon. And every place on which we rest shall be a young universe rejoicing in its strength; the meadows thereof shall be covered with flowers. There shall we rest but a night, and in the morning we shall flee away, comforted.

Now, to myself, I have imagined the chariot of which thee spake, and I look to see who was with me in the chariot. It was an Angel of golden skin, whose eyes were bluer than the sea, whose mouth was redder than the fire, whose breath was ambrosial air. Finer than a spider's web were her robes. And they were of the seven colours.[25]

However, if this particular aethyr had its idyllic aspects, some of the other visionary encounters were more confronting. The most dramatic of these was the tenth aethyr, *Zax*, which included an encounter with the 'mighty devil' Choronzon.

Crowley already knew that the tenth Aethyr was 'accursed' and he marked out a magical circle in the sand dunes, fortifying it with sacred god names to protect his friend. He then traced the triangle in which he would evoke Choronzon, inscribing its sides with the magical names Anaphaxeton, Anaphaneton and Primeumaton — a protection to deter Choronzon from breaking free after he had been evoked.

Crowley and Neuburg made a blood sacrifice within each point of the triangle, cutting the throats of three pigeons which they had brought with them, and taking great care that all the blood was contained within the triangle itself. Neuburg now entered the magical circle with his ritual sword, dagger and writing equipment, while Crowley undertook the much riskier role of entering the triangle where the spirit of Choronzon would be evoked. 'This', writes John Symonds, 'is the only recorded instance of a magician's seating himself in the triangle of exorcism instead of remaining within the protection of the magic circle. It was to invite obsession by the demon when he was evoked into the triangle.'[26]

Crowley made the conjuration and now began to describe to Neuburg what he saw in the topaz. According to the scribe's account, it did not take long for Choronzon to appear from the outermost Abyss. Here are the opening lines of commentary for the tenth Aethyr from *The Vision and the Voice*:

There is no being in the outermost Abyss, but constant forms come forth from the nothingness of it.

Then the Devil of the Aethyr, that mighty devil Choronzon, crieth aloud, *Zazas, Zazas, Nasatanada Zazas.*

I am the Master of Form, and from me all forms proceed. I am I. I have shut myself up from the spendthrifts, my gold is safe in my treasure-chamber, and I have made every living thing my concubine, and none shall touch them, save only I. And yet I am scorched, even while I shiver in the wind. He hateth me and tormenteth me. He would have stolen me from myself, but I shut myself up and mock at him, even while he plagueth me. From me come leprosy and pox and plague and cancer and cholera and the falling sickness. Ah! I will reach up to the knees of the Most High, and tear his phallus with my teeth, and I will bray his testicles in a mortar, and make poison thereof, to slay the sons of men . . .[27]

Unfortunately Neuburg now began hallucinating, seeing within the magic triangle not Crowley but a beautiful Parisian courtesan with whom he had earlier fallen in love. Then, suddenly, Choronzon himself appeared within the triangle:

. . . the terror of darkness, and the blindness of night, and the deafness of the adder, and the tastelessness of stale and stagnant water, and the black fire of hatred, and the udders of the Cat of slime; not one thing but many things. Yet with all that, his torment is eternal. The sun burns him as he writhes naked upon the sands of hell, and the wind cuts him bitterly to the bone, a harsh dry wind, so that he is sore athirst . . .[28]

Choronzon called out to Neuburg for water, but the scribe refused to cooperate. An exchange of taunts now began, with Neuburg summoning the highest god names he knew as a protection. Meanwhile Choronzon proceeded to utter a challenge, apparently unfazed by Neuburg's responses: *I feed upon the names of the Most High. I churn them in my jaws, and I void them from my fundament. I fear not the power of the Pentagram, for I am the Master of the Triangle . . .*

However, from a ritual magic point of view, a more serious event was about to occur. The figure in the triangle – Choronzon or Crowley, Neuburg could hardly distinguish between them now – began throwing sand from the triangle across the defining line of the magical circle, breaking its circumference and thus exposing Neuburg to the conjured devil. 'Choronzon, in the form of a naked savage, leapt from the triangle into the circle, and fell upon Neuburg, throwing him to the ground. "He flung him to the earth," said Crowley, "and tried to tear out his throat with his froth-covered fangs." '[29]

Fortunately, Neuburg was able to ward him off with his magical dagger, although he then transformed once again into the beautiful French courtesan. There was 'an unsuccessful seduction scene' as the bisexual Crowley – or Choronzon – endeavoured to bring the conjuration towards a sense of completion.

Although the ritual finally resolved itself without serious injury, this particular episode was surely a lesson to a novice magician like Victor Neuburg that magical entities like Choronzon were powerful entities, and not to be taken lightly. The Choronzon encounter also provides us with a powerful insight into the experiential realities of ceremonial magic, and shows how unintended changes to forms of ritual protection can produce dramatic and unforeseen effects.

Meanwhile, back in England the Argenteum Astrum was beginning to grow modestly, building on its core membership, which included Captain J. F. C. Fuller and Crowley's old teacher George Cecil Jones. It would in due course initiate around a hundred of Crowley's followers, among them Neuburg's friend and fellow poet Pamela Hansford Johnson, the Australian violinist Leila Waddell, the mathematics lecturer Norman Mudd from Bloemfontein, and the visionary English artist Austin Osman Spare.

Events took a strange turn in 1912 when Crowley was suddenly contacted one evening at his London flat by a man named Theodore Reuss. Reuss identified himself as the head of a German masonic order called the Ordo Templi Orientis (Order of the Temple of the East) and said he was outraged that Crowley had published a statement which revealed the most prized secret of the order's ninth degree – the sacrament of magical sex.

Crowley was initially perplexed by Reuss's accusation and wondered which publication he was referring to. Reuss then reached across to Crowley's bookshelf and pulled down a copy of his recently published work *The Book of Lies*, a collection of magical commentaries and reflections. There, in the section entitled 'The Star Sapphire', were the offending lines: 'Let the Adept be armed with his Magick Rood and provided with his Mystic Rose.'

Crowley was amazed. He pointed out to Reuss that he hadn't actually taken the ninth degree of the OTO, so he could hardly be in a position to reveal its secrets. In 'The Star Sapphire' Crowley had used the Old

English word *rood* to mean a cross, but Reuss had assumed that he was referring to the phallus. As they were speaking Crowley realised intuitively that sexual intercourse between priest and priestess must be a culminating event in the ritual of the OTO's ninth degree, and he now engaged Reuss in a discussion about sex magic which lasted for several hours. The outcome was that Crowley would become the head of a new magical order to be called the Mysteria Mystica Maxima, effectively an English subsidiary of the Ordo Templi Orientis.

In due course Crowley visited Berlin, where he received instructional documents from the OTO. He was also granted the grandiose title 'King of Ireland, Iona and all the Britains within the Sanctuary of the Gnosis' and took Baphomet as his new magical name. Later Crowley would adapt the ninth degree of the OTO so that it identified the priest and priestess as Osiris and Isis, 'seeking Nuit and Hadit through the vagina and the penis'. And he would also develop a series of homosexual magical rituals with Victor Neuburg featuring invocations to Thoth-Hermes. At one point in these rituals – which became known collectively as the Paris Working – Crowley scourged Neuburg on the buttocks and cut a cross on his chest.[30]

If Crowley's magic was becoming debased and increasingly sadistic, his public notoriety still lay ahead. On 1 March 1920, following receipt of a modest inheritance from a deceased aunt, Crowley consulted the *I Ching* – the ancient Taoist oracle – about where he ought to go to start the Great Work, the Law of Thelema. The oracle provided a negative response for Marseille and Capri but seemed to favour Cefalu, a small port in northern Sicily. So on 22 March Crowley set off to his new destination. With him was a French woman, Ninette Shumway, and her young son, and he would soon be joined by Leah Hirsig, who had already become his Scarlet Woman and had borne him a daughter, Poupée. Leah was in London on a financial errand but would soon return.

In Cefalu Crowley learned there was a villa to rent. Set amid olive groves, it was really more like a run-down farm, but the views of Palermo were excellent and there were abundant flowers and fruit trees in the garden. The mighty rock of Cephaloedium lay away to the north and an ancient temple dedicated to Jupiter was also close at hand. So Crowley decided to take the villa and soon began the process of converting it into an Abbey of Thelema. At last he would have a sanctuary where he could explore sex magic in earnest. Crowley referred to it as his *Collegium ad Spiritum Sanctum*.

Five rooms adjoined a central hall which would become the temple of Thelemic mysteries, and Crowley painted a magic circle, superimposed with a pentagram, on the red-tiled floor. In the centre of the circle was a six-sided altar complete with full occult regalia – bell, lamen, sword and cup – and a copy of *The Book of the Law* took pride of place with six candles on each side. Crowley's 'throne of the Beast' was in the eastern quarter of the temple, facing the altar, and another throne for the Scarlet Woman was located in the west. Painted around the inside of the magic circle were Hebrew names of God.

Crowley's quasi-pornographic paintings soon adorned the walls of the other rooms. One was of a naked man being sodomised by the great god Pan while simultaneously ejaculating over the Whore of Stars; another featured a phallic serpent. Crowley maintained that by seeing sexually explicit paintings on the walls, people would in time come to view them indifferently and would therefore lose any inhibitions about sex.

Crowley had by now assumed the grade of Magus – the occult equivalent of Gautama Buddha – and was calling himself Mega Therion 666. Leah was known as Alostrael and Ninette as Sister Cypris, or Beauty. Crowley considered both of them his concubines, although Leah remained his Scarlet Woman.

Nevertheless, there were aspects of daily life in the Abbey that were quite formal. Early each morning Crowley's dictum would be proclaimed: 'Do what thou wilt shall be the whole of the Law', followed by a response from everyone present: 'Love is the Law, love under will.' Then there would be an adoration to Ra in the form of prayers to the Sun. Breakfast began with a series of ritual knocks – three for Saturn, five for Mars, eight for Mercury (these being their numerical equivalents on the Tree of Life) – and then the business of the day would commence. Meals were eaten in silence and in the evening there was a further adoration to the Sun, followed by a reading from *The Book of the Law*. Crowley also planned a routine for newcomers:

1st week: Three days' hospitality. One day's silence. Three days' instruction. The Magical Oath, followed by four weeks' silence and work.

6th week: One day's instruction
7th to 9th week: Three weeks' silence and work
10th week: One week's instruction and repose
11th to 13th week: Three weeks' silence and work[31]

There was a steady stream of visitors to the Abbey. Among them were the American film actress Jane Wolfe (who was much less glamorous than Crowley anticipated); Cecil Frederick Russell, a hospital attendant whom Crowley had met in New York and who had been thrown out of the navy for taking cocaine (Crowley enjoyed discussing different types of drug experiences with him); a Lancashire bricklayer, Frank Bennett (who was also a member of Crowley's A.˙.A.˙.: as well as the OTO); the novelist Mary Butts and her lover Cecil Maitland; and Ninette's sisters Mimi and Helen. It wasn't long before Mary Butts and Cecil Maitland left for Paris. They were quite appalled by what they saw at the Abbey – the main images engraved in their minds being the ritual 'baptism' of a cockerel slain in honour of Ra-Hoor-Khuit, and the extraordinary spectacle of Crowley's Scarlet Woman endeavouring to copulate with a billy-goat.

Maintaining the Abbey was a drain on meagre resources and inevitably Crowley once again began to run short of money. For a brief period he returned to England and while there had the good fortune of meeting the novelist J. D. Beresford, an adviser to the London publisher William Collins. As a consequence Collins signed Crowley up for his first commercial book venture: *Diary of a Drug Fiend*. He also received a contract from Rider to translate *The Key of the Mysteries* by the nineteenth-century French occultist Eliphas Levi. So with some advance royalties and the promise of being able to make an income through writing, he returned to Cefalu.

He now awaited the arrival of a new follower, Raoul Loveday, an Oxford history graduate who had studied *The Equinox* with great interest. Loveday would come with his wife Betty May, an artist's model who had at one time posed for the famous sculptor Jacob Epstein. Having engrossed himself in the works of the Great Beast, Loveday was extremely anxious to meet Crowley in person. Betty was not so enthusiastic, but together they arrived in Cefalu in November 1922.

Loveday immediately fell in love with the surroundings. He warmed to the 'huddle of high lemon-coloured houses lying between the paws of a titanic rock fashioned roughly like a crouching lion' and he felt a sense 'of exultation as [he] stood there inhaling the sweet morning air . . .'[32] Betty, on the other hand, was soon moping about, complaining about the lack of food and the poor sanitation.

Crowley installed Loveday as high priest of the Abbey and was most impressed by his new recruit. Loveday, said Crowley, 'possessed every qualification for becoming a Magician of the first rank. I designated him from the first interview to be my Magical heir.' Crowley gave him the title of Frater Aud, meaning 'magical light'.

Raoul and Betty soon settled in to daily life at the Abbey. Like all male members of the Thelemic group, Raoul had to shave his head, leaving a phallic forelock; Betty, like the other women at the Abbey, was obliged to dye her hair either red or gold to symbolise the magical energy of Horus.

Another of the practices promoted at the Abbey was that only Crowley was allowed to use the word 'I'. His followers had to learn to repress their egos and were supposed to slash their bodies with a cut-throat razor every time they used the offensive word. Loveday's body was soon covered with cuts and it is possible that this caused a serious blood infection. Loveday did not have a strong constitution and another factor that no doubt contributed to his rapid decline in health was the ritual sacrifice of the Abbey's cat Mischette – for Loveday drank some of its blood from a silver cup. Soon afterwards a Palermo physician, Dr Maggio, diagnosed Loveday's condition as an infection of the liver and the spleen. Betty understandably became very alarmed; she felt that her husband had been poisoned.

By 14 February 1923 Loveday's state of health had declined still further – he was now diagnosed with acute enteritis – and two days later he died. Proclaiming the passing of a worthy follower of Thelema, Crowley and the other members of the Abbey presided at his funeral with appropriate magical rites and readings from *The Book of the Law*, and he was buried in the local cemetery.

Loveday's death precipitated a torrent of bad publicity for the Abbey of Thelema. Betty May returned to England, her fare paid by the British consul in Palermo, and she was immediately interviewed by the *Sunday*

Express, which on 25 February ran an explosive headline across its front page: 'New sinister revelations of Aleister Crowley.' Gruesome details were included in the article, many of them inaccurate, and a tide of adverse publicity was building against the Great Beast. It didn't help that Crowley's *Diary of a Drug Fiend* had been released in England just four months earlier, for it too had attracted venomous coverage in the *Sunday Express* and in other sections of the media. Mary Butts had also been interviewed, and spoke of 'profligacy and vice' in the Abbey of Thelema, while *John Bull* added salt to the wound by dubbing Crowley 'the wickedest man in the world'. In England Crowley's name had now became publicly synonomous with bestiality and depravity.

Back in Cefalu, worse was to come: Crowley was summoned to the local police station on 23 April 1923 and told he had to leave Sicily. Italy now had a new leader, Benito Mussolini, and Mussolini didn't approve of secret societies. The Italian authorities had read all about the Argenteum Astrum and the OTO in the London newspapers, and Crowley would have to go immediately.

One can argue that with the demise of the Abbey of Thelema, Crowley's magical career was effectively over. It is true that two years later, in 1925, Crowley was invited by the German occultist Heinrich Traenker to become the international head of the OTO (although a substantial minority of German members rejected both Crowley and *The Book of the Law*[33]) and that the OTO would subsequently take root in Britain and the United States, albeit with different figures in charge. It is also true that Crowley would assist Gerald Gardner in formulating a practical approach to contemporary witchcraft – like Crowley, Gardner was fascinated by sex-magic rituals. But by the end of the 1920s one senses that Crowley's path as a magician was in steady decline. Most of his best writings and his most innovative ideas were now behind him – a notable exception being his work on the Tarot, *The Book of Thoth*, published in 1944, three years before his death.

And yet for all his notoriety, there can be no denying that Aleister Crowley succeeded in making himself an icon of the modern magical revival. His place in occult history is assured – he remains much better known than MacGregor Mathers, whose works he copied and adapted, and he is certainly much more famous than his original teacher Allan Bennett, who introduced him to practical techniques of magic and yoga. One can even argue that Crowleyanity has continued as a minor religion to this day – Kenneth Grant continues to assert the continuity of Crowley's occult vision in the 'typhonic' tradition of the British OTO and in the United States Crowley's influence has even extended to the Temple of Set, the successor to Anton LaVey's Church of Satan. So how can we assess the influence of the Beast?

The Legacy of Aleister Crowley

Among the most enduring aspects of Aleister Crowley's magical perspective are his systematic approach to transcendent levels of magical and mystical consciousness, his emphasis on an ongoing personal commitment to ceremonial techniques and visualisation – the hard work of practical magic – and also his particular focus on self-empowerment. In *The Book of the Law*, in addition to his most famous dictum 'Do what thou wilt shall be the whole of the Law', we also read 'Every man and woman is a star.' According to *The Book of the Law*, all human beings are essentially lights within the firmament, and each of us has an innate obligation to discover our true spiritual purpose in the cosmos, wherever this may take us.

Having said that, one can ask whether Crowley always took his own best advice. Crowley hungered for spiritual illumination – for conversation with his Holy Guardian Angel – and yet he was also a slave to his need for public recognition. He loved spiritual and aristocratic power, assuming grandiose titles and affirming his position over his followers. He was essentially authoritarian, disdained human weakness, and was frequently cruel – especially to those who depended on him. His magical records also reveal that he was a complete chauvinist, regarding women essentially as sex objects rather than as people in their own right.[34]

Nevertheless, by some mysterious process, Crowley managed to mythologise himself as a magical persona. He quickly entered fiction as a character in other writers' novels; for example, he provides the inspirational basis for Oliver Haddo in Somerset Maugham's *The Magician*, for Karswell in M. R. James's *Casting the Runes*, and for Theron Ware in James Blish's science-fiction classic *Black Easter*. And he has entered contemporary popular culture in a way he couldn't possibly

have imagined – his photograph was featured on the collage cover of
the Beatles' legendary *Sgt Pepper* album, and David Bowie referred to
him in his song 'Quicksand': 'I'm closer to the Golden Dawn, immersed
in Crowley's uniform of imagery, I'm torn between the light and dark,
where others see their target, divine symmetry . . .'

Crowley has also been an inspiration for Led Zeppelin's guitarist
Jimmy Page. Page studied Crowley's writings as a schoolboy, purchased
Crowley's former home Boleskine in Scotland, and still owns one of
the largest collections of Crowleyan books and manuscripts in the world.
He also composed a soundtrack for Kenneth Anger's Crowleyan film
Lucifer Rising, before having a dispute with the film director.

Crowley has received strong endorsements in the international counter-culture, from figures such as Timothy Leary – who profiled him as
a key influence in his autobiography *Flashbacks* – and from the popular
writer Robert Anton Wilson, author of *Cosmic Trigger* and the *Illuminatus*
trilogy. And there have been Crowleyan cult-band connections as well,
like David Tibet's Current 93 group, the late Graham Bond's Crowley-
inspired rock albums, and Psychic TV's musical and art association with
the Crowleyan cult the Temple Ov Psychick Youth.[35]

So what exactly is the nature of Crowley's appeal? I believe Gerald
Suster comes close to the mark when he says that the essence of the
Law of Thelema is individualistic libertarianism.[36] This may partially
explain Crowley's continuing popularity, for Crowley was invariably
provocative in thumbing his nose at the status quo and was a fierce
defender of personal freedom – he always emphasised that every person
has it within themselves to change their circumstances and to wrestle
with their own destiny. This has obvious appeal in any era and Crowley
was able to articulate it, loud and clear.

5

Some Other Magical Visionaries

While Aleister Crowley helped revolutionise the modern occult tradition by establishing his own cosmology, he was not alone in exploring the potentials of visionary magic. Dion Fortune, a member of the Golden Dawn, and later the founder of her own magical organisation, would bring a new emphasis to feminine mythological archetypes – especially the so-called Black Isis – and would also help develop the magical concept of 'pathworkings', a method of using guided imagery to explore the visionary imagery of the Tree of Life. Austin Osman Spare would develop a unique approach to trance consciousness involving the use of magical sigils, potent individualised symbols. And during the 1940s and 1950s, the Australian artist Rosaleen Norton would attract both acclaim and notoriety for her fusion of esoteric imagery and pagan, visionary art. All three have had an impact on contemporary occult perspectives and all three are bridging figures between the earlier generations of occult practitioners and the contemporary neopagan movement.

Dion Fortune

Dion Fortune was born Violet Mary Firth on 6 December 1890 at Bryn-y-Bia, in Llandudno, Wales. Her father, Arthur Firth, was a solicitor but for her own reasons Violet liked to emphasise a close connection with the better-known Firth family of Sheffield, who owned a major steel-producing company.

By the time she had reached her teenage years, Violet Firth had already acquired a Christian Science orientation – it is likely that her parents were also devotees, although this has not been established – and she seems to have had an early inclination towards psychism and metaphysics. One of her poems, entitled 'Angels', which appeared in the *Christian Science Journal* in April 1908, alludes to an empty tomb in a garden, and to thoughts of mortality and the fragility of love.[1]

Although details of her early professional life are scanty, it is known that she worked as a therapist in a medico-psychological clinic in east London and later studied psychoanalysis in classes held at the University of London by a Professor Flugel – who was also a member of the Society for Psychical Research. Strongly influenced by the theories of Freud, Adler and Jung, Firth became a lay psychoanalyst in 1918. In Jung's thought, especially, she found correlations between the 'archetypes of the collective unconscious' and a realm of enquiry which would increasingly fascinate her: the exploration of sacred mythological images invoked by occultists during their rituals and visionary encounters.

According to Dion Fortune's biographer Alan Richardson, her first contact with occult perspectives seems to have come through her association with an Irish Freemason, Dr Theodore Moriarty. Firth probably met Moriarty at the clinic where she worked; he in turn was involved in giving lectures on occult theories in a private house in the village of Eversley in northern Hampshire. Dr Moriarty seems to have been a very fascinating individual. His interests were both Theosophical and metaphysical, encompassing such subject matter as the study of psychology and religion, the so-called 'root races' of lost Atlantis, mystical and Gnostic Christianity, reincarnation, and the occult relationship between mind, matter and spirit. He was also interested in the psychic origins of disease, the karmic aspects of pathology, and the influence of black magic on mental health.

It is not clear whether Dr Moriarty had any personal connection with the Golden Dawn magicians – many of whom were also Freemasons. But Violet Firth had a close friend, Maiya Curtis-Webb, whom she had known from childhood and who was also an occult devotee, and through her she was introduced to the Golden Dawn Temple of the Alpha and Omega in 1919. Based in London, this temple was a southern offshoot of the Scottish section of the Golden Dawn headed by J. W. Brodie-Innes. Maiya Curtis-Webb became her teacher at the Alpha and Omega temple, and Firth found the magical ceremonies powerful and evocative. However, there was also a certain gloom about this particular group: 'The glory had departed . . . for most of its original members were dead or withdrawn; it had suffered severely during the war, and was manned mainly by widows and grey-bearded ancients.'[2] Taking her leave a year later, Violet Firth now became a member of a London temple headed by Mrs Moina Mathers, who was continuing the esoteric work of her husband following his untimely death from influenza in the epidemic of 1918.

In the Golden Dawn, Violet Firth took the magical name Deo Non Fortuna – by God and not by luck – which also happened to be the Latin motto inscribed upon the Firth family crest. She now became known in esoteric circles as Dion Fortune, a contraction of her magical name, and in 1922 would form her own meditative group. It was originally known as the Christian Mystic Lodge of the Theosophical Society and would later become the Fraternity of the Inner Light.

This connection with the Theosophical Society is not as surprising as it may seem, because there was a substantial overlap in membership between the Golden Dawn and the esoteric branch of the Theosophical Society in London at this time, and Dion Fortune herself felt a strong psychic and spiritual connection with the Theosophists. In her mind the two organisations did not need to compete with each other, but were complementary. The Christian reference in the name of her mystical group is harder to account for. It can in part be explained by the fact that Dion Fortune's teacher, Dr Moriarty, seems to have been a Gnostic Christian who believed strongly that the Christian Gospels were esoteric allegories.[3] In her book *Applied Magic*, Dion Fortune also reveals that, like Dr Moriarty, she too held an esoteric view of Jesus Christ, describing him as ' a high priest after the Order of Melchizedek' and comparing his spiritual role with that of other 'saviours' like Orpheus and Mithra.[4] Dion Fortune even found her own version of the Golden Dawn Secret Chiefs in a cosmic being called Manu Melchizedek, 'Lord of the Flame and also of Mind', who would become her guiding force on the inner planes.[5]

But there would also be a specific and ongoing connection with the Golden Dawn. According to Dion Fortune's account in the *Occult Review*, the Fraternity of the Inner Light was established by her 'in agreement with Mrs Mathers, to be an Outer Court to the Golden Dawn system . . .'[6]

Dion Fortune seems to have got along reasonably well with Moina Mathers until 1924, when a dispute arose over the publication of Fortune's book *The Esoteric Philosophy of Love and Marriage*. This book put forward the view that a sexual relationship between two people could be considered an energy exchange on many levels of being, not just the physical level. While this now seems reasonably innocuous, and perhaps even obvious, Moina Mathers charged Dion Fortune with 'betraying the inner teaching of the Order'. Fortune protested that she hadn't actually received the relevant degree from Mrs Mathers's temple and she was then 'pardoned'. Nevertheless, the dispute with Moina Mathers continued. Soon afterwards, Fortune writes, 'she suspended me for some months for writing *Sane Occultism*, and finally turned me out because certain symbols had not appeared in my aura – a perfectly unanswerable charge.'[7]

Despite being rejected by Moina Mathers, Dion Fortune persisted in employing the ceremonial and visualisation techniques she had learned in the two Golden Dawn temples, and she set up a temple of her own in Bayswater. Her temple was loosely affiliated with the Stella Matutina which had been formed by Dr R. W. Felkin and other Golden Dawn members following the earlier rift with MacGregor Mathers. However, there would be a more serious turn of events – for she now came to believe that Moina Mathers was attacking her on the inner planes in an act of magical revenge. In her book *Psychic Self-Defence*, Dion Fortune provides a fascinating account of what she believed to be a vicious assault from the astral planes:

My first intimation of the astral attack was a sense of uneasiness and restlessness. Next came a feeling as if the barriers between the Seen and the Unseen were full of rifts and I kept on getting glimpses of the Astral mingling with my waking consciousness. The general sense of vague uneasiness gradually matured into a definite sense of menace and antagonism and presently I began to see demon faces in flashes . . .

Very soon curious things began to happen. We became most desperately afflicted with black cats. The caretaker next door was engaged in pushing bunches of black cats off doorstep and window-sill with a broom, and declared he had never in his life seen so many, or such dreadful specimens. The whole house was filled with the horrible stench of the brutes.

Coming upstairs after breakfast one morning, I suddenly saw, coming down the stairs towards me, a gigantic tabby cat, twice the size of a tiger. It appeared absolutely solid and tangible. I stared at it petrified for a second, and then it vanished. I instantly realised that it was a simulacrum, or thought-form that was being projected by someone with occult powers.

I rose up, gathered together my paraphernalia, and did an exorcism then and there. At the end we looked out of the window again. There was not a cat in sight, and we never saw them again.

The Vernal Equinox was now upon us, and I was obliged to make an astral journey at this season – my attacker knew this as well as I did. My journeys always begin with a curtain of the symbolic colour through whose folds I pass. No sooner was I through the curtain on this occasion than I saw my enemy waiting for me. She appeared in the full robes of her grade, which were very magnificent, and barred my entry, telling me that by virtue of her authority she forbade me to make use of these astral pathways. I replied that I did not admit her right to close the astral paths to me, and that I appealed to the Inner Chiefs, to whom both she and I were responsible. There ensued a battle of wills in which I experienced the sensation of being whirled in the air and falling from a great height and found myself back in my body. But my body was not where I had left it, but in a heap in the far corner of the room, which looked as if it had been bombed.

I recognised that I had had the worst of it and had been effectually ejected from the astral paths; but I also realised that if I accepted this defeat my occult career was at an end. I invoked the Inner Chiefs, and went out once more. This time there was a short sharp struggle, and I was through. I had the Vision of the Inner Chiefs, and returned. The Fight was over. I have never had any trouble since.

But when I took off my clothes in order to go to bed I found that from neck to waist I was scored with scratches as if I had been clawed by a gigantic cat . . .[8]

Dion Fortune clearly believed that Moina Mathers had attacked her magically on the inner planes, and she would later describe the incident in an article in the *Occult Review* entitled 'Ceremonial Magic Unveiled'.[9] While there is no specific evidence to substantiate any evil intent on the part of Mrs Mathers, the alleged encounter spelled the end of their relationship. Dion Fortune now aligned herself more closely with the Stella Matutina before formally establishing her own magical society, the Fraternity of the Inner Light, in 1927.

Although Dion Fortune's earlier magical career was undoubtedly marked by high drama and incident, her unique contribution to esoteric thought really begins with the establishment of the Inner Light. Here she increasingly engaged herself in the mythological dimensions of magic – venturing into what she now came to regard as the collective pagan soul of humanity, and tapping into the very heart of the ancient mysteries. Reversing the male-dominated, solar-oriented tradition which Mac-Gregor Mathers had established in the Golden Dawn, Dion Fortune now committed herself completely to the magical potency of the archetypal feminine, and began exploring goddess images in the major ancient pantheons. Her two novels *The Sea Priestess* and *Moon Magic* contain allusions to what appears to be a Rite of Isis:

Those who adore the Isis of Nature adore her as Hathor with the horns upon her brow, but those who adore the celestial Isis know her as Levanah, the Moon. She is also the great Deep whence life arose. She is all ancient and forgotten things wherein our roots are cast. Upon earth she is ever-fecund: in heaven she is ever-virgin. She is the mistress of the tides that flow and ebb and flow, and never cease . . .

In the heavens our Lady Isis is the Moon, and the moon-powers are hers. She is also priestess of the silver star that rises from the twilight sea. Hers are the magnetic moon-tides ruling the hearts of men . . .

In the inner she is all-potent. She is the queen of the kingdoms of sleep. All the visible workings are hers and she rules all things ere they come to birth. Even as through Osiris her mate the earth grows green, so the mind of man conceives through her power . . .

But there was a different emphasis here as well, for Dion Fortune had begun to explore the symbolic and sexual polarities in magic, including those of the Black Isis. Isis is best known as the great goddess of magic in ancient Egyptian mythology, as the wife of the Sun god Osiris and the mother of Horus. It was Isis who succeeded in piecing together the fragments of Osiris's body after he had been murdered by Set, and it was she who also tricked Ra into revealing his secret magical name. However, Dion Fortune was interested in a different aspect of Isis – a dimension associated with what Kenneth Grant has called the 'primordial essence of Woman (*sakti*) in her dynamic aspect'. While Isis was a lunar goddess and the Moon is traditionally considered passive – a receptacle or reflector of light – the Black Isis was said to destroy all that was 'inessential and obstructive to the soul's development'. This in turn led to an exploration of the magic of sexuality. According to Kenneth Grant, the basis of Fortune's work at this time involved 'the bringing into manifestation of this *sakti* by the magically controlled interplay of sexual polarity embodied in the priest (the consecrated male) and the specially chosen female. Together they enacted the immemorial Rite' and this formed a vortex on the inner planes 'down which the tremendous energies of Black Isis rush[ed] into manifestation.'[10]

If Grant is correct, and he met her in the 1940s around the same time that he knew Aleister Crowley, this was clearly a type of visionary magic which ventured into new realms, encompassing the use of transcendent sexual energies and the fusion, in ritual, of male and female polarities. It seems to have involved some form of Western magical Tantra, and was a clear departure from the Golden Dawn, which tended to downplay the sexual dimensions of magic.[11]

However, while one can only speculate on the sexual aspects of the most secret Inner Light rituals, it is also clear that Dion Fortune's main emphasis was not so much on physical magical activities as on astral encounters with the mythic archetypes of the mind. The Fraternity of the Inner Light continued the experimental work with magical visualisation that had first been undertaken in the Golden Dawn during the

1890s, and the Inner Light magicians now developed a practical approach to magical 'pathworkings' as a direct means of exploring the subconscious mind. An important essay entitled 'The Old Religion', written by an anonymous senior member of Dion Fortune's group,[12] confirms that the Inner Light members believed that astral ventures of this kind could arouse 'ancient cult memories' from previous incarnations. Dion Fortune believed that the key to understanding human life and achievement lay in understanding the nature of reincarnation,[13] and the archetype of the Great Mother, in particular, could be thought of as a symbolic embodiment of the World Memory – a concept which has a parallel in the Theosophical concept of the Akashic Records. Through the universal potential of the Great Mother one could access details of one's earlier lives on Earth, and in this way could divine one's sacred purpose. According to the author of 'The Old Religion':

> Most of the members of these groups have, in the past, served at the altars of Pagan Religions and have met, face to face, the Shining Ones of the forests and the mountains, of the lakes and seas . . . In the course of these experiments it was discovered that if anyone of the members of a group had in the past a strong contact with a particular cult at a certain period, that individual could communicate these memories to others, and could link them with cult memories that still lie within the Earth memories of Isis as the Lady of Nature.[14]

In many mythic traditions the magical journey to the ancient gods and goddesses begins on a path which leads through a gateway to the underworld. We have already mentioned that the Golden Dawn magicians conceived of Malkuth, the tenth emanation upon the Tree of Life, as the doorway to the subconscious mind – and this was like entering the underworld of the human psyche. Utilising classical Roman mythology, members of the Inner Light drew on the imagery of the Cumaean Gates which, according to legend, were located near Naples and were guarded by the Sibyl attending the Temple of Apollo. It was through these gates that Aeneas was said to have passed, after deciphering the labyrinth symbol inscribed upon them. Aeneas sought safe passage in the mythic world by first obtaining the golden bough, which would be given as a gift to Proserpine. He also encountered evil spirits, supernatural monsters and former colleagues, numbered among the dead. Then, having been reunited with his father Anchises, he perceived the 'great vision' – a panorama of past and future Roman history – and was granted access to mysterious secrets of the universe.

The Inner Light members had a special interest in visionary journeys of this sort and incorporated them into their guided-imagery meditations, although under Dion Fortune's leadership they tended to focus primarily on the feminine aspects of the underworld encounter. Reflecting Dion Fortune's early interest in the psychological concepts of Carl Jung, there is more than a hint here of Jung's concept of the animus and anima:

> It is the woman that holds the keys of the inner planes for a man. If you want to pass the Cumaean Gates you must become as a little child and a woman must lead you . . . It was Deiphobe, daughter of Glaucus, priestess of Phoebus, and of the Goddess Three-wayed who, for King Aeneas, opened the keyless door and drew the veil that hides life from death and death from life.[15]

The Inner Light guided meditations helped heighten personal awareness of specific mythic imagery and facilitated a switch of consciousness away from one's waking perception to the symbolic inner locale concerned. The author of 'The Old Religion' describes a series of inner journeys – 'The By-Road to the Cave in the Mountain', 'At the Ford of the Moon', 'The High Place of the Moon' and 'The Hosting of the Sidhe' – the culminating experience being a merging of one's awareness with the ethereal Isis in her 'green' aspect as Queen of Nature.

The following account is given from the viewpoint of a male occultist who is initiated by the feminine archetype:

> As he watched, the green of the beech-leaves and the faint silver colour of the bole seemed to merge in a form that was not the tree, and yet it was the tree. He was no longer seeing the tree with his eyes – he was feeling it. He was once again in his inner, subtler, moon-body, and with it he saw and felt the moon-body of the tree. Then appeared the tree spirit, the deva, the shining one who lives through the trunk and branches and leaves of the beech tree as a

man lives through his torso, limbs and hair. That beech was very friendly and moon-body to moon-body they met, and as his moon-body merged into that of the lady of the beech tree, the sensation of the nature of the season, of the caress of the sunlight, of the stimulation of the bright increase of the waxing moon, and of the sleep-time that comes with the decrease of the waning moon, were his.

'You can merge thus into all life,' he was told; and then he saw, as the fairy sees, the flowers, the waterfalls, the rivers, and the brightly coloured holy mountain of Derrybawn, which means the home of the Shining Ones. He merged himself into the roaring life that was at the summit of that great and sacred mountain – and in so doing he took the initiation of the lady of Nature – the Green Isis – in her temple on the heather-clad hill-top that is above the deep ravine.[16]

Dion Fortune died in 1946 but the approach and techniques of the Fraternity of the Inner Light have continued through the auspices of a contemporary magical order known as Servants of the Light (SOL), whose headquarters are currently located in St Helier on the island of Jersey. The SOL conducts international correspondence courses in Western magic and has members in many countries. Dion Fortune trained the well-known occultist W. E. Butler who, like his teacher, assimilated a vast knowledge of the Kabbalah, mythology and esoteric symbolism into a practical system of magic.[17] In his later years, Butler passed the leadership of the SOL to the present director of the order, Dolores Ashcroft-Nowicki, who has herself produced several important works on the Western magical tradition, including *Highways of the Mind: The Art and History of Pathworking* and *The Shining Paths: An Experiential Journey through the Tree of Life*. The international reach of the SOL and the writings of W. E. Butler and Dolores Ashcroft-Nowicki, which have also been translated into several languages, have ensured that the magical ideas of Dion Fortune continue to have a major impact among devotees of the Western esoteric tradition.

Austin Osman Spare

Austin Spare (1886–1956) provides us with a fascinating example of an artist who was both a magician and a trance-visionary. While the formal structures of the Hermetic Order of the Golden Dawn were fragmenting amid schisms and dissent just before the onset of World War I, Spare was developing a unique system of practical magic through his exploration of ecstatic trance states. Spare was probably the first modern occultist to evolve a self-contained working hypothesis about the nature of psychic energy which could be applied without all the paraphernalia of traditional rituals, grimoires and magical implements. His system of magical sigils showed how an effort of will, when focused on the subconscious mind, could unleash the most extraordinary psychic material.

One of five children, Spare was born in Snow Hill, London, on 30 December 1886, the son of a policeman. The family later moved to south London and Spare attended St Agnes' School in Kennington Park; he would live in this area of the city, in modest circumstances, for most of his life.

Spare showed artistic talent early on, and at the age of twelve began studying at Lambeth Evening Art School. In 1902, when he was sixteen, he won a scholarship enabling him to attend the Royal College of Art, South Kensington, and in 1905 examples of his work were exhibited at the Royal Academy. The president of the Academy, John Singer Sargent, proclaimed Spare to be a genius and he was soon commissioned to illustrate a handful of books, including Ethel Wheeler's *Behind the Veil* (1906) and a book of aphorisms entitled *The Starlit Mire* (1911).

In 1917 Spare enlisted in the Royal Army Medical Corps, and in 1919 visited France as a special war artist documenting the aftermath of World War I – several works based on sketches from this period are included in the collection of the Imperial War Museum. In 1919 Spare also co-founded an excellent illustrated literary magazine called *The Golden Hind*, which included the work of such writers as Aldous Huxley, Alec Waugh and Havelock Ellis.[18]

Although he received a degree of acclaim and recognition during his lifetime – Augustus John proclaimed Spare to be one of the leading graphic artists of his era and he was also praised by George Bernard Shaw – Spare has remained largely unacknowledged in the major art histories. This may be because he was an occultist as well as an accomplished artist: Spare's art teems with magical imagery and he was briefly a member of both the Argenteum Astrum and the Ordo Templi Orientis. When he began to self-publish his illustrated magical books from 1905 onwards, it became evident that his was an eccentric rather than a mainstream artistic talent, and there is little doubt that his unconventionality has pushed him to the sidelines of cultural history. He neverthess remains a legendary figure in the twentieth-century Western esoteric tradition and is one of its truly original thinkers, his approach to trance states and his technique of atavistic resurgence representing a unique contribution to the study of magical consciousness.

Zos and Kia

Spare postulated the existence of a primal, cosmic life force which he termed Kia, and he believed that the spiritual and occult energies inherent in Kia could be channelled into the human organism, which he called Zos. As we will see, his technique of arousing these primal energies – an approach he termed 'atavistic resurgence' – involved focusing the will on magical sigils, which in effect represented instructions to the subconscious. When the mind was in a 'void' or open state – achieved for example through meditation, exhaustion or at the peak of sexual ecstasy – this was an ideal condition in which to direct magical sigils to the subconscious. Here they could 'grow' in the seedbed of the mind until they became 'ripe' and reached back down into the conscious mind. In such a way one could learn to manipulate one's own 'psychic reality'.

How did Austin Spare stumble upon his special approach to magical states of consciousness? Clearly it was no accident. His magic draws on a variety of inspirational sources, encompassing the mythic images of ancient Egypt, a fascination with the sexual energies of the subconscious mind,[19] and his close personal relationship with an unusual psychic mentor whom he always referred to simply as Mrs Paterson.

Spare visited Egypt during World War I and was impressed by the magnetic presence of the classical gods depicted in monumental sculpture. He believed the ancient Egyptians understood very thoroughly the complex mythology of the subsconscious mind:

They symbolised this knowledge in one great symbol, the Sphinx, which is pictorially man evolving from animal existence. Their numerous Gods, all partly Animal, Bird, Fish . . . prove the completeness of that knowledge . . . The cosmogony of their Gods is proof of their knowledge of the order of evolution, its complex processes from the one simple organism.[20]

For Spare, impressions from earlier human incarnations and potentially all mythic impulses could be reawakened from the subconscious mind. The gods themselves could be regarded as a form of internal impetus. 'All gods have lived (being ourselves) on earth,' he wrote, 'and when dead, their experience of Karma governs our actions in degree.'

However, though the classical gods of ancient Egypt made a marked impression on him, Spare learned his actual technique of trance activation from an elderly woman called Mrs Paterson, who was a friend of his parents and used to tell his fortune when he was quite young. Mrs Paterson claimed a psychic link with the witches of the Salem cult and also appeared to have an extrasensory ability to project thought-forms. According to Spare, she was able to transform herself in his vision from being a 'wizened old crone' to appearing quite suddenly as a ravishing siren, 'creating a vision of profound sexual intensity and revelation that shook him to the very core'.[21]

The archetypal female image recurs in all phases of Spare's artistic work — he was a master at depicting the sensuous naked female form — and the Universal Woman would become a central image in his mythology of the subconscious. In his definitive magical credo, *The Book of Pleasure*, he writes: 'Nor is she to be limited as any particular "goddess" such as Astarte, Isis, Cybele, Kali, Nuit, for to limit her is to turn away from the path and to idealize a concept which, as such, is false because incomplete, unreal because temporal.'

Spare employed a technique of ecstasy which frequently combined active imagination and will with the climax of sexual orgasm. Spare believed that his magical sigils — representing symbols of the personal will — could be directed to the subconscious mind during the peak of sexual ecstasy since, at this special moment, the personal ego and the universal spirit, or Kia, were united in a state of blissful, transcendent openness. 'At this moment, which is the moment of generation of the

Great Wish,' writes Spare, 'inspiration flows from the source of sex, from the primordial Goddess who exists at the heart of Matter . . . inspiration is always at a void moment.'

Several of Spare's drawings depict the divine maiden leading the artist into the labyrinthine magical world. One of his central works, *The Ascension of the Ego from Ecstasy to Ecstasy*, shows the goddess welcoming Spare himself, who on this occasion appropriately has wings issuing forth from his head. Spare's 'ego', or persona, is shown merging with an earlier animal incarnation and the two forms transcend each other in the form of a primal skull. Spare clearly believed that he could retrace his earlier incarnations to the universal 'Oneness of Creation', or Kia. According to Kenneth Grant, who knew the artist personally, Spare derived his formula of atavistic resurgence from Mrs Paterson:

> She would visualize certain animal forms and – the language of the subconsciousness being pictographic not verbal – each form represented a corresponding power in the hidden world of causes. It was necessary only to 'plant' an appropriate sigil in the proper manner for it to awaken its counterpart in the psyche. Resurging from the depths it then emerged, sometimes masked in the form to do the sorcerer's bidding.[22]

Undoubtedly, one of Spare's major objectives in using the trance state was to tap energies which he believed were the source of genius. According to Spare, 'ecstasy, inspiration, intuition and dream . . . each state taps the latent memories and presents them in the imagery of their respective languages.' And genius itself was 'a directly resurgent atavism' experienced during the ecstasy of the Fire Snake – Spare's term for magical sexual arousal.

Spare's Magical Cosmology

Spare's unique magical approach took several years to unfold, however, and while ancient Egyptian deities and other pagan entities abound in his drawings, his first book, *Earth: Inferno* – published as a limited edition in 1905 – seems to have been strongly influenced by the Kabbalah and other elements of the Western mystical tradition. Here Spare tends towards dualism, regarding the phenomena of life as generally either positive or negative, spiritual or materialistic, real or delusory. His concept of Kia has a clear counterpart in the transcendent Ain Soph Aur of the Kabbalah, and there is a strong emphasis on the superficial and essentially false nature of appearances. Man, says Spare, should learn to shed his dependency on material security, which inevitably shrouds him in the falsehoods of conventionality. Instead he should search beneath his 'mask' to uncover the potentials of his subconscious.

In *Earth: Inferno* Spare is intent on exploring the relationship between Zos and Kia – between individual awareness and the universal consciousness or primal energy. He concurs with the traditional mystical perspective that the Godhead lies within, and by now has begun to embrace the view that he should follow the beckoning of the Universal Mother of Nature – the 'Primitive Woman' – who can guide him pantheistically back to the source of all being. Spare has also taken a magical name to epitomise his mystical quest: Zos vel Thanatos.

Spare makes it clear that the magical journey is one which is undertaken beyond 'the parapet of the subconscious'. He depicts the world of everyday awareness as a circular pathway along which visionless old men dodder hopelessly, looking to their candles for light while simultaneously remaining unaware of the 'Great Beyond'. Spare also shows us a depraved young man making lustful advances to the Universal Woman in his failure to see beyond her enticing outward appearance. This clearly involves an issue of insight: the Universal Woman is the wise and all-seeing Sophia of the Gnosis and is not to be mistaken for the Scarlet Woman of Babylon. Spare maintains that he himself did not commit this error: 'I strayed with her, into the path direct. Hail! the Jewel in the Lotus!'

Nevertheless, at this stage Spare still finds himself caught between the inner and outer worlds: as he proclaims in his text, 'I myself am Heaven and Hell.' He has begun to encounter the dark night of the soul, and realises that he will have to venture through the illusions of everyday life and the debris of the subconscious in order to experience the transcendence of Kia. Spare talks of this in a reflective way: 'The barrenness of this life but remains, yet in despair we begin to see true light. In weakness we can become strong. Revere the Kia and your mind will become tranquil.'

Spare already believed that every human being is innately divine, though most failed to perceive it. 'I have not yet seen a man who is not God already,' declares Spare provocatively. All man has to do is confront himself as he really is, and he will find God. This in turn involves the death of the ego, for it is the ego that isolates us from the realisation of the unity which sustains all aspects of creation. For Spare, death could even be seen as a positive element because it destroyed the pretence of the personality. 'From behind,' writes Spare, 'Destiny works with Death.' And death is a precursor of enlightenment. In *Earth: Inferno* Spare presents us with a vision which draws on both the Kabbalah and the Major Arcana of the Tarot:

> On entering at the Gates of Life
> Lo, I behold Knowledge the Jester
> Capsizing the Feast of Illusion.
> The drawing aside false Truth
> He shewed us all –
> The World,
> The Flesh
> and
> The Being.
>
> This is the Alpha and Omega.

On the Kabbalistic Tree of Life, Kether is the first emanation from the infinite formlessness of Ain Soph Aur – the first act of Creation 'out of nothing' – and this is the highest level of spiritual awareness any human being can theoretically attain. It is shown symbolically on the Tarot path which leads to Kether as the Jester, or the Fool – the person who knows No-Thing. The Jester is therefore the wisest among all men for he has reached the highest possible state of consciousness. He has experienced Kia, or transcendent reality.

All this involves a relatively orthodox Western mysticism, but Spare was already developing his own individualised philosophy, a system of magical thought which he hoped would be free of dogma or 'belief'. As he saw it, Spare was now liberating his perception from the vices of the world – 'fear, faith . . . science and the like' – and was preparing to plunge into his own personal unknown: his inner self.

With this perspective in mind, he produced a book which would be the magnum opus of his magical and artistic career. Entitled *The Book of Pleasure (Self-Love): The Philosophy of Ecstasy*, it featured many of his finest drawings as well as describing the essence of his new magical approach. *The Book of Pleasure* was privately published in 1913, and included a number of important new concepts.[23]

It is true that before this time a number of occultists had been emphasising the role of the 'will' in magical procedures. The Golden Dawn member Florence Farr had outlined the need for intense mental concentration in her articles in the *Occult Review* (1908), and Aleister Crowley had emphasised the need for both a spiritual and a magical focus in his central dictum 'Do what thou wilt shall be the whole of the Law'. Austin Spare was briefly a member of Crowley's order, the Argenteum Astrum, and he adopted this view too, but only up to a point: he then moved in a different direction.[24]

Sigils and Ecstasy

In *The Book of Pleasure* Spare explored methods of concentrating the will. Since the degree of effectiveness of any action is related to a thorough understanding of the command behind the action, Spare developed a way of condensing his will so that it was more readily grasped as a totality. He did this by writing his 'will' (= desire) in sentence form and by combining the basic letters, without repetition, into a pattern shape, or sigil. This could then be simplified and impressed upon the subconscious mind. Spare describes the process:

Sigils are made by combining the letters of the alphabet simplified. Illustration: the word 'Woman' in sigil form is:

or or etc. The word tiger or . Hat . Come . Moon . It or etc., etc.

The idea being to obtain a simple form which can be easily visualised at will . . .[25]

What was to be done with the sigil once it was arrived at? And what
was the significance of the sigil itself? We must first of all consider
some related ideas.

As has been noted earlier, Spare spoke of Kia as the supreme principle
in the universe: it was akin to a dynamic, expanding vortex of energy,
ever in a state of becoming. Most human beings were unaware of its
full potential simply because they did not let it manifest within themselves ('Are we not ever standing on our own volcano?'). Instead, most
people would shut themselves off by means of the various 'insulating'
devices employed by the ego. The only way in which the cosmic
energy could manifest, or be aroused within, was by thoroughly opening
oneself to it.

According to Austin Spare it was when the individual was in a state
of mental 'vacuity' – or ultimate openness – that Kia became 'sensitive
to the subtle suggestion of the sigil'. This state could be arrived at by
emptying the mind of all its thought-forms in an effort to visualise
nonmanifestation – for example, by meditating on blackness or empti-
ness. This in turn usually involved inducing a state of meditative trance
in which the individual became oblivious of his surroundings as he
focused only on the inner void.

Because we all proceed from the Godhead originally, Spare argued,
it should be possible to track back through the mind to the First Cause.
Like many mystics, Spare believed in reincarnation and he therefore
regarded the subconscious mind as the 'potential' source of all his own
earlier physical embodiments or personalities, right back to the beginning.[26] The psyche, as it were, consisted of a number of different
layers – the resulting impressions of successive lives, most of which
were subconscious. All these were an aspect of the individual's own
'reality'.

Know the subconscious to be an epitome of all experience and
wisdom, past incarnations as men, animals, birds, vegetable life etc.:
everything that has, and ever will, exist. Each being a stratum in the
order of evolution. Naturally then, the lower we probe into these

strata, the earlier will be the forms of life we arrive at: the last is the Almighty Simplicity.

Spare's intention was to gain knowledge of his concealed mental states through 'regression' and eventually to lose his sense of self in an indescribably ecstatic union with Kia, whose energy he had now come to consider as basically sexual. The dark void of the mind, emptied of thought-forms through an act of concentration, could be penetrated by the will by employing a sigil suitable for one's purpose. In theory, and according to one's ability, one could project the sigil to all possible recesses of the subconscious mind and in this way gain access to the entire sphere of the imagination.

In reality this was much harder to achieve than the theory suggests. Obviously, it depended upon a number of crucial factors:

– an ability to derive a suitable sigil
– an ability to prevent random thought-forms from unintentionally disturbing the 'black void' and thus rendering 'impure' the individual's attempt to become a pure vessel for the energies of Kia
– an ability to reach further into the subconscious by totally renouncing the wordly context of one's aspirations. Ultimately this task would involve rejecting one's sense of humanity and eventually destroying the ego altogether – a most unwordly intention!

Naturally the last condition was the hardest to achieve. Spare acknowledged that 'total vacuity' was difficult and unsafe for those 'governed by morality, complexes etc.' – that is to say, for all those governed by the 'superstitions' and intellectual conceptions that most human beings surround themselves with. Indeed, Spare maintained that one would have to cast aside all contrived or finite rationalisations. He therefore tried to think of various situations where a sense of the rational was minimal or absent, and he emphasised three such circumstances.

The first of these was the state of physical exhaustion. If one had a 'desire' or 'concentrated thought' in this situation, Spare argued, the mind would become 'worried, because of the non-fulfilment of such desire, and seek relief. By seizing this mind and living, the resultant vacuity would become sensitive to the subtle suggestion of the sigil.' In other words, by exhausting the body, one made it impossible for normal mental intentions or commands to be carried out physically. The mind would then be forced into manifesting the concepts embodied in the magical sigil. Sheer exhaustion can be brought about in a number of ways, and this includes the climax of sexual orgasm itself. The Tantric yoga technique of using orgasm as the leaping-off point to visionary states of consciousness was well known in Western esoteric circles at the time Spare was writing.

The second method lay in exploiting the mental state of extreme disappointment, experienced, for example, when one lost all faith in a close friend, or when a cherished ideal had been destroyed. Spare felt that this state, too, could provide its own sense of opportunity:

When fundamental disappointment is experienced the symbol enshrining a quota of belief is destroyed. In some cases the individual is unable to survive the disillusionment. But if at such times the moment is seized upon and consciously experienced for its own sake, the vacuum attracts into itself the entire content of belief inherent in the person at the time of disappointment.

Spare is saying, in effect, that when we thoroughly lose faith in a belief or ideal, we are given the option of transcending it, and transcendence of belief can lead to a state of ecstasy as we are drawn into the vortex of Kia.

However, Spare seems to have often preferred a third approach for bypassing the ego, a method which could be used for generalised changes in the personality and also for specifics. This involved a state of self-induced trance in which the body became rigid, ceased to function, and underwent what Spare called 'the Death Posture'. He describes a preliminary exercise designed to bring this about:

Gazing at your reflection (e.g. in a tall mirror) till it is blurred and you know not the gazer, close your eyes and visualise. The light (always an X in curious evolutions) that is seen should be held onto, never letting go, till the effort is forgotten; this gives a feeling of immensity (which sees a small form ⚭ whose limit you cannot reach.

Spare considered that the Death Posture exercise should be practised daily for best effect. 'The Ego is swept up as a leaf in a fierce gale,' he wrote. 'In the fleetness of the indeterminable, that which is always about to happen, becomes its truth. Things that are self-evident are no longer obscure, as by his own will he pleases; know this as the negation of all faith by living it, the end of duality of consciousness.' Here Spare is alluding to the Kia dimension, which is beyond time and space, but which nevertheless represents the central basis for all life and human potential. Spare believed that achieving the state of openness necessary for Kia to manifest would also enable him to direct his magical will into the cosmic memory. By doing this he could acquire a full and detailed knowledge of the earlier life forms which were both an aspect of oneself and of Kia as a whole. The Death Posture provided the possibility of a link; the magical sigil confirmed the possibility.

A sigil, as we have seen, is a visual condensation of the will. However, what we 'will' can often be based on ideas of grandeur and self-deception. Spare points out that even if we imagine ourselves to be great this is not necessarily so, and all the desiring in the world cannot alter the fact. Spare notes: 'Realisation is not by the mere utterance of words . . . but by the living act. The will, the desire, the belief, lived as inseparable, become realisation.' Hoping for something won't help us achieve it; we must must live it and enact it for it to become true. According to Spare,

> Belief to be true must be organic and subconscious. The idea to be great can only become organic (i.e. 'true') at the time of vacuity and by giving it form. When conscious of the sigil form (any time but the magical) it should be repressed, a deliberate striving to forget it; by this it is active and dominates at the subconscious period; its form nourishes and allows it to become attached to the subconscious and become organic; that accomplished is its reality and realisation. The individual becomes his concept of greatness.

In summary, beliefs need to be 'organic', not theoretical; organic realities originate with Kia and lie dormant in the subconscious; we can use a sigil to embody our desire, command our will, and this should relate to what we want to do or become; the sigil can 'grow' in the subconscious but will lose its effect if it is consciously remembered; and, finally, the sigil will eventually manifest as a 'true' aspect of the personality since it comes from within.

Spare also relates this process to the faculty of creativity: 'All geniuses have active subconsciousnesses and the less they are aware of the fact, the greater their accomplishments. The subconscious is exploited by desire reaching it.' This implies that geniuses not born, could be made – an idea he shared with Aleister Crowley.

Spare's system of implanting sigils was capable of different levels of application, and from an occult perspective it could be applied both to high and low magic. Spare often used his sigils to embody transcendent commands, but his system could also be used for comparatively mundane purposes. Kenneth Grant tells of a situation where Spare needed to move a heavy load of timber without assistance. A sigil was required which involved great strength, so Spare constructed a suitable sentence: 'This is my wish, to obtain the strength of a tiger.' Sigilised, this sentence would be:

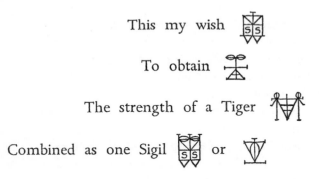

This my wish

To obtain

The strength of a Tiger

Combined as one Sigil or

Grant goes on to say:

Spare closed his eyes for a while and visualised a picture which symbolised a wish for the strength of tigers [i.e. the final sigil above]. Almost immediately he sensed an inner response. He then felt a tremendous upsurge of energy sweep through his body. For a moment he felt like a sapling bent by the onslaught of a mighty wind. With a great effort of will, he steadied himself and directed the force to its proper object. A great calm descended and he found himself able to carry the load easily.

Kenneth Grant makes it clear from his account that first dormant energy was awakened and then it was focused into a specialised activity. This was not always Spare's method, for in his more far-reaching atavistic resurgences he allowed the influx of Kia to obsess him. His mind would become flooded with preternatural influences and there was no semblance of control.[27] Spare himself considered this type of atavistic activity to be an act of bravery:

> Strike at the highest . . . death is failure. Go where thou fearest not. How canst thou be great among men? *Cast thyself forth!* Retrogress to the point where knowledge ceases in that Law becomes its own spontaneity and freedom . . . This is the new atavism I would teach: Demand of God equality – Usurp!

Spare's method is thus clearly an act of stealing fire from heaven. His preferred method, the Death Posture, involved the 'death' of the ego through the negation of conscious thought – a positive but 'unconscious' thrust towards transcendence.

What is unusual about Spare's cosmology and his occult trance techniques is that he believed in regression, rather than in the more conventional mystical concept of 'conscious evolution'. Indeed, he redefines his idea of magical evolution: 'The Law of Evolution is retrogression of function governing progression of attainment, i.e. the more wonderful our attainments are, *the lower in the scale of Life the function that governs them*. Man is *complex*, and to progress, must become simplified.'

This means that because more and more manifestations of Kia are appearing in the world all the time through reincarnation, as the source of Creation expands 'outwards', the true magical direction is 'inwards' or more specifically 'backwards' to the First Cause.

Austin Spare's approach to magical perception is virtually unique within the Western esoteric tradition. Like Aleister Crowley and Dion

Fortune, he has retained an enthusiastic following to the present day. In Spare's case, though, aspects of this renewed interest appear to be of a lower calibre than one might have hoped for. In the United States a group of so-called 'Chaos magicians' now claim to be utilising Spare's sigil methods and an influential work titled *Practical Sigil Magic* by Frater U . ˙ . D . ˙ . , first published in 1990, purports to extend the practical applications of Spare's trance formulations. However, these practitioners appear to fall far short of Spare's magical vision and have seized hold only of its pragmatic 'low magic' applications. While Frater U . ˙ . D . ˙ . writes that 'sigil magic is primarily success magic', Spare is embracing much wider realms than magical self-gratification: his is a unique response to the cosmos. It remains to be seen whether the resurgent interest in Austin Spare will be deflected by a trivialisation of his unique contribution to the exploration of magical consciousness.

Rosaleen Norton

Rosaleen Norton (1917–1979) has been described as Australia's best-known witch, although by now her fame has extended well beyond her native shores. The avant-garde American filmmaker Kenneth Anger, who has had an ongoing fascination with occult mythology and visited Aleister Crowley's Abbey in Cefalu, proposed to make a film about her, and she has also inspired contemporary novels and a play. Rosaleen Norton is certainly one of the most impressive painters of supernatural themes to have emerged in modern times.

Rosaleen lived her last years in a shadowy basement apartment in an ageing block of flats close to the El Alamein fountain in Sydney's Kings Cross district. In one of her rooms she had erected a sacred altar in honour of the horned god Pan, the ancient Greek patron of pastoral life and lord of Nature. However, she kept her deepest beliefs and ideas very much to herself, living like a recluse from the exuberant nightlife which surrounded her.

There was a time when Rosaleen Norton's murals and decorative motifs spanned the walls of several popular coffee bars in Kings Cross, but these are now long gone; the well-known Apollyon yielded to the bypass which now takes the main flow of traffic out to Sydney's eastern suburbs. Her heyday was in fact in the 1940s and 1950s. She was known to the public as an eccentric, bohemian witch-lady who wore flamboyant, billowing blouses and vivid bandannas, puffed on an exotic engraved cigarette holder, and plucked her eyebrows so that they arched in a somewhat sinister curve. Slight in build with long, curly, black hair, she always had a magnetic presence that made her stand out in the crowd.

Rosaleen Norton became known as a controversial painter of provocative half-human, half-animal forms. She depicted naked women wrestling with reptilian elementals or flying on the backs of winged griffins, and gods who were both male and female and whose arms were like wings with claws at the extremities. These days, at a time when fantasy art has brought a vivid array of supernatural and surreal styles to CD covers, posters and T-shirts, Rosaleen Norton's paintings appear more mainstream, but in the decade after World War II they seemed to be an affront to human decency and ran counter to orthdodox religious sensibilities.

Rosaleen Norton was born in Dunedin, New Zealand, in 1917 during a violent thunderstorm which she later claimed was a portent for her love of the night side of life. Even when she was just three years old she was fond of drawing 'nothing beasts' − animal-headed ghosts with tentacle arms − and at the age of five she observed an apparition of a shining dragon beside her bed. These events convinced her of the presence of the spirit world and she found herself developing religious beliefs contrary to those of her more orthodox parents. Rosaleen's father was a captain in the merchant navy and a cousin of the composer Vaughan Williams; her mother was a 'conventional, highly emotional woman, far too absorbed in her family'.

The Nortons migrated from New Zealand in 1925 and settled in the Sydney suburb of Lindfield. Young Rosaleen lived there for the next ten years with her parents but found it increasingly difficult to relate to her mother, preferring the company of her elder sister and a favourite aunt. By the age of fourteen she had decided upon the direction her life should take and was preparing to experience everything she could, 'good, bad and indifferent', engaging both her life and art in the only way that came naturally. A numerologist had earlier worked out her name chart and had arrived at the conclusion that Rosaleen's life and work would lie well off the beaten track − a prediction which certainly came true.

Rosaleen was soon expelled from school under a cloud, her head-mistress writing to her mother indicating that she had 'a depraved nature which would corrupt the innocence of the other girls'. She then studied for two years at East Sydney Technical College under the sculptor Rayner Hoff. During this time she became interested in witchcraft and magic and was soon well versed in the occult writings of Dion Fortune, Aleister Crowley and Eliphas Levi, even though such specialist publications were difficult to obtain in Sydney at the time. After leaving the college she became a pavement artist, displaying her work at the bottom of Rowe Street, near the Sydney general post office. Her subsequent jobs included working as a newspaper trainee, designing for a toy manu-facturer, assisting in a bohemian nightclub, waitressing and modelling. But her work pursuits were becoming increasingly secondary to her occult interests and in 1940 she began to experiment with self-hypnosis as a means of inducing automatic drawing.

Rosaleen was already familiar with the trance methods of the surreal-ists and especially admired the work of Salvador Dalí and Yves Tanguy, who, like the other artists in their movement, had explored techniques of encouraging the subconscious mind to manifest its visionary contents. Sometimes the surrealists drew rapidly so that forms came through unimpeded by the intellect. Others experimented with drugs or docu-mented their dream experiences in great detail in order to develop a greater knowledge of the 'alternative reality' of the subconscious mind.

Rosaleen Norton found that she could shut off her normal conscious-ness by means of self-hypnosis and could transfer her attention to an inner plane of awareness. As she noted in her personal records: 'These experiments produced a number of peculiar and unexpected results . . . and culminated in a period of extra-sensory perception, together with a prolonged series of symbolic visions.' She spent several years after this studying various systems of occult thought, including Buddhist and other examples of Eastern literature as well as standard works on Western magic and mysticism.

During this period she also began to focus more specifically on the magical forces associated with the great god Pan, whose spirit she felt pervaded the entire Earth. Her studies had taught her that the ancient Greeks regarded Pan as lord of all things – symbolising the totality of the elements and all forms of manifest being. He was therefore, in a very real sense, the true god of the world. Pan was a maintainer of the balance of Nature and also had at his command an invisible hierarchy of lesser spirits who could help him in his work of ruling and sustaining the Earth.

Rosaleen painted a large-scale interpretation of Pan, complete with horns, pointed ears, cloven hooves and musical pipes, and mounted it on the wall of her flat. She also conducted magical ceremonies dressed in a tiger-skin robe to honour his presence, and would often experience him as a living reality when she entered a trance state.

Her art continued to reflect the entities she encountered in her visions, including a variety of devilish creatures, half-animal, half-human pagan deities, and various supernatural motifs. Several psychiatrists were fascinated by her style and one of her paintings was bought in the early 1950s by an Adelaide bishop, curious about the source of her inspiration. When the English art critic John Sackville-West arrived in Australia in 1970 he claimed that far too many abstract painters were claiming to be artists when in fact they were really designers; he identified Norman Lindsay and Rosaleen Norton as two of Australia's finest artists, gifted in depicting the detailed human form. Rosaleen was very pleased by this particular praise; she liked to be compared with Norman Lindsay, whom she very much admired and regarded, together with Sir William Dobell, as one of 'Australia's only great artists'. She also admitted to being influenced by Aubrey Beardsley, Leonardo, van Gogh and the etcher Gustave Doré.

The Gods, in Their Own Right

Many occultists have drawn on the Swiss psychoanalyst Carl Jung's concept of the 'collective unconscious' to explain their relationship with the archetypal forces of the mind. As we have seen, Dion Fortune was herself an early enthusiast of Jungian thought. Jung believed that at a deep, collective level of the psyche lay a rich and potent source of sacred archetypal imagery, and that these numinous forms provided the very basis of religious and mystical experience, irrespective of the cultural context involved. In other words, gods and sacred mystical images were really an extension of the universal human experience.

A number of occultists, though, have rejected this view, claiming instead that the gods live apart from the collective minds of humanity and are not merely projected 'thought-forms'. Rosaleen Norton agreed with this latter perspective. In an interview given the year before her death in 1979, she explained to me that she found it egotistical and self-centred for humanity to accord itself a special position in the spectrum of creation. For her, the gods existed in their own right. She knew Hecate, Lucifer and Pan, not as extensions of her own consciousness, but as beings who would grace her with their presence if it pleased them, and not subject to her will. She believed she had discovered some of the qualities of these gods within her own temperament, and that this provided a sense of natural affinity. This made their invocation much easier and more effective than would have been the case had there not been some sort of innate bond. Rosaleen maintained that she went to the realm of the gods on the astral planes – the inner world of spirit accessed through magical trance – and that on different occasions the gods would reveal different dimensions of their own magical potency.

Rosaleen Norton regarded Lucifer, for example, not so much as an embodiment of 'evil' as humanity's natural adversary. He bound and limited man when it appeared that he was growing too big for his boots. He tried to trick man, not out of malice but with the positive intent of exposing the limitations of the ego and revealing the essential falseness of man's pride in his own existence. Rosaleen also regarded Pan as a very significant deity for the present day, a force in the universe which protected and conserved the natural beauty and resources of the environment. For her, Pan was alive and well in the antipollution lobbies and among the Friends of the Earth!

Hecate, on the other hand, she felt to be more imposing – an often frightening, shadowy goddess flanked by cohorts of ghouls and night-forms, a dealer in death and a purveyor of curses. But there was a magical bond to be found there too. Rosaleen regarded magic and witchcraft as her protection and an inspiration in a hostile, ungenerous world. However, her own brand of witchcraft hardly brought her abundance. She lived simply, with few possessions, and certainly without any measure of wealth. If ever she cursed people with 'witch current', she said, it was a means of redressing the balance of events – a legitimate use of the magical art.

Not surprisingly, Rosaleen's paintings show a certain similarity of style to those of Norman Lindsay. But while for Lindsay the world of supernature could only offer decadent and exotic themes for his artmaking, for Rosaleen Norton this realm was a perceptual reality, and this is strongly reflected in her work. There are fire elementals, ablaze with light; devils with dual banks of eyes, indicative of their different planes of perception; cats with magical awareness; horned beings with sensual cheeks and a strange eerie light playing on their brow. Her art was the result of the direct magical encounter. Energies filtered through her, she said, as if she were a funnel. She transmitted the current during a state of self-induced hypnotic trance.[28] If the gods were alive in her, her artistic skills would then allow these gods to manifest, in varying degrees, upon her canvases.

Rosaleen always denied that she portrayed the totality of the god. She could depict only those qualities the god chose to show. The gods existed in their own right, on a plane far removed from the everyday world of human consciousness.

In certain of Rosaleen's paintings and drawings we find creatures which are half human and half animal and these, in many ways, are her most impressive magical images. Several illustrations of this type were reproduced in a volume of the artist's drawings titled *The Art of Rosaleen Norton*, published in 1952 in a limited edition of a thousand copies. The drawings were in black and white, and accompanied a series of poems by Rosaleen's lover Gavin Greenlees.[29]

Greenlees, who died in 1983, was a modest and quietly spoken man for whom the magical view of the world was simultaneously a visionary and poetic expression. In the 1952 edition, Rosaleen Norton's magical images blended superbly with Greenlees's mystical poetry and also provided a type of homage to the major supernatural forces in her magical pantheon.

In his introduction to the book, the publisher Walter Glover noted the parallels between Rosaleen Norton's art and that of certain of the surrealists, and also pointed out that her paintings embodied what he called 'a vision of the night'. Rosaleen Norton would always regard her art as a medium for tapping into a wondrous 'alternative reality'. In an early journal entry she wrote:

There are senses, art forms, activities and states of consciousness that have no parallel in human experience . . . an overwhelming deluge of both Universal and Self Knowledge (often in an allegorical form) from every conceivable aspect – metaphysical, mathematical, scientific, symbolic. These comprise a bewildering and significant relationship to every other facet.

One such experience could be compared with simultaneously watching and taking part in a play in which all art forms, such as music, drama, ceremonial ritual, shape, sound and pattern, blended into one . . .

Rosaleen's artistic output was quite varied and the limited edition remains a hallmark of her stylistic breadth. Her drawings ranged from satirical, but essentially whimsical, parodies of church figures through to semi-abstract vorticist whirlpools of energy and figurative depictions of the great supernatural deities. Her representation of Mars – an obviously warlike entity – shows a powerful human male torso with the winged head of a hawk. The god has a scorpion's tail and clawed feet, and embodies a very tangible feeling of power and aggression. In his right hand he holds a sphere – the puny globe of Earth – asserting his command.

Rosaleen's portrait of Jupiter, meanwhile, shows a proud potentate with a resplendent beam of light issuing from his forehead and a dark, majestic beard lapping down onto his chest. His legs and tail are leonine, and he carries in his right hand a mace, symbolising spiritual authority.

In both these pictures, Rosaleen Norton depicts her deities as an animal-human fusion. For her, animals embodied a dignity which mankind had lost. She was especially fond of cats because of their 'psychic qualities', and the lion, for her, was a supremely appropriate symbol of benevolent authority. Rosaleen felt that, in general, animals had managed to retain their integrity much more effectively than most human beings. Towards the end of her life, she felt an increasing empathy with the animal kingdom, taking great pleasure in her pets, and she began to shun human contact altogether. A believer in reincarnation, she also recalled an earlier 'lifetime' that throws light on her close bond with animals.

In this existence she lived in a rickety wooden house in a field of yellow grass near Beachy Head in Sussex. There were various animals – cows, horses and so on – and she was a poltergeist. She remembered understanding the techniques by which poltergeists made objects move. When 'real' people came near her house, they were offended or frightened by her presence – they could not relate to her poltergeist condition – and she in turn found herself attacking them out of contempt. The animals, however, were no trouble at all. They regarded her as just another cohabitant in their shared universe, as part of the 'natural order'.

Rosaleen's love of animals, and her antipathy towards much of what the human race had come to represent, had a profound influence on her magical conceptions. And yet she acknowledged duelling elements in the animal kingdom as well, for these reflected the important opposing polarities within the cosmos itself. Her preference for animals was not simply a retreat into the world of the nonhuman. On the contrary, she believed that the animal kingdom encompassed a broad range of activities, functions and potentials from which humanity had much to learn.

This recognition of opposing polarities shows itself well in one of her most impressive pictures, *Esoteric Study*. Here an angry demon leers across from the realm of chaos, counterbalanced by a diamond image of white radiance on the other side. A pair of scales rises up from the cosmic egg – a universal symbol of life and new birth – and the superimposition of the artist's face upon the scales suggests that she is the vehicle through which these tides of magical energy must flow. Gavin Greenlees's accompanying poem begins:

> Out of herself, the Earth created by her own Guardian faces
> And using the rule they gave her, out of herself
> She made creatures to serve her – animals, poems,
> Forgotten beings, men, women . . . Out of herself
> She made the grandeur aid its faith, healthy or faded . . .[30]

Another of Rosaleen Norton's key works is *Individuation*, a reference to Jung's concept of spiritual and psychic wholeness. The androgynous figure depicted is a fusion of animal, human and divine and stands astride the zodiac, seemingly drawn down into an accumulation of manifested forms, yet at the same time able to rise transcendent above them.[31] Accompanying the image are these words:

> I speak the birth
> I speak the beginning of presence
> I am inauguration, I am a greeting between friends . . .

Individuation is an important drawing because it embodies the different elements of the magical quest. And while Rosaleen's drawings and paintings so often seem to point to the 'night' side of consciousness, works like this show that she really understood that magical exploration was an encounter with the forces of both darkness and light. One without the other would lead to a state of psychic and spiritual imbalance.

It is fair to say that Rosaleen Norton was frequently misunderstood during her own lifetime. Many remember her more for her exotic public persona as 'the witch of Kings Cross' than for her innovative and often confronting role as a magical artist. And yet, clearly, she was no mere witch. She lived in a world populated by magical beings and astral entities whose presence pervaded her paintings and drawings in varying degrees. For her, the ancient gods were a living presence in the world, and we could fail to heed their call only at our own cost. Like Dion Fortune and Austin Spare before her, Rosaleen Norton was a visionary ahead of her time – an important forerunner of the contemporary occult revival.

6

The Rebirth of the Goddess

Much of the current interest in Western occultism is directly related to the rise and importance of feminism as a contemporary social movement. Witchcraft, or Wicca, and the broader concept of goddess worship – which we will discuss subsequently – both focus on the veneration of a female deity: usually the Nature goddess or the goddess of the Moon. The act of invoking feminine archetypes, reflecting different dimensions of the Universal Goddess, is central to their spiritual perspective.

In this context it is easy to see why Dion Fortune and Rosaleen Norton are bridging figures linking different generations of esoteric practitioners, especially those attracted to feminine mythic imagery. Of course, the feminist movement per se did not exist in their day. Dion Fortune has acknowledged MacGregor Mathers and the Golden Dawn as her main source of occult information, and Rosaleen Norton, coming a little later, was indebted in turn to the writings of Aleister Crowley, Dion Fortune, A. E. Waite and Margaret Murray (author of the controversial *Witchcraft in Western Europe*) as well as Theosophical writers like Madame Blavatsky and Alice Bailey.

It seems extraordinary today, at a time when neopagan perspectives and goddess worship are an important part of the spectrum of 'alternative' spiritual beliefs and practices, that the British Witchcraft Act, dating from 1604, was not finally repealed until 1951. Until this date, books advocating the use of witchcraft rituals could not be released in the United Kingdom. One of the principal figures in contemporary witch-craft, Gerald Brousseau Gardner, had published *High Magic's Aid* in 1949, but it had been portrayed as a work of fiction. It was not until 1954 that Gardner's *Witchcraft Today* would be released, followed by *The Meaning of Witchcraft* in 1959.

Gerald Gardner and the Rise of Modern Witchcraft

Gerald Gardner (1884–1964) had come to magic late in life. Born at Blundellsands, near Liverpool, Gardner was of Scottish descent and his parents were financially secure: his father's family had managed the oldest private timber-trade company in the British Empire. Gardner also had some interesting ancestors. They included Vice-Admiral Alan Gardner, commander-in-chief of the Channel fleet against Napoleon in 1807, and a woman called Grissell Gairdner who was burned as a witch in Newburgh, Scotland, in 1610.

By 1936 Gerald Gardner was a man of independent means, having made a fortune as a rubber planter in Malaya. He was also interested in the history of Malayan civilisation and had written a book titled *Keris and Other Malay Weapons* – a pioneering study of the history and folklore of local armaments.

After his retirement, Gardner and his wife settled in the New Forest area of Hampshire. Just before the outbreak of World War II, he made contact with a group of local occultists headed by 'Brother Aurelius' and Mrs Mabel Besant-Scott, daughter of the well-known Theosophist Annie Besant. Calling themselves the Fellowship of Crotona, they held theatrical performances which they claimed to be Rosicrucian in charac-ter. However, some members of the Fellowship had links with an established witchcraft coven, and secret sabbat meetings were being held at that time in the New Forest. Following his contact with the Fellowship of Crotona, Gardner became an enthusiastic devotee of witchcraft and would soon employ his newly acquired magical know-ledge to support his patriotism and strong sense of Empire. In 1940 he was involved in a major witchcraft ritual conducted on Lammas Day (1 August) in the New Forest – directed against Hitler's threatened invasion of England. At this time a number of covens from southern

Aleister Crowley

Austin Osman Spare, a self-portrait

Austin Osman Spare: 'The Ascension of
the Ego from Ecstasy to Ecstasy', from
The Book of Pleasure (1913)

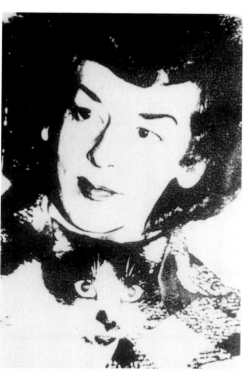

(Left) The Australian witch, Rosaleen Norton, with her pet cat

(Below left) Rosaleen Norton: 'Individuation'

(Below right) Rosaleen Norton: 'The Adversary'

Alex Sanders, photographed in 1985, three years before his death

Alex Sanders's *Book of Shadows*

Janet and Stewart Farrar, in Ireland

Altar in a witches' coven

Olivia and Derry Robertson at Clonegal Castle, Ireland

Initiates at the Fellowship of Isis

A goddess shrine in Clonegal Castle

Z Budapest conducting a goddess meeting in Berkeley, California

Margot Adler, an influential spokesperson for American Wicca

The Temple of Set is one of several magical orders that have revived the ancient Egyptian pantheon. Set is shown seated, holding an ankh. The other deity has a scarab's head – the scarab is associated with the Setian expression *xeper*, which translates as 'I have come into being'

The fantasy artist, H.R. Giger, at home in Zurich

England gathered for what they called Operation Cone of Power, chanting against Hitler and his generals and seeking telepathically to implant the thoughts 'You cannot cross the sea' and 'You are not able to come'.[1] There is no way of knowing, of course, whether this occult 'cone of power' had any influence on the outcome of the war.

Gardner claimed he had been initiated into witchcraft in 1939 by 'Old Dorothy' Clutterbuck, who also participated in the witchcraft ritual directed against Hitler. For many years details about Old Dorothy were hard to come by. However, Doreen Valiente, an authority on witchcraft origins, has established that 'Old Dorothy' was the daughter of Thomas St Quintin Clutterbuck, a captain of the 14th Sikh Regiment. Although the antiquity of her witches' coven, of course, cannot be proven, 'Old Dorothy' herself was hardly the crone her name suggests. Like Gardner, she was well-to-do and when she died in 1951 her estate was valued in excess of £60,000.[2]

Gardner described much of what he experienced in the New Forest coven in his novel *High Magic's Aid*, published in 1949. Two years later, following a campaign by the British spiritualists, the last of the Witchcraft Acts was repealed and the so-called Old Religion was allowed, at last, to come forth from the shadows. Gardner was delighted by this development for he believed passionately that the Craft could not be allowed to die out. Gardner's first nonfiction book on the Craft, *Witchcraft Today*, supported the view that modern witchcraft was a surviving remnant of the organised pagan religion which existed in England during the medieval witchcraft persecutions. It was important for witchcraft to reclaim its place once again as an authentic, Nature-based spiritual tradition.

Gardner maintained that witchcraft should be more accessible in presenting its core perspectives, and could then be presented to a broader public. Gardner believed strongly that the future of witchcraft rested with its appeal to young people and that sharing the tradition with this new generation could even lead to a revival of the old pagan ways. This proved to be an astute observation for, even though Gardner didn't experience it in his own lifetime, witchcraft has since positioned itself at the very centre of the contemporary occult revival.

In 1946 Gerald Gardner and his friend Arnold Crowther called on Aleister Crowley, who had retired to a guesthouse in Hastings.

Crowther had met Crowley during his wartime travels and it was he who arranged for the two occultists to meet. The encounter is significant because modern ceremonial magic, as developed by MacGregor Mathers and Aleister Crowley in the Golden Dawn, and the coven-based witchcraft of the New Forest, were now crossing paths, perhaps for the first time. Gardner and Crowley got on well together and this led to further discussions between the two men until Crowley died in December the following year.

During his meetings with Crowley, Gardner shared many insights with his magical colleague, and Crowley, in turn, made him an honorary member of his sexual magic order, the Ordo Templi Orientis. Repaying the tribute, Gardner began using quotations from Crowley's writings in his ceremonial rites, and it is also likely that substantial sections of Gardner's magical credo were written by Crowley and then fused with a traditional Book of Shadows, a practising witch's personal book of spells and rituals.

Other aspects of Gardnerian witchcraft, however, are quite likely his own invention. One of these is the modern tendency for witches to work naked, or 'sky-clad', in their rituals. Gardner was an enthusiastic naturist and, as Doreen Valiente writes, he had 'a deep-rooted belief in the value of going naked when circumstances favoured it'. For him, 'communal nakedness, sunshine and fresh air were natural and beneficial, both physically and psychologically.'[3] Another possibility is that Gardner may have derived the concept of ritual nudity from the book *Aradia: Gospel of the Witches*, written by American folklorist Charles G. Leland and published in 1889. Leland said he first learned about Aradia from a hereditary Etruscan witch called Maddalena, while he was visiting Italy. Aradia was the daughter of the Roman Moon goddess Diana and Leland's text includes details of Diana's role as queen of the witches. It also mentions that devotees of Diana were instructed to be naked in their rituals as a sign of personal freedom.

While Gardner's approach to nudity seems to have been wholesome enough, other, less appealing sexual tendencies found their way into his witchcraft practices as well. According to Francis King in *Ritual Magic in England*, 'Gardner was a sado-masochist with both a taste for flagellation and marked voyeuristic tendencies. Heavy scourging was therefore incorporated into most of his rituals and what Gardner called the 'Great Rite' was sexual intercourse between the High Priest and the High Priestess while surrounded by the rest of the coven.'[4]

Crowley was an old hand at disguising references to sexual activity in his own ritual writings and had included similar allusions both in his *Book of Lies* and in his principal work, *Magick in Theory and Practice*. It is therefore not surprising that Crowley should have influenced Gardner as much as he did, for these two men obviously had much in common. Crowley's contribution to modern witchcraft, therefore, cannot be underestimated. However, it also has to be said that most forms of contemporary neopaganism are decidedly more respectful to women than Crowley's cult of the Whore of Babalon . . .

A significant modifying factor seems to have been provided by the contribution of Doreen Valiente. Gardner initiated Valiente into his coven in 1953 and she felt that some of the Crowleyian material which Gardner had incorporated was either too 'modern', or inappropriate. Much of this would be written out of the ceremonial procedures between 1954 and 1957, as Gardner and Valiente worked together preparing the rituals which would form the basis of the 'Gardnerian tradition' in contemporary witchcraft.

Following the repeal of the Witchcraft Act, Gardner left the New Forest coven in 1951 and started his own magical circle. He then moved to Castletown on the Isle of Man, where a Museum of Magic and Witchcraft had already been established by an occult enthusiast called Cecil Williamson. Gardner bought the museum from Williamson, became the 'resident witch', and added his own collection of ritual tools and artefacts.

While the Museum of Magic and Witchcraft attracted considerable media attention, so too did the publication of Gardner's later books. The release of *Witchcraft Today* placed him under the media spotlight and the ensuing publicity led to the rise of new covens all across England. Gardner, meanwhile, was dubbed 'Britain's Chief Witch'. However, in his defence it must be acknowledged that this was a title he did not seek or use himself. According to those who knew him well, Gardner was not attracted to the pursuit of power or fame.

Nevertheless, despite Gardner's intentions, a certain degree of fame and influence was now being thrust upon him. In 1963 Gardner met Raymond Buckland, an Englishman who had moved to America.

Gardner's high priestess, Monique Wilson – also known as Lady Olwen – initiated Buckland into the Craft and it was Buckland who would introduce Gardnerian witchcraft to the United States.[5]

Gardnerian witchcraft is now the dominant international tradition in contemporary neopaganism but, as I have mentioned, Gardner himself did not live to see its full impact. He died at sea on 12 February 1964, returning to England from a trip to Lebanon, and was buried the following day in Tunis. In his will, Gardner bequeathed his Museum to Monique Wilson and she ran it with her husband for a short time, before selling it to the Ripley organisation. Unfortunately the contents of the museum are now widely dispersed, but Gardner's writings and occult perspectives – the more important part of his occult legacy – enjoy an ongoing and widespread influence in the international neopagan community. To this extent, Gardner's wish for the continuation of the Craft tradition has been fully realised.

Defining Modern Witchcraft

The practical aspects of modern witchcraft will be discussed in more detail in the following chapter but it is perhaps helpful at this point to summarise some key aspects by way of definition.

Witchcraft is often referred to as Wicca, from the Old English words *wicca* (masculine) and *wicce* (feminine) meaning 'a practitioner of witchcraft'. The word *wiccan*, 'witches', occurs in the Laws of King Alfred (circa 890 CE) and the verb *wiccian* – 'to bewitch' – was also used in this context. Some witches believe that the words connote a wise person, and Wicca is sometimes known as the 'Craft of the Wise'.

Witchcraft in essence is a Nature-based religion with the great goddess as its principal deity. She can take many forms: the Great Mother or Mother Nature, or more specifically Artemis, Astarte, Athena, Demeter, Diana, Aphrodite, Diana, Hathor, Isis or Persephone, among many others. The high priestess of the coven incarnates the spirit of the Goddess in a ceremonial context when the high priest 'draws down the Moon' into her body. In witchcraft, the high priestess is the receptacle of wisdom and intuition and is symbolised by the cup, whereas her consort is represented by a short sword or dagger. Many witchcraft rituals feature the act of uniting dagger and cup as a symbol of sexual union, and there is also a comparable relationship in Celtic mythology between the sacred oak tree and Mother Earth. Accordingly the high priest, or consort, is sometimes known as the oak king – a reference to the oak of the Celts – and at other times as Cernunnos, 'the horned one'. In witchcraft the horned god personifies fertility, and in ancient Greece the great god Pan – the goat-footed god – was a symbol of Nature and the universal life force. There is no connection between the horned god of witchcraft and the Christian horned Devil although, since the time of the witchcraft persecutions of the Middle Ages, this has been a common error.

Wiccan covens vary in size although traditionally the membership number is thirteen – consisting of six men, six women and the high priestess. When the group exceeds this number, some members leave to form a new coven. Wiccans take special magical names which they use in a ritual context and they meet for their ceremonies at specific times of the year. The meetings held through the year at full moon are known as esbats and these are essentially monthly gatherings of the witches' coven. These are smaller meetings than the major gatherings – the so-called greater sabbats of the witches' calendar – which are related to the changing seasons of Nature and traditional times for harvesting crops.

The four greater sabbats are:

Candlemas (2 February), known by the Celts as *Imbolc*
May Eve (30 April), or *Beltane*
Lammas (1 August), or *Lughnassadh*
Halloween (31 October), or *Samhain*

In addition, there are four minor sabbats: the two solstices at midsummer and midwinter, and the two equinoxes in spring and autumn.

In pre-Christian times, Imbolc was traditionally identified with the first signs of spring; Beltane was a fertility celebration when the sacred oak was burned, mistletoe cut, and sacrifices made to the gods, and Lughnassadh was related to autumn and the harvesting of crops and celebrated both the gathering-in of produce and the continuing fertility of the earth. Samhain represented the transition from autumn to winter and was associated with bonfires to keep away the chilly winter winds.

Samhain was also a time when the spirits of the dead could return to Earth to be once again with their loved ones.

Contemporary witches still meet in their covens to celebrate these Celtic rites, although in the southern hemisphere most Wiccan practitioners adjust the sabbats to fit the appropriate season. Sabbats are a time for fellowship, ceremonial and initiation, and after the rituals have been performed there is feasting, drinking and merriment.

Wiccan ceremonies take place in a magic circle which can either be inscribed upon the floor of a special room set aside as the 'temple', or marked on the earth at a designated meeting place – for example, in a grove of trees or on the top of a sacred hill. The earth is swept with a ritual broomstick for purification and the four elements are ascribed to the four directions: earth in the north, air in the east, fire in the south and water in the west. The altar is traditionally placed in the north. Beings known as the 'lords of the watchtowers' are believed to govern the four quarters and are invoked in rituals for blessings and protection.

Within the circle and present on the altar are the Wiccans' Book of Shadows (a personal book of rituals and invocations), a bowl of water, a dish of salt, candles, a symbolic scourge (representing will and determination), a bell, a cord to bind candidates in initiation, and consecrated symbols of the elements: a pentacle or disc (earth, feminine), a cup (water, feminine), a censer (fire, masculine) and a wand (air, masculine). The high priestess has her own *athame*, or ritual dagger, and the sword of the high priest rests on the ground before the altar.

Contemporary Wicca recognises three initiations. The first confers witch status upon the neophyte, the second promotes a first-degree witch to the position of high priestess or high priest, and the third celebrates the bonding of the high priestess and high priest in the Great Rite – either real or symbolic sexual union.[6] It is also generally the rule that a man must be initiated by a woman and a woman by a man, although a parent may initiate a child of the same sex. Most covens do not admit anyone under the age of twenty-one.[7]

There is an emphasis in Wicca on the threefold aspect of the Great Goddess in her role as maid (youth, enchantment), mother (maturity, fulfilment) and crone (old age, wisdom). This symbolic personification of the phases of womanhood are represented, for example, by the Celtic triad Brigid – Dana – Morrigan, the Greek goddess in her three aspects Persephone – Demeter – Hecate, or by the three Furies, Alecto (goddess of beginnings) – Tisiphone (goddess of continuation) – Megaera (goddess of death and rebirth); and these threefold aspects are particularly emphasised by feminist Wicca groups in their development of 'women's mysteries'. As the American neopagan Z Budapest writes in her *Holy Book of Women's Mysteries*: 'Images of the Mother Goddess, female principle of the universe and source of all life, abound . . . [for she is] the goddess of ten thousand names.'

It should also be mentioned that in Wicca, as in other contemporary forms of esoteric practice, magic is usually classified as 'black' or 'white' and this has to do with intent. Black magic is pursued in order to cause harm to another person through injury, illness or misfortune, and it also aims to enhance the personal power of the magician in bringing about this result. White magic, on the other hand, seeks a beneficial outcome and is often associated with rites of healing, with eliminating evil or disease, and with the expansion of spiritual awareness.

The Influence of Alex Sanders

Alongside Gerald Gardner, Alex Sanders (1916–88) is regarded as the most influential figure in the early phase of the contemporary witchcraft revival. He even has an entire Wiccan tradition named after him, for so-called Alexandrian witches – by virtue of a play on the words of his name – are those descended from his initiatory covens in the late 1960s and early 1970s. This period was undoubtedly his heyday, for he was then a very public figure and, accompanied by his former wife Maxine, provided witchcraft with a certain ceremonial glamour.

By his own account Sanders was born in Manchester in 1916. Appropriately, since he would later help revive the worship of the lunar goddess in modern times, it is clear that women rather than men played a formative role in his upbringing. His mother, sister and grandmother were the significant forces in his early life, his often drunken and wayward father a much lesser figure. According to his biographer June Johns, Sanders was raised on bread and dripping as a youth, and the family had to struggle to make ends meet. Sanders' mother Hannah was a cleaner, his father an itinerant musician. But it was his Welsh grandmother, Grandma Bibby, who would determine his future occult career.

One day when he was seven Sanders paid her an unannounced visit and came upon her naked, 'with wrinkled belly and match-stick thighs', engaged in a witchcraft ritual in her kitchen. Sanders recalls that 'a number of curious objects surrounded her. These were swords, a black-handled knife, a sickle-shaped knife and various bowls lying around on the floor: other odd objects lay on a large Welsh dresser.'[8]

Frightened at first by this unexpected encounter, young Sanders was sworn to secrecy by his grandmother and told he would be duly initiated. Grandma Bibby now ordered him to remove his clothes, step forward into the magical circle, and bend over with his head between his thighs. Taking the sickle-knife in her hands, she nicked Sanders's scrotum with it, drawing blood. 'You're one of us now,' she told him, and Sanders realised he was destined to be a witch. Later Grandma Bibby explained to her grandson that she was descended from a line of witches dating back to the fourteenth-century Welsh chieftain Owain Glyn Dwr (Owen Glendower), who had worshipped the Great Goddess and kept the ancient Celtic traditions alive.

Over the next few years a strong bond developed between Sanders and his grandmother, as she instructed him in making love potions and good-luck charms and also showed him the ceremony of 'drawing down the Moon' – a ritual in which the high priestess is transformed ceremonially into the living lunar goddess. Sanders also learned how to write his own Book of Shadows, so called because its contents relate to the 'other world' of gods and spirits. All practising witches write by hand their individual assortment of occult lore, ceremonies, invocations and charms.

According to Wiccan tradition the Book of Shadows is burnt when the dying witch 'passes over'.

When Grandma Bibby died in 1942, Sanders destroyed her Book of Shadows but retained her black-handled knife, her ceremonial sword and other items of ritual equipment. Before her death she had initiated Sanders into the third degree, which included token sexual intercourse with her – an act symbolising the union of the fertility goddess and her consort.

Sanders now had an exotic occult pedigree to offer the world. However, his initial forays into occult covens were characterised by material-istic self-advancement. By his own admission, Sanders engaged in ritual magic with the aim of attracting prosperity and sexual success – and in his case it appeared to work. Sanders was taken up by a wealthy couple who for several years treated him as their son, bestowing gifts and riches upon him, and he also found himself attracted to a frivolous, fun-loving group of promiscuous party-goers. However, this phase passed and Sanders realised that he had more serious esoteric matters to attend to. He resolved to develop several witchcraft covens in the Manchester area and continue the work passed on to him by his grandmother.

It was during this time that Sanders met Maxine Morris, an attractive young woman who had been raised as a devout Roman Catholic and educated at the local convent. Her mother was a committed Christian but Maxine herself had had childhood visions of merging with the earth and sky and Sanders was convinced she was a natural witch. Although they were not initially drawn together, they gradually realised a shared purpose and married in 1967. Eventually Maxine would become known in English neopagan circles as the 'witch queen'.

In this same year, Sanders and his wife moved to Notting Hill Gate and established the witchcraft coven that in due course would attract Stewart and Janet Farrar – who in turn would later become influential figures in the international neopagan movement. By now Sanders had established himself as the leading public witch in Britain. Just a few years earlier he had been endorsed by a group of 1,623 practising Wiccans as 'king of the witches'. He was also becoming a media celeb-rity. There were numerous television appearances, late-night talks on the BBC, record albums of his rituals, and even a film, *The Legend of the Witches*, based loosely on his pagan activities.

Sanders was also emphasising an apparent point of superiority over Gerald Gardner – for Sanders had gained a third-degree initiation from his grandmother whereas Gardner had only received a first degree from Old Dorothy. It is a point of distinction which still rankles in some occult circles when witchcraft pedigrees are discussed, for both Sanders and Gardner continue to retain a substantial neopagan following and questions of 'authenticity', 'tradition' and 'lineage', as always, produce factionalism and rivalry.

Sanders and his wife separated in 1973. Maxine Morris continued running her coven in London with a new consort and a much more low-key public presence. Sanders, meanwhile, drifted towards semi-retirement and moved to Bexhill in Sussex, where he lived until his death in 1988.

However, issues of lineage and authenticity resurfaced once again with the departure of Alex Sanders from the scene, and several highly respected witches in Britain let it be known that they did not promote the public witchcraft endorsed by Alex Sanders and his group. The influential English witch Patricia Crowther – whose husband had introduced Gerald Gardner to Aleister Crowley in 1946 – was one of those who objected to Sanders's public style. Patricia Crowther had been initiated by Gardner on the Isle of Man in June 1960 and later established a coven with her husband in Sheffield. She took the initiation of high priestess in October 1961 and has been considered by many to be Gardner's natural successor. When I discussed the issue of occult secrecy with her in the mid-eighties, she told me that she was strongly opposed to witches who 'break their oaths' and release too much information to the public. For her, the 'old school' of witches – including Doreen Valiente, Lois Bourne and Eleanor Bone – were authentic, whereas many of the more public witches had not been properly initiated.[9]

Janet and Stewart Farrar

The issue of how much authentic Wiccan information could be presented to the public was one which also had to be addressed by Janet and Stewart Farrar, both of whom had been initiated in Alex Sanders's coven.[10] The Farrars are among the most visible practitioners of contemporary witchcraft, and by the late 1970s had already assumed a leadership role in London's neopagan community. They have written several major works on neopaganism, including *Eight Sabbats for Witches*, *The Witches' Way*, *The Witches' Goddess* and *The Witches' God*, published both in Britain and the United States, and through their writings and advocacy have strongly influenced neopagan thought and practice on both sides of the Atlantic. The rituals, spellcraft and specific conjurations described in these books represent a working guide to practical witchcraft and provide the sort of information Patricia Crowther believes should remain restricted to the inner circle.

Janet Farrar (née Owen) was born in 1950 and was raised in east London in a strictly Christian family: her grandfather was a church councillor in their Anglican parish. However, she began to drift away from Christianity during her adolescent years and later became briefly involved in Transcendental Meditation. She worked for a while as a model and then became a secretary in the Beatles' London office.

Around this time Janet visited Alex and Maxine's coven in Notting Hill Gate. She was impressed by Wicca as a spiritual path and decided to join the circle. It was here that she met her husband Stewart.

Stewart had a very different background from hers. Born in Essex in 1916, he had been raised as a Christian Scientist but later became an agnostic – a position he maintained until becoming a devotee of witchcraft. He studied journalism at University College, London, during the 1930s, served as an anti-aircraft gunnery instructor during World War II, and later worked for several years as an editor for the news agency Reuters. He also produced several radio drama scripts for the BBC before becoming a feature writer for the weekly men's magazine *Reveille* in 1969. It was in his capacity as a journalist that Stewart Farrar had been invited to Sanders's coven – he had come simply to write an account of a Wiccan initiation. He did not realise at the time that he himself would become a dedicated convert to neopaganism.

Despite the substantial difference in their ages – thirty-four years – Janet Owen and Stewart Farrar were drawn together as magical partners. In December 1970, a few months after taking their initiations, they left Sanders's group to form a coven of their own. They married five years later in a traditional Wiccan handfasting ceremony and in 1976 moved to Ireland, where Stewart was able to gain tax relief as an author of science-fiction novels, his other major interest. For a time the Farrars ran a coven in a secluded farmhouse near Drogheda, north of Dublin, before returning to England in 1988.

Like Gerald Gardner and Alex Sanders before them, the Farrars emphasise that they are supporting an authentic Celtic tradition. In their major ceremonies, Janet, as high priestess, becomes the archetypal embodiment – a ritual incarnation – of the lunar goddess. In the Wiccan invocation ritual I was allowed to attend as an observer, she wore a skirt of silver, a crown of bright jewels, and was naked to the waist. Proclaimed within the coven's rituals as 'Our Lady, Goddess of the

Moon', Janet is always the focus of the group and plays the paramount role – for Wicca is a matriarchal religion. Stewart, despite his seniority in years, serves only as consort to the reigning 'queen'. In his role as high priest of the coven, he wears a horned crown, symbolic of the Celtic deity Cernunnos, and invokes the god of the sacred oak: *Thou God of old, thou mighty Horned One, thou who dwelt upon the waters and wert the first light of dawn – return to us again. Come at our call by rushing winds and leaping flame . . .*

The role of high priestess and high priest are nevertheless seen here as complementary, for one could not exist without the other. For Janet Farrar the essential aim of witchcraft is a spiritual fusion of male and female polarities, and the restoration of the sacred bond with Nature:

> Once a woman realises her own psychic potential, she becomes fully mature and can reunite man with herself in a way that mankind hasn't seen for aeons. We don't want to replace a male-dominated culture with a female-dominated one. We want to make the two work in perfect harmony . . .
>
> The world at the moment needs an injection of the pagan outlook. This means relating to the Earth, relating to the environment, relating to our fellow creatures. We are in danger of losing that contact and the balance needs restoring. Culture, religion and society have been male-dominated for two thousand years or more, and life has got out of balance. We need to recover the feminine aspect – the Goddess.[11]

Feminism and the Goddess

While contemporary witchcraft lineages have spread their networks far afield, and both Gardnerian and Alexandrian covens now abound not only in Britain but also in other parts of Europe and in the United States, Canada and Australia, the broader concept of goddess worship has also established itself as a major neopagan perspective. Goddess worship extends beyond the structure of coven-based witchcraft and its rituals are broader in scope, more diverse, and less bound by the traditional Wiccan concept of a threefold initiation. Many goddess wor-shippers do not refer to themselves as witches at all for, in its broadest definition, this form of neopagan belief is a universal feminist religion, drawing on mythologies from many different ancient cultures. And while contemporary Wicca has characteristically British roots, reflecting its Celtic origins, goddess worship first emerged in the American feminist movement as a spiritual perspective clearly at odds with mainstream, patriarchal religion.

In her book *Changing of the Gods: Feminism and the End of Traditional Religions*, published in 1979, Naomi Goldenberg spoke of creating a 'powerful new religion' focused on the worship of the goddess,[12] while around the same time the influential thinker Mary Daly was talking of a new feminist witchcraft in which woman's nature could be considered as innately divine. For neopagan women it would not be a matter of reflecting the goddess so much as *becoming* the goddess, or *being* the goddess,[13] and this was a sacred potential in which all women could share. As Mary Farrell Bednarowski and Barbara Starret have observed:

> Feminist witchcraft elevates woman's nature above man's nature in its life-giving abilities . . . Feminist witches describe themselves as committing a 'political act' when they replace the Father with the Mother: The image of the Mother does not lose its old connotations of earth, intuition, nature, the body, the emotions, the unconscious etc. But it also lays claim to many of the connotations previously attributed to the father symbol: beauty, light, goodness, authority, activity etc. The feminist witch claims both sun and moon, both heaven and earth, and she invokes the goddess in herself and in other women in her efforts to make it possible.[14]

This is a feminist concept of self-empowerment. For over twenty years American feminist goddess worshippers have focused on 'sisterhood' – close bonds between women – and for some devotees this has involved taking the goddess tradition beyond the male domain altogether. As Judy Davis and Juanita Weaver expressed it in the mid-1970s:

> Feminist spirituality has taken form in Sisterhood – in our solidarity based on a vision of personal freedom, self-definition, and in our struggle together for social and political change. The contemporary women's movement has created space for women to begin to per-

ceive reality with a clarity that seeks to encompass many complexities. This perception has been trivialized by male dominated cultures that present the world in primarily rational terms . . . [Feminist spirituality involves] the rejoining of woman to woman.[15]

A leading advocate of this position within the American neopagan movement is Z Budapest (pronounced Zee), whose goddess groups exclude men altogether. Z Budapest has even gone so far as to develop a 'self-blessing ritual', conceived as a means of 'exorcising the patriarchal policeman, cleansing the deep mind, and filling it with positive images of the strength and beauty of women'.[16]

Zsuzsanna Budapest was born in Hungary in 1940, the daughter of a psychic medium. Zsuzsanna's mother, Masika Szilagyi, composed poems and invocations while in trance and seemed at times to speak in an ancient Egyptian tongue. She was also an artist, poet and Tarot-card reader and earned recognition in Budapest as a sculptress – often featuring pagan and goddess themes in her motifs. Most importantly for Z, her mother also had an impeccable pedigree as a shamaness and could trace her mystical lineage back to the fourteenth century.

At the age of nineteen, Z came to Illinois from Vienna, where she had been studying languages, and now renewed her interest in German literature at the University of Chicago. Later she worked in theatre in New York, studying techniques of improvisation, before moving to Los Angeles in 1970.

It is on the American west coast that Z Budapest has made most of her impact, proclaiming her pagan heritage and stimulating interest in 'women's mysteries' within the feminist movement. Soon after arriving in Los Angeles she opened a now legendary occult shop, the Feminist Wicca, on Lincoln Boulevard in Venice. This store served as a 'matriarchal spiritual centre', dispensing candles, oil, incense, herbs, jewellery, Tarot cards and other paraphernalia, and it also emerged as a meeting place for women wishing to perform rituals together. Soon there were groups of neopagan women meeting for ceremonies on the equinoxes and solstices. As Z has said, 'feminist spirituality had been born again'.[17]

Among the best known of her friends at this time was Miriam Simos, a softly spoken Jewish woman who had rejected traditional Judaism and Buddhism as 'male authoritarian'. After graduating from UCLA and studying feminism, Simos heard about Z's centre and became interested in the public rituals to the goddess Diana which were being performed there. Now best known by her magical name Starhawk, Miriam Simos has since written several highly regarded books, including *The Spiral Dance*, *Dreaming the Dark* and *The Pagan Book of Living and Dying*, all of which are considered key works in the revival of goddess worship and neopaganism. Starhawk lost contact with Z for a time after moving north to form her own magical group in San Francisco. Meanwhile Z was attracting a new type of fame through the media.

On 10 February 1975, Z was arrested and charged with fortune-telling after giving an undercover policewoman a Tarot-card reading. Prior to going on trial in West Los Angeles, she announced at a press-club meeting that her supporters would be burning two thousand candles 'on altars throughout the city'. Describing herself as the 'first witch to go on trial for her beliefs in three hundred years', Z proclaimed herself to be a religious leader and demanded her right to freedom of belief under the First Amendment. This was partly to rebuke her legal charge, since fortune-telling was forbidden under the municipal code unless performed by a religious leader. Z maintained strongly that she deserved this exempt status, noting that she was now high priestess of the Susan B. Anthony #1 Coven – a group named after a controversial nineteenth-century suffragette.

The trial resulted in a $300 fine and a probation order, forbidding Z to read Tarot cards, so she turned instead to supplementing her income by teaching classes in the Tarot, divination and witchcraft – a change of emphasis allowed for under the law.

Z's brush with the authorities did nothing to diminish her outspokenness, however, and many people who had heard of her through the media were now intrigued to know what sort of religion she practised. In a lengthy interview with journalist Cheri Lesh, published shortly after the trial, Z explained that Wicca was not an inverted form of Christianity but represented the remnants of a much older, matriarchal system of worship which recognised the feminine as the creative force in Nature.[18] In the interview, Z spoke of the bloody transition from a matriarchal society to a patriarchal form, in which roaming bands of warriors ravaged the great queendoms of Anatolia, Sumer and Thrace and fragmented the 'Great Goddess' into a number of minor deities. This led to a much diminished status for the goddesses, who then had confined and restricted roles as a consequence. In Greek mythology, for example, Aphrodite became simply a goddess of love and sexuality, while Artemis represented hunting and Athena wisdom. Hera, Amphitrite and Persephone, meanwhile, became adjuncts to Zeus, Poseidon and Hades.

As Z pointed out in her interview with Cheri Lesh, such a transition was a major cultural disaster:

> Mythology is the mother of religions, and grandmother of history. Mythology is human-made, by the artists, storytellers and entertainers of the times. In short, culture-makers are the soldiers of history, more effective than guns and bombers. Revolutions are really won on the cultural battlefields.

Z maintained that the impact was far-reaching:

> Women understand this very well, since we became aware of how women's culture had been ripped off by the ruling class. This resulted in a stunted self-image of women which resulted in insecurities, internalizing the cultural expectations of us created by male culture-makers. Most of the women in the world still suffer from this spiritual poverty.

It is hardly surprising that Z's practice of Dianic worship excludes men altogether. She acknowledges that there are men who wish to discover the 'inner woman' within themselves but adds that there are other occult groups that cater for this. The women's mysteries, in her view, must be kept pure and strong, and men have no place in them. As she told me when I interviewed her for a television documentary: 'We have women's circles. You don't put men in women's circles – they wouldn't be women's circles any more. Our goddess is life, and women should be free to worship from their ovaries.'[19]

Z now favours an equal mix of lesbian and heterosexual women in her circles to 'balance the polarities' in her rituals. She is a practising lesbian herself, although she has not always been so inclined. Formerly married, with two sons – one a physicist, the other a fighter pilot in the marines – she has since adopted a strongly feminist position and has chosen to deliberately avoid what she calls the 'duality' of man and woman. Her emphasis on women's mysteries allows the different phases of womanhood to be honoured in their own right: the young, the mature and the older woman each have much to offer, and in Z's group ceremonies are performed for each of these phases of life.

If it is fair to say that Z Budapest adopts a somewhat confrontational style in defending the Dianic mysteries, her friend Starhawk has earned widespread acclaim for her less strident and often eloquent public advocacy of goddess mythology. Starhawk works as a psychotherapist and teacher and was a founding member of an organisation called Reclaiming: A Center for Feminist Spirituality and Counseling, in San Francisco. For a time in the mid-1980s she was also on the teaching faculty of Matthew Fox's postgraduate institute at Holy Names College in Oakland, exploring the common ground between her own neo-paganism and Fox's renegade Roman Catholic-based Creation-centred spirituality.[20] While Starhawk continues to regard herself as a political activist, she has also been able to convey the essence of the contemporary neopagan perspective in a poetic and lyrical fashion. In an interview with the Toronto-based writer Alexander Blair-Ewart, Starhawk explained that for her:

> what's important about witchcraft and about the pagan movement is, essentially, that it's not so much a way of seeing reality, as it's a different way of valuing the reality around us. We say that what is sacred, in the sense of what we are most committed to, what determines all our other values, is this living Earth, this world, the life systems of the Earth, the cycles of birth and growth and death and regeneration; the air, the fire, the water, the land . . .[21]

In her own writings Starhawk has referred specifically to the nurturing and revitalising power of the goddess-energy:

> The symbolism of the Goddess has taken on an electrifying power for modern women. The rediscovery of the ancient matrifocal civilizations has given us a deep sense of pride in woman's ability to create and sustain culture. It has exposed the falsehoods of patriarchal history, and given us models of female strength and authority. The

Goddess – ancient and primeval; the first of deities; patroness of the Stone Age hunt and of the first sowers of seeds; under whose guidance the herds were tamed, the healing herbs first discovered; in whose image the first works of art were created; for whom the standing stones were raised; who was the inspiration of song and poetry – is recognized once again in today's world. She is the bridge, on which we can cross the chasms within ourselves, which were created by our social conditioning, and reconnect with our lost potentials. She is the ship, on which we sail the waters of the deep self, exploring the uncharted seas within. She is the door, through which we pass to the future. She is the cauldron, in which we who have been wrenched apart simmer until we again become whole. She is the vaginal passage, through which we are reborn . . .[22]

Starhawk remains one of the leading advocates of the goddess tradition in America. She continues to write and lecture, and was also featured in the National Film Board productions *Goddess Remembered* and *The Burning Times*.

Further Afield

If contemporary goddess worship has its origins in the American feminist movement, it is also true that its seeds have been scattered to far-off shores and it now has a voice around the world. Two distinctive examples, among many, include the Temple of the Mother in Perth, Western Australia, and the Fellowship of Isis in Ireland – both of which have extended their scope well beyond the structures of traditional witchcraft.

The Temple of the Mother is headed by Levanah, a woman of German and Maori extraction, who emigrated to Perth from her native New Zealand. Raised as a Roman Catholic, Levanah recalls that when she was about six years old her father would take her away from the convent in Wanganui on weekends, and they would spend time together watching the full moon. Even then Levanah felt that the Moon was a 'sacred being', and she wondered in her innocent way whether it might somehow be possible to connect the Moon with the Virgin Mary and the Holy Ghost.

When she was sixteen she joined the Rosicrucians, while also continuing her allegiance to Roman Catholicism and attending Mass every
morning. After a period of overseas travel she immersed herself in New
Zealand politics, working as a publicist for the National Party. She later
married and worked with her husband in a civil engineering firm. After
a sudden decline in the company's business fortunes, Levanah and her
husband were forced to make a completely new start, and they decided
to establish themselves in Western Australia.

It was during a visit to Egypt, while still based in Perth, that Levanah
met a Muslim 'spiritual master' who worked in a mosque in Heliopolis.
This man clearly had a deep and special connection with the magical
traditions of this ancient land. Levanah says that it was through him
that she first became attuned with Isis, the mother goddess. And it was
also through him that she discovered that Egypt 'had her heart':

> We spent many, many days in the desert together, and as he spoke
> to me I realised he was describing a system that I had within me —
> that he was awakening my ancient self. As a person he was very,
> very beautiful. He radiated much love and light, and his teachings
> often came like a vibration from within him — it was almost like
> clairvoyant pictures before my eyes, an unveiling of knowledge.[23]

Levanah returned to Perth eager to put the Egyptian mysteries into
practice. Around this time she also met Peter Barwick, an Alexandrian
witch who was running the Magic Circle bookshop in Perth. With
him, Levanah explored the roots of traditional witchcraft, but she also
felt instinctively that she wanted to encompass a broader spiritual terrain.
She in turn instructed Barwick in the mysteries of Egyptian magic,
showing him how to draw on the *neters* — the ancient Egyptian god-
energies — as a means of developing his self-awareness. Not surprisingly,
the Temple of the Mother has developed as a fusion of the two traditions, blending ancient Egyptian magic and contemporary witchcraft
while seeking to pay special homage to the divinity of the mother
goddess in all her aspects.

Within the Temple itself there is an inner circle of thirteen members
— a reflection of the traditional coven structure — but the outer order
of the Temple is much broader, with around forty members at any

given time. Many of the members have belonged formerly to witchcraft covens or have explored a variety of other esoteric traditions. They come to the Temple to learn authentic Egyptian invocations, to perform the ancient songs and dances, and to relive the old ways. The Temple's ceremonies include ritual dances and invocations to Isis, Osiris, Nepthys and Anubis, but the Great Goddess clearly takes pride of place. Levanah explains her central role in invoking the goddess:

> Magic gives me vitality. It feeds me. It makes me constantly aware of change. It makes me constantly aware that I'm part of this universe and everybody else is part of it too. I actually do feel like I am the Great Mother. I feel like I am the earth. I'm sea, I'm everything feminine. And the priest and priestesses before me – as I look into their eyes and they look into my eyes, there is a most incredible openness that one doesn't find in the mundane world. We can only experience that within the sacredness of a ritual where we have worked to invoke the neters within ourselves, opening ourselves to learning. And as they kneel in front of me during the Full Moon, I have this feeling of being dissolved and being part of them, and of them being part of me, and of everything dissolving, all of Nature – everything dissolving around us, all of us becoming one.[24]

Although it is a unique expression of goddess worship in Western Australia, the Temple of the Mother is not alone in its pursuits. Thousands of miles away, in the little Irish village of Clonegal, a similar revival of goddess worship is taking place.

One comes to Clonegal by a meandering country road, flanked by hedgerows and rolling fields. The closest township is Bunclody, with its charming market square and sloping main street. Away to the north, some two hours' drive away, lies the clutter of Dublin, but here the mood is tranquil and timeless. The narrow road into Clonegal passes across a humped stone bridge, veers to the right, and proceeds between a cluster of modest houses. Hidden behind these dwellings is Clonegal Castle.

Clonegal Castle is the home of Lady Olivia Durdin-Robertson and, until his recent death, her brother Lawrence, the 21st Baron of Strathloch, also lived here. Lawrence – who preferred to be known as

Derry – was born in England in 1920 and grew up in Ireland from the age of five. After a stint in the Irish army he decided to pursue a more peaceful career in the Church and studied for three years at the Wells Theological College in Somerset, just after World War II. After his ordination he became parish rector at Aghold, County Wicklow, and then spent five years as rector in East Bilney, Norfolk. By now he had become interested in comparative religion and the more unorthodox realms of spiritualism, theosophy and the occult. Then, in 1966, he experienced the revelation that the feminine aspect of deity was all-important, or, in his own words, 'that God was female'. Accordingly, on the vernal equinox in 1976, Derry and Olivia formed the Fellowship of Isis, a magical order 'dedicated to spreading the Religion of the Goddesses throughout the world'. The family castle would be the head-quarters of the new magical order.

Clonegal Castle is an authentic Jacobean castle and dates from 1625 – it was one of the last buildings of its type erected in Ireland. Long before the castle was built, there was an abbey on the site, and before that, an ancient Druid community worshipped on the land. The sacred well used by the Druids is now incorporated within Clonegal Castle itself, and is used during ceremonies to the Goddess.

Derry and Olivia Robertson converted the basement of their castle into what they called the Temple of the Stars – a series of rooms and passageways housing several shrines and chapels. There are twelve such shrines, one for each sign of the zodiac, and each has symbols and motifs of the Universal Goddess appropriate to that astrological motif. The Temple of the Stars includes statues and paintings of Isis, Aphrodite, Diana and Hathor, among many other female deities, and provides the setting for the ritual ordination of priests and priestesses within the Fellowship of Isis.

According to Olivia Robertson, the first phase of priesthood involves obedience and service to the nominated goddess – candidates are free to choose which goddess they will dedicate their lives to – and this is expressed through hymns of praise and the quest for salvation. The second phase is more of a visionary leap forward: the individual now identifies totally with the specific deity and becomes a human channel for the spiritual presence of that sacred being. Because women are 'naturally psychic and intuitive', they are ideally suited to this type of religious expression, and the Fellowship of Isis sees its role as assisting such spiritual transformation. Olivia calls the Temple 'a half-way house between this world and the other'.

In rites of ordination, candidates are presented for the priesthood and take vows to serve the Goddess and express themselves through her. Usually a sizeable group of devotees assembles for each ordination ceremony; there may be as many as fifteen or twenty Fellowship members on each occasion.

Fully robed in ceremonial regalia, the candidates enter the castle from the gardens and walk along an avenue of ancient yew trees. The group then makes its way down the steps into the Temple of the Stars and gathers around the ancient well, which is sacred to the Irish goddess of prosperity, Brigid. Here holy water is presented to the candidates, who drink it to enhance the spiritual vision and healing in their lives. The group now moves further on into the Temple to confront the Dark Mother – a symbolic embodiment of the dark side of the soul.

A Fellowship member personifying Morrigan, the Celtic queen of demons, now presents herself to the group from the castle dungeon. She wears dark robes and a formidable, if somewhat gruesome, tribal mask. The idea is to present the least attractive aspect of the Goddess as a counterpoint to the beauty, love and happiness she also bestows. Here is the Goddess in her most menacing form – a hag, a potential destroyer. The candidates are asked in turn if they fear her, but attuned to the spirit of the occasion, they offer their love and submission. Morrigan now removes her mask and reveals herself as the radiant goddess of the Moon – a force of life and light transcending the darkness and restriction of the castle dungeon.

Moving still further into the Temple, past the many shrines and chapels that similarly reveal different aspects of the divine feminine, the candidates come to the high altar. Offerings are now made to the Goddess and Olivia asks the new initiates which aspect of the feminine deity they have chosen to dedicate themselves to. Perhaps they will follow Isis, Aphrodite or Diana – or perhaps the more local goddesses like Dana, mother of the Tuatha de Danaan, or Cesara, Banba or Fodhla. Olivia, as priestess, now anoints the head, heart and hands of each candidate and presents them each with a crown and wand. As she does so, she makes a blessing over them: *With this crown I dignify thy head, with this stole I hallow thy heart, with this wand I strengthen thy will for good. . . may you be blessed by the Goddess.*

The candidates are now accepted into the priesthood and make their first invocations as initiates, each in turn calling on the Goddess to enrich their lives and those about them. The ceremony ends with a symbolic 'coming forth from the womb' as members of the Fellowship of Isis emerge from the castle and proceed into the gardens once again.

An important aspect of the Fellowship of Isis is that it transcends denominational boundaries. Catholics, Protestants, Buddhists, Hindus, Muslims, neopagans – all are welcome and come to Clonegal Castle regularly. Others communicate by letter, sharing rituals and broadening their range of contacts via the *Isis* newsletter.

The Fellowship of Isis continues to maintain one of the largest neopagan networks in the world, with representatives from over eighty countries, including the United States, Canada and Australia as well as Britain and several other European nations. A large number of members also come from Africa, especially Nigeria, Ghana and the Ivory Coast. Olivia Robertson believes that traditional African religious beliefs are quite compatible with the aims of the Fellowship of Isis since both, at heart, are polytheistic, or multidimensional. The rites at Clonegal Castle thus provide a framework for developing old religious ideas within a modern context while also bringing diverse peoples together. Olivia Robertson's perspective on the Goddess and the neopagan revival – a view shared by her late brother – is essentially similar to that of their American feminist counterparts:

> The upsurge in the occult comes from within. It cannot find containment in the existing western religions so it has to find expression in some other form. The old religions, and paganism if you like to call it that, make far more allowance for spiritualism and the occult than orthodox Christianity, which is basically patriarchal. The patriarchal religions have a certain fixed framework and their followers must believe within those limits. They don't allow for spontaneous inspiration or revelation.[25]

Starhawk and Z Budapest, I feel sure, would wholeheartedly agree with these thoughts.

7

Neopagan Pathways

There is, of course, no single pathway in neopaganism. Some neopagans are highly structured in their ceremonial response to the mythic universe, while others are much more spontaneous. Some emphasise lineage and authority within their covens, others are more egalitarian. And as I have already mentioned, clear differences have already emerged between contemporary neopaganism in Britain – where the rebirth of witchcraft first gathered momentum – and its American counterpart, which is grounded in the feminist counter-culture. Accordingly, there is considerable diversity, and some dissension, about what is sacred and what is significant upon the neopagan path. We will deal here with some of the central practices and perspectives, while recognising the potential for almost infinite variations on a theme.

Some Points in Common

It may be useful to start by considering issues on which most neopagans agree – for these shared perspectives point to core elements in their beliefs and practice.

Clearly, Wiccans venerate the Goddess of Nature in all her manifest aspects and most celebrate the cycle of the seasons which follows the path of the Sun and the various phases of the Moon. Wiccans also believe that whatever magic they do indeed engage in involves dealing

168

with natural forces and energies – they do not perceive their magic as being in any way 'supernatural'. In focusing especially on the feminine principle, associated with intuition and inner knowing, they are also inclined to consider their individual magical prowess as part of a natural innate potential. Wiccans place great emphasis on learning how to manipulate psychic energy and develop their powers of magical visualisation as adjuncts to their work in rituals and spellcraft.

Wicca has also developed its own code of conduct and ethics. The Wiccan *Rede* states a simple principle which all Wiccans are asked to adhere to: 'And it harm none, do what you will.' One is reminded immediately of Aleister Crowley's dictum 'Do what thou wilt shall be the whole of the law; love is the law, love under will' – although 'harm none' adds an element missing in Crowley. And in more recent times the Pagan Federation in London has expanded upon the Wiccan *Rede*, issuing a statement which reflects in more detail what many neopagans accept as a basic philosophy of life:

Love for and Kinship with Nature: rather than the more customary attitude of aggression and domination over Nature; reverence for the life force and the ever-renewing cycles of life and death.

The Pagan Ethic: 'Do what thou wilt, but harm none'. This is a positive morality, not a list of thou-shalt-nots. Each individual is responsible for discovering his or her own true nature and developing it fully, in harmony with the outer world.

The Concept of Goddess and God as expressions of the Divine reality; an active participation in the cosmic dance of Goddess and God, female and male, rather than the suppression of either the female or the male principle.[1]

Both the *Rede* and the Pagan Federation statement are reminders to practising Wiccans that they are obliged to be fully aware of the consequences of their behaviour. Many Wiccans believe that any misplaced or ill-intentioned action is likely to rebound with threefold strength upon the perpetrator.

Responding to the Goddess

Beliefs and ritual practices inevitably reflect individual perceptions and there are numerous approaches to the Goddess, whose sacred presence defines the very heart of the Wiccan perspective. Nevertheless, most Wiccans relate to the Goddess of the Moon as a triple goddess – a reference to her symbolic association with the female fertility cycle. As the waxing Moon she is seen as the maiden, as the full moon she is the mother, and as the waning Moon she is the crone. She is also widely considered as a goddess of the here and now – a goddess who permeates our very being and existence. As Starhawk has put it, 'The Goddess is around us and within us. She is immanent and transcendent . . . the Goddess represents the divine embodied in Nature, in human beings, in the flesh.'[2]

For Starhawk, it is also clear that the encounter with the Goddess should be based on personal experience, and not on religious belief:

> In the Craft, we do not *believe* in the Goddess – we connect with Her; through the moon, the stars, the ocean, the earth, through trees, animals, through other human beings, through ourselves. She is here. She is within us all. She is the full circle: earth, air, fire, water and essence – body, mind, spirit, emotions, change.
>
> The Goddess is first of all earth, the dark, nurturing mother who brings forth all life. She is the power of fertility and generation; the womb, and also the receptive tomb, the power of death. All proceeds from Her, all returns to Her.[3]

Some Wiccans, in considering the all-encompassing nature of the Great Goddess, describe their spiritual perspective as monotheistic, while others acknowledge an innate dynamism between the female and male polarities in the mythic universe. Dion Fortune – who in many ways anticipated the feminist perspective in contemporary Wicca – believed that all of the goddesses in the various mythic pantheons are really manifestations of the one Great Goddess whose identity is the universal feminine spirit of Nature. And Margot Adler, a well-known spokesperson for American neopaganism, has similarly claimed that many Wiccans regard the Goddess as essentially One – a perspective she herself endorses. However, Adler has also acknowledged that other Wiccans distinguish between the goddess of the Moon, Earth and sea, and the god of the woods, hunt and animal realm, in a type of 'duotheism'.[4] The British Wiccan authority Vivianne Crowley responds to the issue in a different way when she says: 'All Gods are different aspects of the one God and all Goddesses are different aspects of the one Goddess . . . ultimately these two are reconciled in the one divine essence.'[5]

Vivianne Crowley's evaluation reminds us that Wicca offers very different potentials for men and women upon the neopagan path, and Starhawk also makes this point: 'For women, the Goddess is the symbol of the inmost self, and the beneficent, nurturing, liberating power within woman . . . For a man, the Goddess, as well as being the universal life force, is his own, hidden, female self.'[6]

Profound reflections on the complementary relationship between female and male potentials can be found in the following Wiccan tract, which has been passed informally between different covens in Australia:

Silence preceded everything. And within the silence was the natural spark of life, inherent in all things, the creative magical current which was both male and female, equal with each other.

The male and female energies united with love, bringing together two essential sparks of life. Then there was light, within which all was true and balanced. She was Water and Earth. He was Fire and Air, and together they were Spirit.

They once again united and created all on Earth, not one before the other. All life was created out of the essential elements of Water and Earth, Fire and Air, and Spirit: animals, plants, insects, rocks, man and woman. Man and woman came together, became one in sexual union, with the spirit of magic within them.

He was the Lord incarnate upon the Earth, and She was the Great Earth Mother.[7]

The Magic Circle and the Cone of Power

As we saw earlier in the chapter on the Golden Dawn, the magic circle is a symbol of sacred space. This is also true in the Wiccan tradition, but here it has added significance. In Wicca it is a symbol of the womb of the Goddess, and represents containment, totality, and a sense of transcendent wholeness. Margot Adler calls the sacred circle a 'microcosm of the universe', and Starhawk says that it 'exists on the boundaries of ordinary space and time; it is "between the worlds" of the seen and unseen . . . a space in which alternate realities meet, in which the past and future are open to us.'[8]

In Wicca the magic circle is usually marked by the four cardinal points and these in turn are linked to the four elements. North is associated with earth (symbolising the physical body), east with air (associated with thoughts and communication), south with fire (energy and will) and west with water (emotions and feelings). The centre of the circle represents spirit – for in spirit we find a resolution of the four elements and a true sense of unity.

Many neopagan rituals begin by drawing the circle with a stick or with chalk. Alternatively, one may stand within an existing circle, if a special space has already been prepared. However, the circle has to be marked off ritually as sacred, distinguishing the ritual space within its confines from the everyday world beyond. The four elements are then invoked at the cardinal points, followed by invocations to the Goddess.

Wiccans also focus on the image of the magic circle to build what they call 'the cone of power' – a vortex of collective magical energy which can be directed towards the specific ritual at hand. In building the cone of power, coven members run clockwise around the circle holding hands, at the same time focusing their attention on the central altar candle. Often this is accompanied by 'The Witches' Rune', a colourful chant written by Gerald Gardner and Doreen Valiente, which has since become part of international Wiccan folklore:

> *Eko, Eko, Azarak*
> *Eko, Eko, Zamilak*
> *Eko, Eko, Cernunnos*
> *Eko, Eko, Aradia*

Darksome night and shining moon,
East, then south, then west, then north;
Hearken to the Witches' Rune —
Here we come to call ye forth!
Earth and water, air and fire,
Wand and pentacle and sword,
Work ye unto our desire,
Hearken ye unto our word!
Cords and censer, scourge and knife,
Powers of the witch's blade —
Waken all ye into life,
Come ye as the charm is made!
Queen of heaven, Queen of hell,
Horned hunter of the night —
Lend your power unto the spell,
And work our will by magic rite!
By all the power of land and sea,
By all the might of moon and sun —
As we do will, so mote it be;
Chant the spell, and be it done!
Eko, Eko, Azarak
Eko, Eko, Zamilak
Eko, Eko, Cernunnos
Eko, Eko, Aradia

Interestingly, this chant first appeared in Gerald Gardner's *High Magic's Aid* and may have come to his attention through an article on the black arts written by Captain J. F. C. Fuller, one of Crowley's most loyal disciples. Here is an earlier version of the chant, which was first published in 1921 in *Form* — an arts magazine established by Austin Osman Spare:

Eko! eko! Azarak
Eko! eko! Zomelak
Zod-ru-kod e Zod-ru-koo
Zon-ru-koz e Goo-ru-mu!
Eo! Eo! Oo . . . Oo . . . Oo . . . !

In Wiccan ceremonies it is common for witches to work sky-clad, or naked. We have already mentioned Gardner's preference for ritual nudity and this remains the preferred procedure in Wiccan ceremonial today. However, robes are often worn by the high priest and high priestess as a sign of symbolic rank during major initiations, and there are some neopagan groups whose members prefer to work fully robed at all times.

The Tools of Witchcraft

As in the magic of the Golden Dawn, certain magical implements define the very nature of Wiccan ritual practice. On the witch's altar the chalice represents the element water, salt represents earth, and the censer both air and fire. The pentacle represents earth and is also used as a receptacle for the 'mooncakes' which are eaten in communion at the close of the ritual. Also on the altar are the communion wine, an altar candle, and the witch's personal tools and 'weapons'. The basic implements of witchcraft are as follows:

The *sword* is a symbol of power and authority and is used to cast the circle. It is also a potent symbol of protection.

The *athame* is a double-edged black-handled knife, sometimes with symbols on its hilt, which is used to direct magical power. It can also be used to cast the magic circle. The *athame* should ideally have an iron blade representing the will and an ebony handle representing steadfastness. A white-handled knife called a *boline* may also be located on the altar but its use is purely utilitarian.

The *dagger* is employed in ceremonial rites for invoking and banishing spirits associated with the element air.

The *cup* or *chalice* is a ritual object associated with the element water and is also a symbol of the womb of the Goddess. When the *athame* is inserted into a chalice filled with liquid, it represents the sacred marriage of the God and Goddess: 'As the *athame* is to the male, so the chalice is to the female, and when conjoined become one.' The cup is also used as a receptacle for the ritual wine.

The *wand* is used to direct the will and to summon and control spirits. It must be held with both hands, with its point well away from the body, and is usually made from willow, birch, hazel, oak or elder.

Wiccans go into the woods to find an appropriate piece of wood which can then be fashioned into a wand.

The *brass thurible*, which stands on three legs or alternatively hangs from three chains, is the container for the incense. In Wiccan ceremonies it is taken around the edge of the circle to purify the sacred space with the elements of fire and air.

The copper *pentacle* or disc is a symbol of the element earth. It is used to call earth spirits and may also be used to cast the magic circle by rolling the disc around the circumference.

A *three-pronged candelabra* is also placed on the altar. Depending on the nature of the lunar cycle or the nature of the ritual itself, it will contain a white candle (the Goddess as maiden), a red candle (the Goddess as mother) or a black candle (the Goddess as crone). The black candle represents age and wisdom and is not symbolic of the 'black arts'!

Sometimes a *scourge* is also used in Wiccan rituals. Intended primarily as an aid to spiritual purification in initiation ceremonies, it is generally used for mild forms of self-flagellation and is only rarely used for punishing offenders within the coven.

The *altar cloth* is usually black or white and resting upon it, of course, are containers for the salt and the water which are used to purify the circle with the elements earth and water. Some altars also display *images of the Goddess and the God*; for example, small figurines considered appropriate to the specific ritual in question.

Other items employed in Wiccan rites include the *besom* – a broom fashioned from six different woods (birch, broom, hawthorn, hazel, rowan and willow) – which is used to clean the ritual area, and the *cauldron*, a female symbol made of cast iron. It has three legs, representing the three faces of the Goddess (maiden, mother and crone), and is used to generate a safe ceremonial fire during indoor rituals.

And, of course, every witch needs a *Book of Shadows*. This is the witch's personal collection of rituals, spells, herbal remedies and other details of occult lore. As the anthropologist Dr Lynne Hume has noted:

> the idea of a 'Book of Shadows' is attributed to [Gerald] Gardner. Doreen Valiente believes that it was around 1949 that Gardner first thought of calling a witch's book of rituals and magical information

a Book of Shadows and that he only used this term after his own book, *High Magic's Aid* was published . . . Material from Gardner's Book of Shadows . . . comes from various sources including Rudyard Kipling, Charles Leland, the Key of Solomon, the Order of the Golden Dawn and Aleister Crowley. It contains rituals for all Wiccan occasions and is meant to be handcopied by each witch after she or he has been initiated.[9]

In groups where robes are worn, the specific colours and symbolic embellishments are likely to vary considerably. The most common ritual attire is a black hooded robe, large enough to allow ample room for movement and dancing. High priests and high priestesses are often robed during major initiations and may choose to wear symbolically coloured cords around their waists. This cord is called the cingulum and is traditionally three feet six inches long, to ensure that a traditional witches' circle of at least nine feet in diameter can be easily measured. The cingulum may also be used when candidates are ritually bound during initiation ceremonies.

The Nature of Ritual

Ceremonial ritual is the outer enactment of an internal event. In all magical religions, from ancient shamanism to contemporary Wicca, those performing a ritual believe that what they are doing is not simply theatrical, but accords with some sort of sacred, inner reality. For a time the participant in the ritual will feel caught up in a mystical drama, perhaps involving union with a goddess or a god, identification with a source of spiritual healing, or the act of embodying some sort of transcendent power. In this way the person engaging in the ritual is tapping into a dimension which is much larger and more awesome than the world of familiar everyday reality. It is participation in a mystery – engaging with the sacred nature of the cosmos itself.

It has been said that rituals move participants towards a sense of transcendence. They may also involve rites of passage. Whatever the circumstance, we can recognise that the magical ritual should be a *transformative* experience. As one American neopagan practitioner put it: 'I want to learn something, I want to be moved, I want to feel renewed, I want to feel like I've had some sort of participation in something bigger than myself.'[10]

It is also widely acknowledged in Wiccan circles that 'good ritual' doesn't just happen by itself. It involves a blend of effective planning and spontaneity, a mix of balanced intent and inspiration. Like a good story, a ritual should also have a beginning, a middle and an end. The Wisconsin-based witch Selena Fox similarly divides rituals into three parts: preparation and orientation; the work or focus of the ritual itself, and the closure and assimilation. Wiccans recognise that sacred energy must be 'grounded' at the close of a ritual, thereby enabling participants to return to the 'real' world of everyday activities. Sometimes a group will share 'cakes and wine' as part of the closure and there will also be a parting blessing:

> *The circle is open but never broken*
> *Merry meet, merry part, and merry meet again . . .*

Drawing Down the Moon

The invocation known as Drawing Down the Moon is central to Wiccan practice. Here the high priest invokes the Goddess into the high priestess as part of the opening ceremony:

> *I invoke Thee and beseech Thee, O Mighty Mother of all life and fertility. By seed and root, by stem and bud, by leaf and flower and fruit, by life and Love do I invoke Thee to descend into the body of this thy servant and High Priestess.*[11]

This may be preceded by what Wiccans refer to as the 'fivefold kiss', an act of psycho-spiritual arousal performed by the high priest:

> First he ceremonially kisses her from the feet up to the crown of her head by way of the knees, womb, breasts and lips. Next he visualises links between the chakras (energy centres) of his own body with those of the priestess – beginning at the base of her spine and working up. When the two are connected, linked like electrical circuits, and the energy is flowing between them, he envisages the form of the

Goddess behind the priestess. Then the Goddess is asked to 'descend into the body' of the priestess. It is not unknown for other participants in the ceremony to see changes in the priestess as she becomes inspired, filled with the Goddess . . .[12]

The Wiccan priestess and writer Vivianne Crowley has described the experience of having the Goddess drawn down into her by her high priest:

Andy, as High Priest, knelt before me and began the invocation to the Goddess. There was a stillness and silence within me. Then the flow of the power came, down through my crown chakra, down to my feet and out into the circle. She had come . . .

I was far away, deep into samadhi; that state of consciousness whereby there is no longer any 'I and other', 'this and that', 'far and near', only a sense of oneness with the universe. As though from a long way off, I heard Andy's voice stop. The power of the Goddess flowed through me once more and I made ready to respond . . .[13]

Once the high priestess has incarnated the Goddess, she then utters what is known in Wicca as the Charge. Here, in effect, the Goddess herself is speaking directly to her followers. First the high priest addresses the coven: *Listen to the words of the Great Mother; she who of old was called among men Artemis, Astarte, Athena, Dione, Melusine, Aphrodite, Cerridwen, Dana, Arianrhod, Isis, Bride, and by many other names.*

The high priestess now speaks to the group as the Goddess incarnate:

Whenever ye have need of anything, once in the month, and better it be when the moon is full, then shall ye assemble in some secret place and adore the spirit of me, who am Queen of all witches. There shall ye assemble, ye who are fain to learn all sorcery, yet who have not won its deepest secrets; to these will I teach things that are yet unknown. And ye shall be free from slavery; and as a sign that ye be really free, ye shall be naked in your rites; and ye shall dance, sing, feast, make music and love, all in my praise. For mine is the ecstasy of the spirit, and mine is also joy on earth; for my law is love unto all beings. Keep pure your highest ideal; strive ever towards it; let naught stop you or turn you aside. For mine is the secret door which opens up the Land of Youth, and mine is the cup of the wine of life, and the Cauldron of Cerridwen, which is the Holy Grail of immortality. I am the gracious Goddess, who gives the gift of joy unto the heart of man. Upon earth, I give the knowledge of the spirit eternal; and beyond death, I give peace, and freedom, and reunion with those who have gone before. Nor do I demand sacrifice; for behold, I am the mother of all living, and my love is poured out upon the earth.

The high priest now briefly interpolates: *Hear ye the words of the Star Goddess; she in the dust of whose feet are the hosts of heaven, and whose body encircles the universe.*

And then, once again, the Goddess addresses the coven through the high priestess:

I who am the beauty of the green earth, and the white Moon among the stars, and the mystery of the waters, and the desire of the heart of man, call unto thy soul. Arise and come unto me. For I am the soul of Nature, who gives life to the universe. From me all things proceed, and unto me all things must return; and before my face, beloved of Gods and men, let thine innermost divine self be enfolded in the rapture of the infinite. Let my worship be with the heart that rejoiceth; for behold all acts of love and pleasure are my rituals. And therefore let there be beauty and strength, power and compassion, honour and humility, mirth and reverence within you. And thou who thinkest to seek for me, know that seeking and yearning shall avail thee not unless thou knowest the mystery; that if that which thou seekest thou findest not within thee, thou wilt never find it without thee. For behold, I have been with thee from the beginning; and I am that which is attained at the end of desire.[14]

Esbats and Sabbats

Wiccans honour both the lunar and the solar cycles of Nature. Esbats are monthly meetings of the coven held at the time of full moon, whereas the solar cycle is marked by eight sabbats referred to collectively as the Wheel of the Year: these are the solstices, equinoxes and the four points between. As Margot Adler has observed, these meetings and festivals renew a sense of living communion with natural cycles, and with the changes in the seasons and the land.[15]

There are thirteen months in the lunar calendar, and therefore there are usually thirteen esbats each year. Wiccans believe that esbats are marked by a sense of heightened psychic awareness resulting from the lunar energy of full moon, and many Wiccans like to perform their specific magical workings at this time. Esbats are a time for invocations, love magic and healing ceremonies but they are also a time for dancing, drinking and feasting – the word 'esbat' itself is thought to derive from the Old French word *s'esbattre*, meaning 'to frolic and amuse oneself'.[16]

Each of the esbats has its own name and this is linked symbolically to the time of the year in which it occurs. The first occurs in October just before the festival of Samhain (All Hallows' Eve, or Halloween) and is called Blood Moon. It is traditionally associated with the slaughter of animals for food before the onset of winter and is therefore represented by the colour red. Snow Moon rises in November and is associated with the first falls of snow. Oak Moon is the full moon in December. It is linked to the colour black and to the oak – sacred symbol of the Dark Lord aspect of Cernunnos – since it is his wood that is burned at Yule. Ice Moon, represented by the colour purple, comes in January, followed by Storm Moon in February – a time when the ice and sleet may turn to rain. This full moon is linked to the element water, and to the colour blue. March brings the Chaste Moon, the return of spring from the depths of winter, and is represented by the colour white. In April, Seed Moon is a time when the seeds in the earth bring forth new life, and this esbat is represented by the colour green. Hare Moon rises in May and is dedicated both to the Goddess and to fertility. Its colour is pink, symbolic of love. June brings the Dyad Moon and, as Gwydion O'Hare notes, this name alludes to 'the visible presence of the God and Goddess reflected in the bright sun and green fields'. The associated colour is orange, 'the colour of the summer sun'.[17] The Mead Moon comes in July and is a time for dancing and revelry. Traditionally this is the time when honey mead was made for the harvest celebrations and accordingly its symbolic colour is yellow. August brings the Wort Moon – a reference to the dark-green abundance of harvest time – and September is the month of the Barley Moon. This is the season when grain is harvested: brown is the symbolic colour for this esbat. Finally, Wine Moon is the esbat which arises as a consequence of the difference between the solar and lunar calendars. Unlike the twelve-month cycle of the solar calendar, any given year usually has thirteen full moons, and this esbat is the thirteenth. It honours the sacrament of wine and its colour is burgundy red. Wine Moon precedes Blood Moon, and so the lunar cycle continues.[18]

Esbats are sometimes referred to as 'lesser' Wiccan celebrations. As Doreen Valiente has put it, 'the esbat is a smaller and less solemn occasion than the sabbat'.[19] The major sabbats, on the other hand, are celebrations which link contemporary Wicca directly with festivals honoured by the Celts and Druids.[20] The four so-called greater sabbats are those of Candlemas (2 February), May Eve (30 April), Lammas (1 August) and Halloween (31 October), and the traditional Druidic names for these celebrations are Imbolc or Oimelc, Beltane, Lughnassadh and Samhain respectively. The lesser sabbats are those marked by the mid-summer and midwinter solstices and the equinoxes in spring and autumn. Considered as a whole, the Wheel of the Year represents not only the cycle of the seasons but more specifically the cycle of Nature's fertility. This is also reflected in the major Wiccan initiations, which culminate with the sacred marriage of the God and Goddess, whose union brings forth new life.

The Wheel of the Year

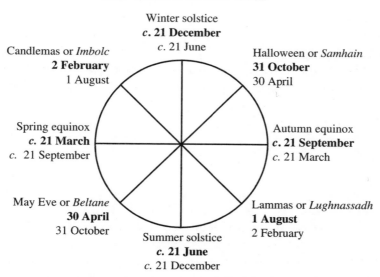

Winter solstice
c. 21 December
c. 21 June

Candlemas or *Imbolc*
2 February
1 August

Halloween or *Samhain*
31 October
30 April

Spring equinox
c. 21 March
c. 21 September

Autumn equinox
c. 21 September
c. 21 March

May Eve or *Beltane*
30 April
31 October

Lammas or *Lughnassadh*
1 August
2 February

Summer solstice
c. 21 June
c. 21 December

Northern hemisphere dates are in **bold type** with southern hemisphere corresponding dates given beneath

The symbolic associations of the greater sabbats are as follows, commencing with Halloween – the traditional beginning of the pagan year:

Halloween/Samhain

This is a celebration to honour the dead. Samhain means 'summer's end' and it is a time of grieving, as the dying sun passes into the netherworld. However, this is both an ending and a beginning, for the Sun god will be reborn with the passage of the seasons. Halloween is said to be the time of the year when the thin veil between the everyday world and netherworld is most transparent, allowing Wiccans to communicate more readily with the spirits of the departed. Halloween is also a time to reflect on one's own mortality. Mythologically, this is the season during which the dying god sleeps in the underworld awaiting rebirth. At the same time the seed of new life gestates within the womb of the Great Mother – who in this cycle is regarded as the queen of darkness.

Candlemas/Imbolc

This sabbat has been described as 'the quickening of the year, the first stirrings of Spring within the womb of Mother Earth'.[21] *Imbolc* means 'in the belly' and this is a fertility celebration. The focus is on light and new life, as opposed to the darkness of winter which has now receded. Imbolc is sometimes known as the Feast of Lights. Mythologically, the Goddess has become a virgin.

May Eve/Beltane

Beltane marks the beginning of summer and is also a fertility celebration. The name of this sabbat may come from the Celtic deity Bel or Balor, god of light and fire, for in ancient times 'bel-fires' were lit on the hilltops to celebrate the return of life and fertility to the world.[22] Wiccans often celebrate Beltane by dancing round the maypole and celebrating the love between men and women. Mythologically, Beltane honours the mating of the Sun god with the fertile Earth goddess. The Goddess is now pregnant.

Lammas/Lughnassadh

The word *lammas* is thought to mean 'loaf-mass' and this is the time of year when the first corn is harvested. Known to the Druids as Lughnassadh, this sabbat marks the season of autumn and was traditionally a celebration to Lugh, the Celtic Sun god. Lughnassadh is associated with the waning power of the Sun – in mythic terms the god has begun to die – but it is also a season in which one can reflect upon the fruits of the earth. Wiccans gather at Lammas to celebrate the gifts of abundance which have come forth from the womb of the Goddess. Mythologically, Lughnassadh represents fulfilment – the reaping of all that has been sown.[23]

So, while Wicca is primarily a religion of the Goddess, it is clear from the mythic cycle of the greater sabbats that the role of the Sun god is also very important. The Celts acknowledged that just as the Goddess waxed and waned through her lunar cycles as maiden, mother and crone, so too did the Sun god pass through death to rebirth. In Wicca the god of fertility is also thought to have two personas, representing the god of the waxing year and the god of the waning year. The Oak King represents expansion and growth and is associated with the time of the year when the days grow longer. The Holly King represents withdrawal and rest, and is associated with the time when the days grow shorter. They are two further examples of the rich mythology associated with the traditions of contemporary Wicca.

The Three Initiations of Wicca

Esbats and sabbats are collective celebrations which involve the entire Wiccan coven. However, there are other special occasions – the three Wiccan initiations, or degrees – which relate to the spiritual development of the individual. We have already mentioned that magical rituals, by their very nature, are intended to evoke a sense of personal transformation. Wiccan initiations are in this tradition for they are rites of passage – specific milestones upon the spiritual path of the neopagan.

The First Initiation

Many covens will ask candidates for this initiation to fast for several days before the ceremony itself. They may also be advised to spend time meditating on Nature, thereby opening their inner being to the spiritual energies of the world around them. Immediately before the first initiation takes place, the candidate will be asked to bathe and will then be brought naked and blindfolded to the sacred circle. Usually the hands are bound with ritual cords. The state of nakedness in itself represents a casting-aside of the old persona. The individual is about to become an initiated first-degree witch and has therefore taken an all-important first step upon the magical path. In a symbolic sense the first-degree candidate is about to become an entirely new person.

While the new initiate-to-be waits outside the circle, the Great Goddess and horned god are invoked into the high priestess and high priest for the duration of the rite. For all new coven members the Charge of the Great Mother is used to open the initiation ceremony.

At the outer rim of the circle, the candidate is challenged at the point of a sword: this is intended to heighten the candidate's sense of vulnerability and exposure. However, once the new candidate has been accepted within the circle as a sincere seeker after truth, he or she is welcomed by the initiator, who kneels and bestows kisses upon the new candidate:

> *Blessed Be thy feet that have brought thee in these ways*
> *Blessed Be thy knees that shall kneel at the sacred altar*
> *Blessed Be thy phallus/womb without which we would not be*
> *Blessed Be thy breasts formed in beauty and in strength*
> *Blessed Be thy lips that shall utter the sacred names.*

As Vivianne Crowley has put it, 'the body is honoured and reverenced' and the essential message of the First Initiation is one of acceptance.[24]

First-degree witches are introduced during the ritual to the practical tools of witchcraft. They are also shown how to cast a magical circle and how to call the watchtowers of the four elements from north, east, south and west. Following their initiation, they will also be expected to develop an increasing familiarity with the principles and philosophy of witchcraft. Well-known texts like Janet and Stewart Farrar's *Eight Sabbats for Witches*, Vivianne Crowley's *Wicca: The Old Religion in the New Millennium* and Starhawk's *The Spiral Dance* are often recommended, but each coven will have its own reading list. The new initiate may also take a magical name and will be known by this name among other coven members.

The Second Initiation

The next step in Wicca is to become a high priestess or high priest but this is not bestowed lightly: some Wiccan covens require three years of ritual work before they grant the second degree to one of their members. In the second degree a stronger connection is made between the initiator and the initiated, and candidates will need to find an opposite-sex partner with whom they can work compatibly in partnership.[25]

The high priestess Vivianne Crowley has described the second initiation in Wicca as essentially a journey into the depths of the unconscious mind. An important feature of the second-degree rite includes the mystery play called *The Legend of the Goddess*, in which the initiate and other coven members enact the descent of the Goddess into the underworld. Here the Goddess encounters the God in his role as the Dark Lord of Death.

Male and female participants can expect to respond differently to this ritual because issues of the animus and anima – the polar opposites within the psyche – are clearly involved. According to Crowley, for a man to find his true self he must encounter the divine feminine. For a woman it is about overcoming passivity and purposefully seeking experience. In the legend the Goddess goes forth into the underworld to seek an answer to the question: Why dost thou causeth all things that I love and take delight in to fade and die?[26]

The answer lies within – for here we are talking of self-knowledge, of tapping the spiritual depths of who we really are. If the first degree was about vulnerability and exposure, says Crowley, the second degree is about overcoming the fear of annihilation. It can be a fear of physical death or a fear of surrendering one's sense of self. It is also about encountering the sexual opposites within the psyche. At the end of the ritual, though, there is an opportunity for the fear to be transformed into something positive, for the candidate is now presented with a new revelation: that from the dark world of the unconscious and the land of death may come rebirth. Janet and Stewart Farrar have transcribed this part of the ritual text as follows:

> There are three great events in the life of man: Love, Death and Resurrection in the new body; and Magic controls them all. For to fulfil love you must return again at the same time and place as the loved one, and you must remember and love them again. But to be reborn you must die and be ready for a new body; and to die you must be born; and without love you may not be born . . .[27]

The Legend closes with the God and Goddess instructing each other in these mysteries. She teaches him the mystery of the sacred cup which is the cauldron of rebirth, and in return he gives her the necklace which is the circle of rebirth.[28]

The rite concludes with the initiator announcing to the four quarters that the initiate has been consecrated as a high priest or priestess. Some Wiccan candidates take a new magical name after attaining the second degree.

The Third Initiation

The third degree represents the culmination of the Wiccan initiatory process, and only practitioners who are themselves third-degree coven members are allowed to participate in it as initiators. Wiccans wishing to take the third degree must not only be skilled in the ways of witchcraft but must also know how to enter an altered state of consciousness, for they must be able to 'draw down' the God or Goddess into their partner. Experienced Wiccan practitioners emphasise that candidates for the third degree need to be psychically and spiritually balanced because in this initiation they are invoking powerful archetypal forces – and these sacred energies must be harmonised once they have been summoned.

The third degree is bestowed upon a couple together, and involves what is known as the Great Rite. The ritual itself is essentially a sacred marriage – the ritual union of the Goddess and the God. However, from a mystical perspective the Great Rite is not only about sexual congress – it also points towards transcendence. For in the sacred marriage between Goddess and God, duality – or the polarity of opposites – has ceased. The two have become one.

During the first part of the ritual the Goddess and the God are invoked into the high priestess and high priest by their initiators. However, in the second part they are acting as incarnate deities themselves: 'they themselves have the Divine forces invoked into them so that the Sacred Marriage may be performed between the Goddess and the God.'[29]

Wiccans engaging in the third degree do not necessarily consummate their ritual union physically. When the union is symbolically enacted – for example, by ritually plunging the *athame* into the chalice – it is said to be performed *in token*. But when two partners taking the role of God and Goddess wish to physically enact their sacred sexual union, the Great Rite is performed *in true*. Essentially the partners bestow the initiation upon each other, the high priest offering the third degree to his partner in token, and the high priestess returning it to him in true. The following account by a female witch initiated into the Great Rite by Alex Sanders provides an insight into the sanctity of the occasion:

> My Great Rite was, for me, a most holy and sacred experience. It all has to do with will, intent, and the correct use of energy. It has to do with the flow and use of energy. Physicality is only a very small part. Sex, as sacred sex, creates a lot of energy but is very misunderstood. What occurs in the Great Rite is the persons engaging in sex become the God and Goddess – if it is done properly. You have to think that inside the person is the God/Goddess. You don't see it as being unfaithful to your own partner or as having merely physical sex . . .[30]

The Great Rite is regarded as a sacred act in Wicca. It is not taken lightly nor indulged in for its own sake, and is performed in private after other coven members have left the circle. The initiation closes with the following salutation from the high priest as the God and Goddess lie in union:

Make open the path of intelligence between us;
For these truly are the Five Points of Fellowship –
Foot to foot,
Knee to knee,
Lance to Grail,
Breast to breast,
Lips to lips,
By the great and holy name Cernunnos;
In the name of Aradia;
Encourage our hearts,
Let the light crystallise itself in our blood,
Fulfilling of us resurrection.
For there is no part of us that is not of the Gods.[31]

Clearly the essence of Wicca revolves around concepts of fertility and the sacred union of the Goddess and the God. Everything in Wicca points in this direction for it is a religion of male and female polarities, of Moon and Earth and Sun. Its devotees are willing participants in sacred processes revealed through the symbolic language of myth, legend and song. Their celebrations are aligned with the natural flow of the seasons and they are keen to see these cycles reflected in the mirror of their own being. It is Mother Nature who opens her door to the sacred, the Goddess of the Moon who inspires and illumines through the power of dreams and intuition. Ultimately the Wiccans are urging us to honour the divine Goddess as the Queen of All Being. While she has her consort in the Sun god, it is the Goddess herself who shines forth from the heart of Creation. For the neopagan it is the Goddess to whom we must ultimately return.

8

Dark Forces

In the popular imagination witchcraft and satanism have meant much the same thing. Both are frequently assessed – especially by fundamentalist Christians – as belonging collectively to the realm of the black arts, and both are seen as a form of 'Devil worship'. Quite apart from the inaccuracy of such an evaluation, it is also one which both witches and satanists themselves reject. As we will see, satanists look askance at any form of worship involving 'protective transcendental deities' – whether this worship is addressed to a god or a goddess. And several witches have also been outspoken on the issue of confused identity. As Z Budapest has put it, in her characteristically colourful style:

> Witchcraft is a universal, joy-oriented, artistic kind of religious practice that celebrates the earth and its journey around the sun. Now, we got a bad rap from the Christians about this. We have been told that we worship Satan, the Devil. Well, the Devil is a Christian god. We have never heard of the Devil. Many of us got burned [in the Middle Ages] because we didn't know who they were talking about . . . so many died. Many were going to their death still wondering who the Devil was . . .[1]

If we are to understand contemporary satanism, we need to explore the origins and philosophy of the Church of Satan and its successor, the Temple of Set, for they occupy a central position in the world of contemporary black magic. However, as will become clear, the Church of Satan and the Temple of Set offer quite different perspectives – the first based primarily on hedonistic indulgence or sins of the flesh, the second on metaphysical revelations from the ancient Egyptian entity Set. The now defunct Church of Satan was always in one sense an offshoot of Californian show business – a form of institutionalised party revelry. The Temple of Set, on the other hand, continues to encompass a much broader esoteric domain and is based on carefully considered philosophical responses to the magical universe.

Anton LaVey and the Church of Satan

From the very beginning the Church of Satan was conceived as a religion of self-indulgence. Its founder, Anton LaVey (1930–1997), was a carnival performer and musician, and his new religion was intended to shock conservative mainstream America out of its complacency and moral double standards. LaVey would soon become known to his followers as the 'Black Pope' and would parade as an intentionally sinister figure sporting a pointed goatee beard and wearing a black cloak and inverted pentagram. An intimate of celebrities like Marilyn Monroe and Jayne Mansfield, and a close friend of Sammy Davis Jr, he would later star as the Devil in Roman Polanski's film *Rosemary's Baby*. As an orchestrator of occult extravaganzas, he had no peer.

Born in Chicago on 11 April 1930, Anton Szandor LaVey was of French, Alsatian, German, Russian and Romanian descent and had Gypsy blood as well. His parents Joe and Augusta apparently sought to instill useful middle-class values in their son without pressing any particular religious dictates upon him but he was attracted to the occult path from an early age. He learned about vampires from his maternal grandmother Luba Kolton, and also immersed himself in reading occult and fantasy literature like Bram Stoker's *Dracula* and the popular magazine *Weird Tales*. By the age of twelve he was familiar with the medieval magical grimoires of Albertus Magnus.

The LaVey family moved to the San Francisco Bay area shortly after Anton was born and it soon became apparent that he was a rebellious and unusual child, with a mind and will of his own. As a child, LaVey regarded school as a place 'to escape from' and at the age of sixteen, he gave up on formal education and left his home in Oakland to join the Clyde Beatty Circus as a cage boy, later becoming an assistant lion tamer. To begin with, LaVey's role at the circus was to feed and water the big cats, but he soon discovered a real affinity with them. Within a year he was putting the cats through the hoops, handling eight Nubian lions and four Bengal tigers at once, and frequently performing alone with the cats in the big cage.

LaVey travelled with the Beatty Circus through California, Oregon, Washington, Nevada, Arizona and New Mexico before leaving at the end of the circus season in October 1947. He then worked in the Pike Amusement Park in Long Beach, California, playing a steam calliope. Later he expanded his range, working for travelling shows on the Pacific coast and playing a calliope, a Wurlitzer band organ or a Hammond organ in a variety of carnival settings. It was here that he got his first taste of what he regarded as Christian hypocrisy:

> On Saturday night I would see men lusting after half-naked girls dancing at the carnival, and on Sunday morning when I was playing the organ for tent-show evangelists at the other end of the carnival lot, I would see these same men sitting in the pews with their wives and children, asking God to forgive them and purge them of their carnal desires. And the next Saturday night they'd be back at the carnival or some other place of indulgence. I knew then that the Christian Church thrives on hypocrisy, and that man's carnal nature will out![2]

Although it seemed that Anton LaVey would make his career as an entertainer, he was inspired by his first wife to study criminology at San Francisco City College and then, for a brief period, became a photographer with the San Francisco Police Department. It was here that he observed the gruesome side of urban life: 'people shot by nuts, knifed by friends, kids splattered in the gutter by hit-and-run drivers. It was disgusting and depressing.'[3] These grim events had a strong impact on LaVey's spiritual perspectives. He concluded that violence was a part of the divine and inscrutable plan of God, and he turned away from God altogether as a source of inspiration and benevolence.

After leaving his position as a police photographer, LaVey continued to play the organ for his livelihood, immersing himself still further in his study of the occult and parapsychology. Soon he was holding weekly classes on various esoteric topics, and these were attended by a diverse range of people, including the novelist Stephen Schneck and the avant-garde film producer Kenneth Anger. The so-called Magic Circle meetings were held in his tightly shuttered house at 6114 California Street and included lectures on vampires, werewolves, haunted houses, extra-sensory perception, zombies and other related subjects intended to stir the imagination. LaVey also lampooned the Catholic Church with a 'Black Mass' which involved desecrating the Host, using an inverted cross and black candles, and reciting prayers backwards.[4]

LaVey was fascinated by the concept of Sir Francis Dashwood's eighteenth-century Hellfire Club – where establishment figures would meet for an evening of revelling and debauchery – and it occurred to him that the Magic Circle could provide the basis for a modern-day equivalent. Finally, in a typical act of bravado, LaVey shaved his head and announced the formation of the Church of Satan on the most demonic night of the year, Walpurgisnacht, traditionally associated with the ascendancy of the powers of darkness. LaVey declared 1966 to be Year One, Anno Satanas – the first year of the reign of Satan. The Age of Fire had begun . . .

LaVey also made a pronouncement about his new church: 'Satanism is the only religion in which a person can "turn on" to the pleasures around him without "dropping out" of society.' This was an emphatic rephrasing of the hippie dictum 'Turn on, tune in and drop out' then being advocated by the counter-culture guru Timothy Leary. LaVey was opposed to any notion of drug-based escapism; instead he emphasised sensual indulgence and personal empowerment. LaVey believed, essentially, that man is God and God is man. The ceremonies of the Church of Satan would become a means for channelling magical power into a full expression of human carnal desire.

At 6114 California Street the ritual altar room was completely black with an inverted pentagram mounted on the wall above the fireplace. This particular pentagram represented the sigil of Baphomet, a symbol adapted from the Knights Templars in the fourteenth century. Services began and ended with satanic hymns and a ritual invocation to Satan.

A naked woman – a symbol of lust and self-indulgence – was used as an 'altar'. Here is an account of a typical ceremony at the Church of Satan:

> A bell is rung nine times to signal the beginning of the service, the priest turning in a circle counterclockwise, ringing the bell to the four cardinal points. The leopard-skin cover is removed from the mantelpiece, revealing the nude body of the female volunteer altar for the evening. The purification is performed by one of the assistant priests, who sprinkles the congregation with a mixture of semen and water, symbolic of creative force. LaVey then takes a sword from its sheath, held by Diane, his wife and high priestess, and invokes Satan in his cardinal manifestations. Satan, in the South, represents Fire; Lucifer in the East, is symbolic of Air; Belial, in the North, represents Earth; and Leviathan, in the West, is his watery aspect. The officiating priest then drinks from the chalice, which is filled with any liquid he may desire, from lemonade to 100-proof vodka, making a symbolic offering to Satan. The chalice is then placed on the pubic area of the girl-altar, where it stays for the remainder of the evening.[5]

The rituals themselves would vary from week to week, but invariably involved some form of personal wish-fulfilment:

> Members of the congregation are led forward into the center of a circle formed by the hooded priests and are asked what they desire. Accompanied by eerie organ music, the high priest touches the member's head lightly with a sword, in a kind of knighting gesture, and asks the Devil to grant the man's request. The member and the priests focus all their emotional powers on that which has been named. The request might be for material gain, for the acquiring of a mate, for the acquisition of a physical or emotional quality.
>
> Whatever the wish, the purpose of the ritual is to have the participant focus his powers inward, to enable him to visualize and achieve his objective. After each member of the congregation goes through this process and all are returned to their seats, the proceedings are brought to a close, the bell being run, nine times clockwise, while the organ plays the satanic hymns.[6]

LaVey certainly believed in celebrating Christian 'sins' as virtues and formulated the following satanic statements as the quintessence of his approach:

> Satan represents indulgence instead of abstinence.
> Satan represents vital existence instead of spiritual pipe dreams.
> Satan represents undefiled wisdom instead of hypocritical self-deceit.
> Satan represents kindness to those who deserve it instead of love wasted on ingrates.
> Satan represents vengeance instead of turning the other cheek.
> Satan represents responsibility to the responsible instead of concern for psychic vampires.
> Satan represents man as just another animal . . . who, because of his 'divine spiritual and intellectual development' has become the most vicious animal of all.
> Satan represents all of the so-called sins as they all lead to physical, mental or emotional gratification.
> Satan has been the best friend the Church has ever had, as he has kept it in business all these years.[7]

LaVey also developed what he called the Eleven Satanic Rules of the Earth, which were effectively a guide to negotiating one's path through the 'human jungle':

> Do not give opinions or advice unless you are asked.
> Do not tell your troubles to others unless you are sure they want to hear them.
> When in another's lair, show him respect or else do not go there.
> If a guest in your lair annoys you, treat him cruelly and without mercy.
> Do not make sexual advances unless you are given the mating signal.
> Do not take that which does not belong to you unless it is a burden to the other person and he cries out to to be relieved.
> Acknowledge the power of magic if you have employed it successfully to obtain your desires. If you deny the power of magic after having called upon it with success, you will lose all you have obtained.

Do not complain about anything to which you need not subject yourself.

Do not harm little children.

Do not kill non-human animals unless attacked or for your food.

When walking in open territory, bother no-one. If someone bothers you, ask him to stop. If he does not stop, destroy him.[8]

LaVey's dictums combine parental authoritarianism with a sense of streetwise wariness and a willingness to enter into physical and magical confrontation. However, while on one level LaVey was presenting a clear challenge to the conventional Christian mores of Middle America – there was no place in his credo for humility, weakness or 'turning the other cheek' – he did not regard either himself or his church as specifically anti-Christian. For him Christianity was simply irrelevant. It did not address humanity's basic emotional needs, it denied man's basic carnal nature, and it placed its devotees in a position of dependence on a god who apparently had 'little concern regarding any suffering which we may encounter'. LaVey also had no illusions about vows of poverty as a means of gaining spiritual redemption. For him magic was essentially about power – and wealth was a type of power. LaVey reserved the right to channel funds accruing to the Church of Satan in any way, and for any purpose, he saw fit. However, some of his fellow practitioners had other views on this matter, and this particular issue would eventually lead to a split in the church leadership.

The Birth of the Temple of Set

By 1975 it was becoming clear that all was not well within the Church of Satan. In the words of LaVey's magical colleague Michael Aquino, editor of the church's newsletter, the *Cloven Hoof*, the church was now starting to attract far too many 'fad-followers, egomaniacs and assorted oddballs whose primary interest in becoming Satanists was to flash their membership cards for cocktail-party notoriety'.[9] More to the point, LaVey was finding that he couldn't survive as a full-time magician on the ten-dollar annual fee levied for church membership, and it was this realisation that brought about a crisis.

In early 1975, LaVey sent out advice in the church newsletter advising that, forthwith, all higher degrees of initiation would be available for contributions in cash, real estate or valuable objects of art. The effect, according to Aquino, was shattering:

> If there had been a single unifying factor that had brought us to Satanism, it was the Church's stand against hypocrisy. So when we learned of this policy, our reaction to it was that Anton LaVey was betraying his office, betraying everything that he had worked for, for so many years.[10]

However, there was no way of firing the leader – the Church of Satan to all intents and purposes was vested in him. The only alternative was for the priesthood to leave. In June 1975 an act of mass desertion took place. Key members of the priesthood resigned from the Church of Satan, at the same time making it clear that they were not leaving the priesthood itself. 'In fact,' says Aquino, 'we had a sacred responsibility to take it with us.'

A graduate from the University of California at Santa Barbara, with a strong interest in comparative religion and philosophy, Michael Aquino had joined the Church of Satan in 1969.[11] He was now a priest of the fourth degree and the senior member of the splinter group. However, it was clear that new guidelines were required from Satan himself. On the evening of 21 June 1975, in a ritual magic ceremony, Aquino summoned the Prince of Darkness 'to tell us what we may do to continue our Quest'. The result, according to Aquino, was an act of automatic writing, 'a communication from a god to a human being'.

In a document known as *The Book of Coming Forth by Night*, Satan now revealed himself as the ancient Egyptian god Set, and named Michael Aquino as LaVey's replacement. Aquino was described in the script as the successor to Aleister Crowley, and Magus, fifth degree, of the new Aeon of Set. Gone were all references to the Christian Devil. *The Book of Coming Forth by Night* also identified a new name for both church and deity: 'Reconsecrate my Temple and my Order in the true name of Set. No longer will I accept the bastard title of a Hebrew Fiend.'

There were also other instructions for the new magical epoch:

When I came first to this world, I gave to you my great pentagram, timeless measure of beauty through proportion. And it was shown inverse, that creation and change be exalted above rest and preservation.

With the years my pentagram was corrupted, yet time has not the power to destroy it. Its position was restored by the Church of Satan, but its essence was dimmed with a Moorish name, and the perverse letters of the Hebrews, and the goat of decadent Khar. During the Age of Satan I allowed this curious corruption, for it was meant to do me honour as I was then perceived.

But this is now my Aeon, and my pentagram is again to be pure in its splendour. Cast aside the corruptions, that the pentagram of Set may shine forth. Let all who seek me be never without it, openly and with pride, for by it shall I know them.

Let the one who aspires to my knowledge be called by the name Setian.[12]

In conclusion, Set also announced a sacred magical word for the new era: 'The Word of the Aeon of Set is *Xeper* – become.'

A New Magical Direction

Michael Aquino says that this revelation led the priesthood of the former Church of Satan into completely new areas of enquiry:

The founders of the Temple of Set knew very little about Egyptology and we had to go and find out who Set was, and why something like this should be happening. We found out some very interesting things. The usual understanding of Set is that he was an evil god in the old Egyptian system – the benevolent father-god being Osiris and his evil antagonist, Set, who murdered him.

In our research we discovered that this was in fact a much later corruption, and that the initial identity of Set had been that of the god of night, of the darkness, as opposed to the god of the day, the sun. Set symbolised the isolated psyche, the spark of life within the self, a creative force in the universe rather than an enemy figure, an inspiration for the individual consciousness.[13]

The magical word *xeper* (pronounced *khefer* and translated as 'I have come into being') would also become central to the philosophy of the Temple of Set. Its associated symbols were the scarab beetle and the dawning Sun. In a recent statement exploring the significance of *xeper*, Temple Magus Don Webb has written that this word 'generates the Aeon of Set, and is the current form of the Eternal Word of the Prince of Darkness. To know this word is to know that the ultimate responsibility for the evolution of your psyche is in your hands. It is the Word of freedom, ecstasy, fearful responsibility, and the root of all magic.'[14]

Webb describes *xeper* as 'the experience of an individual psyche becoming aware of its own existence and deciding to expand and evolve that existence through its own actions'. And since the Temple of Set reveres the magical potential of the individual, the focus of the entire organisation reflects this orientation. All Setians are on an individual magical journey, and where this will take them is essentially up to them.

While there are various initiatory degrees within the Temple of Set, there are no prescribed rituals or dogmas, and no specific vows. According to Lilith Sinclair, Aquino's wife and fellow priestess in the Temple of Set, the rituals in the Church of Satan used to be presented 'on a very self-indulgent, materialistic level' and Satan himself was 'more a symbol than an actual reality'. However, that is not the case now. Lilith says that within the context of the Temple of Set her personal contact with the Prince of Darkness has been both tangible and powerful – 'a very quiet, serene, beautiful touching of minds'. She emphasises that there is no pact signed in blood, as popular folklore would have it, but instead a type of private vow: 'It's done on an individual basis, and it's something that I myself wanted to do.' While most forms of mysticism and neopagan religion advocate the final surrender of the ego in a state of transcendence, in the Setian philosophy awareness of the personal self is maintained at all times. When communicating with Set, says Lilith, 'you retain your individuality . . . but at the same time you are linked with the essence of the Prince of Darkness. It's a natural exchange and flow of energy, of mind awareness.'[15]

The Structure of the Temple of Set

During the latter years of the Church of Satan, Anton LaVey and his wife Diane tired of holding meetings solely in their own home and decided to sponsor other branches of the church, both in San Francisco and in other cities across the nation. Known as 'Grottos', these branches were established as far afield as Louisville, Kentucky; Santa Cruz; San José; Los Angeles; Denver; Dayton, Ohio; Detroit; Washington, DC; and New York, and were mostly centred on charismatic individuals intent on spreading the word. LaVey had titled himself High Priest of Satan and there were five initiatory degrees: Apprentice Satanist I°, Witch or Warlock II°, Priest or Priestess of Mendes III°, Magister IV° and Magus V°. Even within these grades, however, the satanic quest was considered something personal – a developing relationship between the individual and the Prince of Darkness.

The Temple of Set has a somewhat comparable structure of initiatory degrees, although the Grottos have now been replaced by 'Pylons'. A key to the thinking behind this terminology is contained in Michael Aquino's privately published volume on the Church of Satan: 'Humanity is like a tall building. It needs stage after stage of scaffolding. Religion after religion, philosophy after philosophy; one cannot build the twentieth floor from the scaffolding of the first . . .'[16] A more recent statement from the Temple of Set also makes it clear that the reference to Pylons derives from the massive fortified gateways of the temples of ancient Egypt.[17] The very concept of Pylons is of course much more substantial than that of Grottos and moves the thrust of the Temple away from an organisation based primarily on self-indulgence to one focused more specifically on the evolving Setian philosophy. The intent is clearly more serious than it was in earlier times, although the core attitude remains the same: man is God, or a potential God. As the present high priest of the Temple of Set, Don Webb, has expressed it: 'The mission of the Temple of Set is to recreate a tradition of self-deification.'[18]

The Temple of Set has authorised the establishment of Pylons in a number of towns and cities across the United States as well as in such countries as Australia, Britain, Germany and Finland, although the extent of its membership is not publicly revealed.[19] Just as Grottos could only be established by second-degree members of the Church of Satan,

Pylons are similarly sponsored by a senior Setian – in this case a third-degree member known as a 'Sentinel'. Pylon meetings are generally held in individual members' homes and their purpose is to 'provide a focus for the initiate, a place to internalise knowledge'.[20] However, Setians clearly regard the Pylon as not just a meeting place but as a type of sacred metaphor. Webb refers to the Temple of Amen-Ra at Luxor by way of illustration:

> The gateway presents a passage to the outside world, a narrow gateway within, and serves as a secure wall to the persons within. This is a good metaphor for what a Pylon should be . . . The gateway to Pylons is narrow; it is easily guarded by one man or woman. The role of the Sentinel is a guardianship role . . .[21]

However, the Setian commitment itself remains essentially a private and internal process:

> The gateway to your own initiation is in your heart, but often hidden there by circumstance and habit. External gateways are symbols you can use in making your rites of passage. Most of the rites of passage you need in your life, you will have to create yourself. Pylons are one such gateway. Real initiation doesn't come from texts, it passes from mouth to ear . . .[22]

Nevertheless, as we have seen, the Temple of Set does recognise initiatory degrees and has a similar structure to the Church of Satan. After Michael Aquino retired from the high priesthood of the Temple in 1996, Don Webb assumed the role of high priest, or Magus V°. There are also different orders within the Temple dedicated to different types of magical research. One of these is the Order of the Trapezoid, whose particular focus is the rune magic of northern Europe – work specifically associated with a senior Temple scholar, Dr Stephen Flowers. Dr Aquino now has a type of emeritus position within the Temple of Set – he is an Ipsissimus VI° – and continues to be active as an individual member within the organisation.

The Setian Perspective

As the first high priest of the Temple of Set, Dr Aquino remains its principal formulator, and the Temple reflects his intellectual background and his emphasis on rational thought.

Aquino divides the manifested universe broadly into three levels of reality. In the everyday world – the so-called 'natural order' – we observe cause-and-effect relationships, and the scientific method and technology are based on this. At another level further removed, and exemplified by Plato – whom Aquino much admires – is philosophic thought. This is characterised by the processes of deduction and induction: the power of reason buttressed by observable fact. And beyond this, at an even more profound level, is the world of magical reality. There is a spiritual and psychic dimension to the human condition, says Aquino, and this transcends the more mundane levels of existence. However, where he differs from Christians, mystics and pagans – whom for this purpose he groups together – is in his belief that the psychic dimension separates mankind from the rest of Nature. For him, mystics and occultists alike are generally content to subsume their individual selfhood within the flow of cosmic consciousness – essentially an act of surrender to a higher force. Christians, meanwhile, are oppressed with feelings of guilt and hypocrisy and find themselves endorsing 'hackneyed moral standards' in an effort to appease God.

For Aquino, satanism is unique because it advocates personal behaviour that is self-determined:

> All conventional religions, including the pagan ones, are simply a variation on the theme of reunion and submergence of the self within the natural universe. So from our point of view, it really makes no difference whether you pray to a Father god or to a Mother goddess – or to an entire gaggle of gods and goddesses! You are still wishing for their acceptance. You are waiting for them to put their arms around you and say: 'You belong. You are part of us. You can relax. We will take care of you. We approve of you. We endorse you . . .' The satanist, or black magician, does not seek that kind of submergence of the self. We do not seek to have our decisions and our morality approved or validated by any higher god or being. We take responsibility unto ourselves.[23]

This, of course, begs the question of how the satanist stands in relation to Set, who is presumably regarded as a being on a higher plane of existence. According to Michael Aquino:

> We do not pray to the Devil or Satan or Set. We have no desires or wishes that we expect to be granted by some sort of divinity. We consider Set to be our activating force and the entire notion of good and evil is something which is determined by human beings themselves. We cannot pass the responsibility to *any* god, whether it is a so-called benevolent god or a so-called evil god.[24]

Those who have explored the many different branches of self-development within the human-potential and transpersonal movements will recognise here the self-actualising philosophy served up in a different form.[25] As Werner Erhard, founder of est, emphasised in his workshops and seminars, we should all learn to take responsibility for our own being and in so doing we are then able to create our own reality. Others within the personal-growth movement have similarly emphasised that we should 'own our own lives' and become independent psychic powers in a universe essentially of our own making. All of which implies, of course, that man has the potential to become a god. However, Lilith Sinclair is inclined to put this position somewhat more emphatically: 'We regard ourselves very highly because we feel we are superior beings. We feel that we are gaining the knowledge of a deeper universe.'

Both Michael Aquino and Don Webb endorse this view too. According to Aquino, the Temple of Set has introduced a new philosophical epoch – a 'state of mental evolution'. And from Webb's perspective:

> If we want to participate in the cultural revolution/evolution of the New Cycle, the best method is to transform ourselves. To actively seek, every day, those experiences and perform those deeds that lead to wisdom. If the magician transforms himself or herself, the actions of the magician lead to a transformation of the world around them. If one becomes as a god, one's words and deeds will have the effect of gods.[26]

Nazis, Death and Necromancy

In its most benign aspects one could consider the Temple of Set simply as a magical organisation dedicated to exploring the full potential of the individual – a type of magical self-help institution. However, it is certainly much more than this, for it advocates the deification of its individual members. This brings with it the associated mythology of the spiritual illuminati – a doctrine of the elect that some have associated with mystical fascism. It comes as no real surprise, therefore, that Michael Aquino has acknowledged a strong attraction to certain aspects of the former Nazi regime.

The specific links between the Setian philosophy and the magical practices of the esoteric Nazi group led by Heinrich Himmler are difficult to trace but are present, nevertheless. Although Dr Aquino states very clearly that there are many aspects of the Nazi era which are repugnant to him, he is also convinced that the Nazis were able to summon an extraordinary psychic force which was misdirected – but need not have been. Associated with the Setian quest for the superman, or initiated man, is the implication that as a god, the magical adept would gain the means to live forever, becoming a bright star in the firmament.

In an article in his Temple newsletter *Runes*, Aquino makes the comment that 'the successful magician must develop and ultimately master the ability to make himself the *constant*, and everything else *variable*, subject to his Will' (my italics).[27] This means the magician 'moves gradually towards an existence in which time becomes your servant and not your master'. It will also, says Aquino, 'enable you to conquer death'.

Aquino quotes from the well-known classic of Egyptian thought, *Her-Bak*, which includes a sage's answer to the young priest Her-Bak's enquiry about life and death:

> What is life? It is a form of the divine presence. It is the power, immanent in created things, to change themselves by successive destructions of form until the spirit or activating force of the original life-stream is freed. This power resides in the very nature of things . . . It is the spiritual aim of all human life to attain a state of consciousness that is independent of bodily circumstance.

Aquino believes that the Nazis tried to transfer the life-consciousness from the individual to the state, but that members of Himmler's esoteric group understood the process on a deeper level:

> Most Nazis were able to achieve [the transfer of consciousness] only in a mundane sense – in a kind of ecstatic selflessness created and sustained by propaganda. But the 'monk-knights' of the pre-war SS could disdain, even willingly embrace, the death of the individual human body because the consciousness had been transferred to a larger life-form – that of the Hegelian state – and individual sacrifice towards the strengthening of that life-form would actually contribute towards one's immortality. All of the individual-death references in the SS, such as the *Totenkopf* insignia and ritual pledges of 'Faithfulness unto death' were in fact arrogant affirmations of immortality.[28]

This leads us to a magical ceremony undertaken by Michael Aquino in a chamber in Wewelsburg Castle, beneath the Marble Hall used by Himmler's magical order, the Ahnenerbe. Wewelsburg Castle is located in German Westphalia, on the site of ancient Saxon fortifications. The castle in its present form was constructed by Archbishop Theodore von Fürstenberg in 1604–07 but was damaged by Swedish artillery during the Thirty Years' War. In 1815, the north tower was struck and nearly destroyed by lightning, and the castle fell into neglect. However, in 1933 the SS acquired Wewelsburg as its inner sanctum and Himmler began a programme of reconstruction. One of his innovations was to build a circular chamber known as the *Marmorsaal* (Marble Hall) to replace the original chapel of the castle. According to Aquino, it was inspired by the Hall of the Grail created by Alfred Roller, on Hitler's instructions, for the 1934 production of the opera *Parsifal* at Bayreuth.

Set in the red Italian marble floor is a dark-green marble disc from which extend twelve rune motifs. The design as a whole, while usually categorised as a 'solar symbol', is actually a secret magical sigil from an esoteric order, the Westphälischen Femgerichte, usually known as the Vehm. As such, the room was an ideal meeting place for the Ahnenerbe, who believed they were part of the same magical tradition.

Michael Aquino clearly perceives the inner group of priests and priestesses of the Temple of Set to be the magical successors, in turn, to the Ahnenerbe and Vehm. It was beneath the Marble Hall, in a secret chamber known as the Hall of the Dead, that he chose to perform another ritual invocation to the Prince of Darkness in 1982.

We do not have the details of Aquino's invocation for, as with his earlier revelation from Set, there are aspects which remain strictly private. What we do know, however, is that during the ceremony Aquino confirmed his belief that magically man stands apart from the universe. In his own words, 'The Wewelsburg working asserts that Life is conceptually contrary to Nature . . . and "unnatural" in its very essence.'[29]

For Aquino, then, the essential task of the magical initiate is to evolve to godlike proportions, subjecting the 'natural' universe to his will. Man owes his special status on Earth to 'the deliberate intervention of a non-natural intelligence [known as Set] and the respect accorded to the Prince of Darkness is simply an acknowledgement that he inspires man to strive ever higher in his quest for dominance'.

Included in this pursuit, as mentioned earlier, is the attempt to conquer death. Whereas most mystics believe they must surrender their individuality to the godhead – Nirvana, Sunyata, Ain Soph Aur – Aquino maintains that this is ill-advised: 'We would simply say that what they have is a sort of sublimated death-wish of the self and that we, unlike them, do not want to die.'[30]

The key to Michael Aquino's philosophy of cheating death is also contained in the *Runes* newsletter. More intriguing even than the potentials of genetic engineering, this involves manipulating the actual animating force in living things. Aquino believes that the psyche is neither dependent on, nor imprisoned by, the body, and that the mind of the magician is capable of reaching out 'towards the limitlessness of its conscious existence'. This, for Aquino, is what *xeper* really means. For the master Setian, the conscious universe literally has no boundaries.

Aquino developed this idea from a statement contained in the Book of Lucifer in Anton LaVey's *Satanic Bible*:

If a person has been vital throughout his life and has fought to the end for his earthly existence, it is this ego which will refuse to die, even after the expiration of the flesh which housed it . . . It is this . . . vitality that will allow the Satanist to peek through the curtain of darkness and death, and remain earthbound.[31]

The broader implication, of course, is that the satanist can meddle with life forces governing the principles of birth, death and creation – manipulating the processes of Nature for his own ends.

An additional insight into satanic approaches to life and death is provided by a bizarre and rather unwholesome experiment in necromancy undertaken by Aquino and LaVey. This took place in August 1973, when the two occultists were still working together, and represented an attempt to bring a dead person back to life. In this case the corpse was none other than that of ill-fated movie star Marilyn Monroe – with whom LaVey had had a brief sexual relationship when he was eighteen.[32] The aim of the sorcery was to summon her anima to take form once again from the natural elements into which her life force had dissipated. There had been rumours of foul play by the CIA following Monroe's clandestine sexual escapades with President Kennedy and his brother Robert, who at the time was Attorney General of the United States. LaVey suspected that Monroe's 'accidental suicide' was nothing of the sort – that she had been expertly murdered to silence her threatened revelations.

Both Aquino and LaVey were interested in a 'psychic evaluation' of the events leading up to the actress's death in August 1962, and with this purpose in mind the two men descended into the ceremonial Council Room of the Church of Satan and sat before the trapezoidal altar. Aquino describes their necromantic experiment in his book *The Church of Satan*:

> Anton asked that we both direct our thoughts to the bedroom of the house in the Brentwood cul-de-sac . . . it was in this bedroom that Marilyn's corpse had been discovered. For perhaps 15 minutes there was no change in the still atmosphere. Then I noticed that the chamber, already cold, seemed even more chill. Gazing slowly about the room, I saw that a change of a more material type had also taken place: the top of the low bed was now distorted with uneven indentations along its right side . . . Within the impressions on the bed there gradually appeared the nude body of a woman, face-down, contorted, and irregularly streaked or blotched with what seemed to be blood . . . The materialisation of this body was accompanied by

a mental sensation of 'queasiness' — as though one had encountered something corrupt or unclean.

Anton LaVey may have known the details of Marilyn Monroe's death, but I myself did not. The following year, when Robert Slatzer's book *The Life and Curious Death of Marilyn Monroe* was published, I learned that the actress's body had been discovered nude and face down on her bed. Suspicion had been aroused by how uncontorted the body was — not characteristic of death by barbiturate poisoning — and of course there was no visible blood. It was the contorted and bloodied state of the anima that told Anton what he wanted to know.[33]

Clearly both within the Church of Satan and, more recently, within the Temple of Set, there has been an unusual view of death — a perception that the skilled magical initiate can overcome the normal limitations of physical mortality. LaVey and Aquino believed that even eleven years after Marilyn Monroe's tragic death they could still summon a magical impression of her last moments as a living being. Both men have also expressed the view that the satanist who has developed a potent sense of vitality and willpower is capable of projecting the individual psyche beyond the normal dissolution of death. Whether these beliefs, fantastic as they are, simply represent delusory thinking or a type of occult conceit is for the reader to decide — such views are certainly uncharacteristic of the other magical traditions considered in this book.

This issue aside, we also need to ask how we can distinguish 'black' magic from its 'white' counterpart. Are we dealing here with a fundamental distinction between good and evil, or are such distinctions purely arbitrary and a matter of cultural preference? Is evil simply a matter of intent, or are deeper issues involved? And more specifically still, do we have anything to fear from the satanist or Setian?

Why Is Black Magic Black?

Members of the Church of Satan and the Temple of Set have described themselves as 'black magicians', and yet their idea of black magic is clearly different from that which prevails in the popular imagination.

For most people, the idea of black magic, or sorcery, involves magic of harmful intent, magic intended to do serious injury to another person or group of people, or magic intended to damage property – that is to say, magic which is basically destructive. But in their defence, this is not how the Setians themselves view the terrain. Leon Wild, editor of the *Ninth Night* – an Internet journal committed to Setian principles – has recently drawn a clear distinction between what he calls 'the myth of Satanic crime' and the core *raison d'être* of the black magician. From his perspective, legitimate satanists do not kill or injure people or animals, do not engage in rape or human sacrifice, do not burn or desecrate the churches of other religions, and do not interfere with burial grounds – even though they are frequently accused of all these things.[34]

And yet it is precisely issues of this type that come to mind when one considers the nature of black magic. In addition, there are psychopaths in all walks of life, many of whom are attracted to the self-empowering philosophies presented by the occult traditions. Many such people – Charles Manson and his followers included – have committed horrendous crimes through their deranged advocacy of the black arts. So one is obliged to ask whether all 'black magicians' are necessarily psychopaths or deviants.

There can be little doubt that for the nine years of its existence the Church of Satan was an organisation dedicated to licentious self-indulgence, but it is equally apparent that the Temple of Set presents a more cerebral and philosophical perspective. Dr Aquino's interest in Himmler's esoteric practices provides a natural cause for concern, but it would seem that the appeal here is more associated with notions of immortality and superhuman aspirations than with flagrant evil as most of us would understand it.

Nevertheless, it has to be said that Anton LaVey was certainly not above reproach in the Church of Satan. Blanche Barton's biography reveals that Anton LaVey placed a curse on Jayne Mansfield's attorney, Sam Brody, and then warned Mansfield to stay away from him. Both subsequently died in a horrific road accident in June 1967. Whether the curse actually created the fog which descended upon Highway 90 near Lake Pontchartrain, causing Mansfield's vehicle to crash into the rear of a tank truck, is of course open to speculation. But it is certainly the case that harmful intent was involved. LaVey was using a magical invocation to rid Jayne Mansfield – a participating member of the Church of Satan – of the intrusive jealousy of her attorney. Elsewhere, as we have seen, LaVey specifically mentions in his Eleven Rules of Satanism that one may legitimately destroy an offender. Proclamations of hate and vengeance were certainly a feature of the Church of Satan.

And yet, for the most part, the Church of Satan seems to have been primarily concerned with the full expression of human sexual indulgence – advocating uninhibited revelry in 'sin' rather than a full-blown engagement in 'evil'. Its anti-Christian antics are hard to take seriously, offensive though they must have been to many practising Christians.

One is left to conclude that for black magicians themselves, the so-called 'left-hand path' in magic would seem to mean something else altogether. Leon Wild distinguishes between white magic – which tends finally towards the sublimation of egoic awareness in an act of transcendence – and black magic, which is based on 'the acceptance and exultation of the Self'.[35] Here the Setian is proclaiming the aspiration of the human being as a potential god – an aspiration, which according to one's perspective, could simply be seen as an arrogant assertion or a vain deceit. However, as we have seen, Satanists and Setians make no secret of the fact that they believe that man has limitless potential and may even attain conscious immortality. For them the exploration of this sacred potential is a rational goal which carries its own justification. As Don Webb has written:

> The tradition of spiritual dissent in the West has been called Satanism . . . [and is] a rationally intuited spiritual technology for the purpose of self-deification. We choose as our role model the ancient Egyptian god Set, the archetype of Isolate Intelligence, rather than the somewhat limiting Hebrew Satan, archetype of the Rebel against cosmic injustice. As part of our practice we each seek the deconstruction of the socially constructed mind, so we begin in rebellion. We do not worship Set – only our own potential. Set was and is the patron of the magician who seeks to increase his existence through expansion . . . Black Magic is to take full responsibility for one's actions, evolution and effectiveness.[36]

What, then, of the darkness itself? Setians regard the image of Set — the Egyptian god of the night — as a dynamic force for change. He is the 'separator' or 'isolator' — the God who 'slew' stasis (represented by Osiris) and overcame chaotic mindlessness (represented by Apep). In this context Set represents the elimination of obsolete thought patterns and social conditioning — a 'dethroning of those internal gods that we have received from society'. To this extent the Setian approach is one of open rebellion against the concepts of the status quo, and in this way the Setians, like many other magical practitioners, seek to steal the fire from heaven. However, there is an important difference. As we have seen, for members of the Temple of Set, the journey is also one of achieving personal immortality. As Don Webb explains in his essay on the sacred word *xeper*, the magical quest, as he sees it, is 'to become an immortal, potent and powerful Essence'.[37]

In Egyptian mythology Set was the only god who overcame death. For Setians this is of special significance, for they seek an infinite future, opened to them through the magical will. For these magicians, darkness represents infinite potential. It is nothing less than *xeper* — the black void that may yet yield its secrets.

9

Mythologies of the Spirit

In one respect the Temple of Set is characteristic of many other contemporary magical groups — in the sense that its members aspire to be like gods. In his *Ritual of the Mark of the Beast* Aleister Crowley proclaims:

I am a God . . . very God of very God; I go upon my way to work my will . . . I am Omniscient, for naught exists for me unless I know it. I am Omnipotent, for naught exists save by Necessity my soul's expression through my will to be, to do, to suffer the symbols of itself. I am Omnipresent, for naught exists where I am not, who fashioned space as a condition of my consciousness of myself . . .[1]

Here Crowley is imagining the cosmos from the perspective of a creator god, but the revealing point is that he should even have conceived of this possibility in the first place. Crowley was doing what many occultists do — identifying with the god-form. There has always been an assumption in the world of magic that like mirrors like — as above, so below. The magician who imitates the god, becomes the god.

Margot Adler, a leading spokesperson for American neopaganism, confirms this as well: 'The fundamental thing about the magical and pagan religions is that ultimately they say, "Within yourself you are the god, you are the goddess — you can actualise within yourself and create whatever you need on this earth and beyond."'[2]

Part of this thinking has to do with the core concept in spiritual humanism that each individual has deep within their being a divine potential, a sacred source of vitality. There is only a slight shift of emphasis between acknowledging that each of us has a sacred link with the spiritual universe as a whole, and identifying with that divinity from an egoic perspective by asserting: I have become the god. The first viewpoint is a statement of connection, the second a statement of dominance. The first is founded on humility, the latter on arrogance. Unfortunately, arrogance has been a common feature of magical groups, especially among their leaders. The main problem occurs, it seems to me, when occult leaders assume the role of sacred illuminati and combine identification of the god image with unresolved personal issues of ego and power. The history of Western occultism is fraught with such examples – including MacGregor Mathers, who asserted autocratic spiritual authority in the Golden Dawn, and Aleister Crowley, who rebelled against Mathers and Yeats before establishing his own religious cosmology in Cairo in 1904.

And yet the first viewpoint mentioned above – the idea that we all have within us a sacred potential – would seem to have much to commend it. One can trace its origins back to Gnosticism itself and more recently to Carl Jung and his concept of the archetypes of the collective unconscious, for this is a framework of the psyche widely endorsed by practising occultists.

Carl Jung and the Mythic Unconscious

Jung believed that deep within the psyche, beyond the biographical and sexual components of the unconscious mind, one could find mythic 'archetypes' which provided the core impetus for visionary and religious experience. According to Jung, these archetypes transcended personal and cultural variables and were manifested in numerous symbolic forms around the world, invariably having a profound impact on those visionaries fortunate enough to encounter them first-hand in dreams, mystical visions, or acts of creative inspiration.

Jung was making the momentous point that divinity is not external to humanity but lies within – that it is an aspect of our 'humanness' which we all share and can have access to. In parting company with

Freud, whose view of the unconscious was essentially biological, Jung would increasingly emphasise that the sacred depths of the psyche provided the origin of all religious and mystical experiences. To this extent he was advocating an essentially Gnostic approach to spiritual knowledge. For Jung, it was not so much a matter of believing in a 'God up there', external to human events, as recognising the sacred potentiality within every human being. Furthermore, the encounter with the archetypes was not simply an act of grace bestowed by God. One could facilitate the process of spiritual awareness oneself – through dreamwork and visualisation techniques, as well as through other techniques like meditation and yoga.

Jung recognised that the unconscious mind seemed to contain a vast storehouse of imagery which was much greater than the repressions of the individual ego. It also seemed to him that to a certain extent the unconscious appeared to act independently of the conscious mind. He also discovered that there were certain motifs within dreams which did not seem to be a part of the individual psyche. The study of these symbols is what led him to formulate the concept of the 'collective unconscious':

> There are many symbols that are not individual but collective in their nature and origin. These are chiefly religious images; their origin is so far buried in the mystery of the past that they seem to have no human source. But they are, in fact, 'collective representations' emanating from primeval dreams and creative fantasies. As such, these images are involuntary spontaneous manifestations and by no means intentional inventions.[3]

What Jung was saying, in effect, was that at a certain psychic level, motifs common to the whole of humanity were capable of manifesting in dreams. These motifs were a symbolic expression of 'the constantly repeated experiences of humanity'. That is to say, they were derived from observations about Nature (the sky, changes of the seasons and so on) which had become embedded in the psychic patterns of the whole species. Jung called these primordial images 'archetypes' and gave the following example of how an archetype is formed:

One of the commonest and at the same time most impressive experiences is the apparent movement of the sun every day. We certainly cannot discover anything of this kind in the unconscious, so far as the known physical process is concerned. What we do find, on the other hand, is the myth of the sun hero in all its countless modifications. It is this myth and *not the physical process* that forms the archetype.[4]

Jung came to regard the archetype as an anthropomorphic rendition of a force in Nature. Its potency derived from the fact that the observation of the Sun's movement constituted one of the universal, fundamental experiences of existence, and was something which man could not change – a power beyond human manipulation. The Sun therefore became an object of mystical veneration, one of a number of archetypes with which to identify in religious or ritual acts of transcendence.

Naturally, different cultures would conceive of the Sun hero in a different form; for example, as Apollo-Helios in classical Greece and Rome, or as Ohrmazd in ancient Persia. Jung regarded all these variables as patterns on a theme – the core principle common to all of the cultural representations being the archetype itself. And there was another side to the archetype as well: its awe-inspiring vibrancy and its apparent autonomy, or ability to appear separate. As Jung notes:

> The 'primordial images', or archetypes, lead their own independent life . . . as can easily be seen in those philosophical or gnostic systems which rely on an awareness of the unconscious as the source of knowledge. The idea of angels, archangels, 'principalities and powers' in St Paul, the archons of the Gnostics, the heavenly hierarchy of Dionysius the Areopagite, all come from the perception of the relative autonomy of the archetypes.[5]

Furthermore, said Jung, an archetype contains within it a certain type of power or influence. 'It seizes hold of the psyche with a kind of primeval force.'[6] This perception forced Jung to regard the deepest regions of the psyche as profoundly spiritual, and he gradually embraced the view that the essential aim of personal development was to move towards a state of wholeness by integrating the conflicting contents and archetypal processes of the unconscious. He called this process 'individuation'.

Jung distinguished different aspects of the personality. These included the persona, the face we present to the world, and the ego, which included all the conscious contents of personal experience. However, Jung also believed that men and women should accommodate opposite gender polarities within their consciousness – he termed these the 'anima' for men and the 'animus' for women – and he talked of the 'shadow', an embodiment of memories and experiences repressed from consciousness altogether. The shadow would often appear in dreams and nightmares as a dark, repellent figure. Jung argued that if material from the shadow was acknowledged and allowed back into consciousness, much of its dark, frightening nature would disappear. Dealing with the dark side of the psyche remains an important aspect of all Jungian forms of psychotherapy.

Jung regarded the self as the totality of the personality, including all the aspects of the psyche mentioned above. He also considered the self to be a central archetype, personified symbolically by a circle or mandala, representations of wholeness. The thrust of all individual self-development was therefore towards wholeness of being. Self-realisation, or individuation, simply meant 'becoming oneself' in a true and total sense.

Jung described the process of personal growth in his essay 'The Relations Between the Ego and the Unconscious' (1928):

> The more we become conscious of ourselves through self-knowledge, and act accordingly, the more the layer of the personal unconscious that is superimposed on the collective unconscious will be diminished. In this way there arises a consciousness which is no longer imprisoned in the petty, oversensitive, personal world of objective interests. This widened consciousness is no longer that touchy, egotistical bundle of personal wishes, fears, hopes and ambitions which always has to be compensated or corrected by unconscious countertendencies; instead, it is a function of relationship to the world of objects, bringing the individual into absolute, binding and indissoluble communion with the world at large.[7]

Jung's impact on contemporary forms of spiritual practice has been considerable. His concept of the collective unconscious has encouraged many to look at myths, fables and legends for insights into the human condition, and also to relate the cycles of symbolic rebirth, found in many of the world's religions, to the process of personal individuation.

Another aspect of Jung's approach is his emphasis on individual trans-formation. According to Jung, we hold our spiritual destinies in our own hands. This is a profoundly Gnostic attitude, quite different from the spiritual message which emanates from most forms of Western institutional religion. However, it resonates strongly with modern esoteric belief. According to Jung, the archetypes of the collective unconscious provide spiritual milestones along the awe-inspiring path-way which leads to the reintegration of the psyche – and where this journey takes us is really up to us.

I think it is clear that many of Jung's principal ideas correlate with themes found in the esoteric traditions. Here too we have the idea of personal spiritual growth through various forms of self-knowledge, initiation and rites of passage. We find the polarities of the animus and the anima reflected in the second of the three Wiccan initiations and also in the mythic imagery of alchemy. Indeed, Jung himself was fasci-nated by these correlations. And the concept of Jungian individuation, too, is mirrored by the magical journey through the various archetypes found on the Kabbalistic Tree of Life, with Tiphareth – symbolic of spiritual rebirth and wholeness – at their centre. Occultists have long sought to explore the visionary potentials of their inner being, and their invocations and visualisations are intended to call the gods forth into consciousness. Magic is essentially about stealing the fire from heaven – and then integrating the flame within.

The Rise of Sacred Psychology

Following the development of the personal-growth movement from the late 1960s onwards – a movement based substantially on the self-actualising ideas of Abraham Maslow – many people in the spiritual counter-culture became increasingly attuned to the idea of an inner mythology of the god or goddess within. One of the bridging figures who continued the direct legacy of Carl Jung and who also served as a spiritual mentor to many in the personal-growth movement was the American writer and teacher Joseph Campbell. Campbell had visited Jung in Zürich in 1953 and was enthusiastic about Jung's interpretation of the universal themes in world mythology. And he was a distinguished scholar in his own right, producing a number of authoritative but accessible studies on Oriental, indigenous and Western mythology, and many insightful essays on the symbols of comparative religion.

Campbell's special skill was his ability to relate the themes of mythology to the human condition. In his seminars at the Esalen Institute and elsewhere he would explain, 'Mythology helps you identify the mysteries of the energies pouring through you . . . Mythology is an organisation of images metaphoric of experience, action, and fulfilment of the human spirit in the field of a given culture at a given time.'[8] He also rejected fundamentalist concepts of creator gods, regarding them as archetypes of one's inner being. According to Campbell, 'Your god is a manifestation of your own level of consciousness. All of the heavens and all of the hells are within you . . .'[9]

Campbell remained primarily a scholar and a teacher during his long career and probably would not have considered himself part of the personal-growth movement, even though he knew many of its key figures. And yet one aspect of Joseph Campbell's credo has had enormous impact and is widely quoted in alternative mystical circles: *Follow your bliss*. In saying this, Campbell was endorsing the idea that we should all follow what he called a 'path with heart', a path that defines our place in the cosmos and on this Earth. Campbell was not alone in articulating this view but he helped endorse it, and since his time there has been a substantial resurgence of interest in the role mythology can play in contemporary human life. Several key figures in the personal-growth movement, among them Dr Jean Shinoda Bolen and Dr Jean Houston, have helped develop Campbell's approach and have played a prominent role in exploring practical and inspirational ways of introducing archetypal mythic realities into everyday consciousness.

Dr Bolen is a Jungian psychiatrist and the author of such works as *Goddesses in Everywoman*, *Gods in Everyman* and *The Tao of Psychology*. For many years she has supported the view that all individuals can apply the archetypal energies of the gods and goddesses in their everyday lives. Bolen trained as a doctor, was strongly influenced by the women's movement in the 1960s and taught a course on the psychology of women at the University of California's San Francisco campus. She is now clinical professor of psychiatry at the University of California Medical Center and believes, like Jung, that myths are a path to the deeper levels of the mind:

> Myth is a form of metaphor. It's the metaphor that's truly empowering for people. It allows us to see our ordinary lives from a different perspective, to get an intuitive sense of who we are and what is important to us . . . Myths are the bridge to the collective unconscious. They tap images, symbols, feelings, possibilities and patterns – inherent, inherited human potential that we all hold in common.[10]

Although myths sometimes seem to have an archaic quality removed from the everyday world, Bolen argues that mythic or archetypal awareness can provide a real sense of meaning in day-to-day life:

> If you live from your own depths – that is, if there is an archetypal basis for what you're doing – then there's a meaningful level to it that otherwise might be missing . . . When people 'follow their bliss' as Joseph Campbell says, their heart is absorbed in what they're doing. People who work in an involved, deep way are doing something that matters to them just to be doing it, not for the paycheck, not for someone saying to them: 'What a good job you're doing.'[11]

In her personal life, despite her Japanese ancestry, Jean Shinoda Bolen has identified with the ancient Greek goddesses. She told the interviewer Mirka Knaster that the goddesses who had most reflected in her life were Artemis, Athena and Hestia, who represented the 'independent, self-sufficient qualities in women'. Artemis, goddess of the hunt, seemed to embody her Japanese family's frequent moves around the United States in the 1940s, to avoid being detained in an American concentration camp; Athena, goddess of wisdom, seemed present in her decision to train as a medical doctor, and Hestia, goddess of the hearth, epitomised her present love of 'comfort in solitude'. However, in her role as a writer and lecturer she has also felt drawn to Hermes as an archetype of communication.

Bolen emphasises that we can all embody both the gods and goddesses in our lives, not just the archetypes of our own gender. And, most significantly, she sees such mythic attunement as opening out into greater planetary awareness. Bolen echoes the sentiments of the Wiccan devotees Margot Adler and Starhawk, whose perspectives we discussed earlier:

> The current need is a return to earth as the source of sacred energy. I have a concept that I share with others that we're evolving into looking out for the earth and our connection with everybody on it. Women seem more attuned to it, but increasingly more men are too. I believe that the human psyche changes collectively, when enough individuals change. Basically, the point of life is to survive and evolve. To do both requires that we recognise our planetary community and be aware that we cannot do anything negative to our enemies without harming ourselves.[12]

Dr Jean Houston, also a leading advocate of goddess psychology, takes much the same position and is similarly attuned to the new 'Gaia consciousness'. 'The Earth is a living system,' she says. 'That is why women are now being released from the exclusivity of a child-bearing, child-rearing role. This is also a time when the Earth desperately needs the ways of thinking and being that women have developed through thousands of years.'

Houston is the former president of the Association of Humanistic Psychology and a director of the Foundation for Mind Research in Pomona, New York, but her talents also extend into many forms of creative expression. An award-winning actress in Off-Broadway theatre, she has developed numerous training programmes in spiritual studies which include the enactment of themes from the ancient Mystery traditions. Her many methods include visualisation, chanting, storytelling and rituals – and she believes strongly that myths can shape and transform consciousness. In an interview published in *Magical Blend* she explained her own role in this process: 'My task is to evoke people into that place of identifying the god or goddess or archetype that is personal to them and allowing that being to speak for them . . .'[13]

Houston is personally interested in a broad range of myths, especially those which describe sacred journeys of transformation. She is also fascinated by archetypal figures like Parsifal and the Holy Grail, St Francis of Assisi, Odysseus, Christ, Isis and Osiris – for all of these are examples of how we may undertake a quest of spiritual renewal. For Houston, myths and archetypes are of central concern in our daily lives:

> Myths may be the most fundamental patterns in human existence. They're source patterns, I think, originating from beneath us, behind us, in the transpersonal realm . . . yet they are the key to our personal and historical existence. That's why I often say they're the DNA of the human psyche . . .[14]

She also believes that not only mythologically, but also quite literally, our origins are in the cosmos:

> Earlier peoples saw archetypes in Nature and in the starry Heavens – in the Sun, the Moon, the Earth, the vast oceans – implicitly realising our descent from these primal entities. Everyone and every-thing derives from the stars – those fiery solar generators of the primary elements of beingness. The sediments of Earth make up our cells, and the briny oceans flow through our veins and tissues. Our ancestors storied this deep knowing into tales of the community of Nature: the marriage of Heaven and Earth; the churning of the ocean to create the nectar of life; the action of the wind upon the waters to bring form out of chaos. In these mythic tellings, our forerunners located higher reality and its values in the larger community – in the things of this world, shining reflections of the community of arche-types. They clearly perceived that the pattern connecting both world and archetype was the essential weave that sustains all life.[15]

And it is precisely because myths and archetypes are so primal, and because they help define our relationship with the cosmos, that they are of such vital importance today. For Houston our present era – a time on the planet when many feel gripped by a sense of existential crisis – is characterised not simply by a sense of 'paradigm shift' but by a 'whole system transition, a shift in reality itself'. We live in a time of a 'radically changing story', and sacred psychology – with its lessons of transformation and renewal – will play a vital role in this transition. For Jean Houston the hallmarks of the age are an increasing sense of 'planetisation', the rebirth of the archetypal feminine, the emergence of new forms of science, new understandings of the potential for extending human capacities and the 'ecology of consciousness', and an emergence, overall, of a global spiritual sensibility.[16]

During the early 1980s Houston used a variety of experiential techniques to take participants into mythic states of being. One of these was to invite participants to learn 'shape-shiftings' by relaxing and identifying with different god and goddess identities, thereby helping them to acquire archetypal perceptions. This could involve, for example, meditating on such figures as the Great Mother, the wise old king, the young redeemer, the trickster or the divine child. Houston now believes that visualisations in themselves, while helpful, are not enough. It may well be that some sense of personal conflict is required to spur one on in the spiritual quest. Personal growth, she feels, can often follow from a sense of being 'wounded' – expressed, perhaps, in the feeling of being abandoned or hurt in some way. 'God may reach us through our affliction,' she says; 'we can be ennobled and extended by looking at this wounding in such a way that we move from the personal particular to the personal universal.'[17]

An Archaic Revival – the Rediscovery of Shamanism

Shamanism is the world's oldest religion, but it too has been revived within the personal-growth movement as a visionary approach to the cosmos. Shamanism is not only the earliest but also the most widespread spiritual tradition in human culture and extends back to the Palaeolithic era. Remnants of it are still found as far afield as Siberia, the United States, Mexico, Central and South America, Japan, Tibet, Indonesia, Nepal and Aboriginal Australia.

Anthropologists and archaeologists associate the first dawnings of human spiritual awareness with Neanderthal cave sites in Europe and

Central Asia. In a cave at Le Moustier in France the bones of a dead youth were discovered, laid in repose and accompanied by a selection of tools and bones of animals, which suggests a belief that such implements could assist the youth in his life after death. Similarly, in a grave in Uzbekistan a circle of ibex horns had been placed reverently around the body of a dead child.

But it is at other locations like the Franco-Cantabrian cave of Les Trois-Frères that the shamanic bond with Nature can more clearly be seen. Here, cave art dating back some 15,000 years reveals the quite specific figure of the hunter-shaman armed with a bow and disguised as a bison amid a herd of wild animals. From earliest times, shamans have mimicked birds and animals in their rituals, have revered sacred plants, and have developed what we in the twentieth century would call a holistic relationship with the cosmos.

Shamanism, though, is more than just imitative magic. It can be regarded as an animistic approach to Nature and the cosmos, which utilises visionary states of consciousness as a means of contacting the denizens of the spirit world. The shaman – who can be a man or a woman, depending on cultural determinants – is essentially a magical practitioner who, through an act of will, can enter into a state of trance, and who then journeys to the land of the gods or perhaps, closer to home, divines by visionary means the causes of sickness and malaise.

Underlying all forms of shamanism is the notion that the universe is alive with gods and spirits. The shaman's role is to divine the presence of harmful or malicious spirits which are causing individual illness or 'cursing' members of the tribal group. The shaman or medicine man is thus an intermediary between the natural and metaphysical worlds, meeting the spirits on their own territory.

As a phenomenon, shamanism first attracted widespread attention in the late 1960s and early 1970s through the magical writings of Carlos Castaneda (1925–1998). For many devotees of the new spiritual perspectives then surfacing in the American counter-culture, Castaneda and his 'teacher', the Yaqui shaman don Juan Matus, were the first point of contact with the figure of the shaman. Even after his recent death, Castaneda's influence and fame continue to spread, alongside that of his equally controversial female counterpart, Lynn Andrews.[18] Casteneda's more recent works are now regarded substantially as fiction, but his early writings did appear to be grounded in more solid shamanic research and had a core authenticity.

Castaneda was always a highly private person and only sketchy details of his personal history are known. However, it has been established that between 1959 and 1973 he undertook a series of degree courses in anthropology at the University of California, Los Angeles. Although his real name was Carlos Arana or Carlos Aranha, and he came from Lima, São Paulo or Buenos Aires, he adopted the name Carlos Castaneda when he acquired United States citizenship in 1959. The following year, having commenced his studies, he apparently travelled to the American Southwest to explore the Indian use of medicinal plants. As the story goes, a friend introduced him to an old Yaqui Indian who was said to be an expert on the hallucinogen peyote.

The Indian, don Juan Matus, said he was a *brujo*, a term which connotes a sorcerer or one who cures by means of magical techniques. Born in Sonora, Mexico, in 1891, he spoke Spanish 'remarkably well' but appeared at the first meeting to be unimpressed with Castaneda's self-confidence. He indicated, however, that Castaneda could come to see him subseqently, and an increasingly warm relationship developed as the young academic entered into an 'apprenticeship' in shamanic magic.

Carlos Castaneda found many of don Juan's ideas and techniques strange and irrational. The world of the sorcerer contained mysterious, inexplicable forces that he was obliged not to question, but had to accept as a fact of life. The apprentice sorcerer would begin to 'see' whereas previously he had merely 'looked'. Eventually he would become a 'man of knowledge'.

According to Castaneda's exposition of don Juan's ideas, the familiar world we perceive is only one of a number of worlds. It is in reality a description of the relationship between objects that we have learned to recognise as significant from birth, which has been reinforced by language and the communication of mutually acceptable concepts. This world is not the same as the world of the sorcerer, for while ours tends to be based on the confidence of perception, the *brujo*'s involves many intangibles. His universe is a vast and continuing mystery which cannot be contained within rational categories and frameworks.

In order to transform one's perception from ordinary to magical reality, an 'unlearning' process has to occur. The apprentice must learn how to 'not do' what he has previously 'done'. He must learn how to transcend his previous frameworks and conceptual categories and for a moment freeze himself between the two universes, the 'real' and the 'magically real'. To use don Juan's expression, he must 'stop the world'. From this point onwards, he may begin to see, to acquire a knowledge and mastery of the mysterious forces operating in the environment which most people close off from their everyday perception.

'Seeing,' said don Juan, was a means of perception which could be brought about often, although not necessarily, by hallucinogenic drugs – among them *mescalito* (peyote), *yerba del diablo* (Jimson weed, or datura) and *humito* (psilocybe mushrooms). Through these, the *brujo* could acquire a magical ally, who could in turn grant further power and the ability to enter more readily into 'states of non-ordinary reality'. The *brujo* would become able to see the 'fibres of light' and energy patterns emanating from people and other living organisms, encounter the forces within the wind and the sacred waterhole, and isolate as visionary experiences – as if on film – the incidents of his earlier life and their influence on the development of the personality. Such knowledge would enable the *brujo* to tighten his defences as a 'warrior'. He would know himself and have complete command over his physical vehicle. He would also be able to project his consciousness from his body into images of birds and animals, thereby transforming into a myriad of magical forms and shapes while travelling in the spirit vision.[19]

Although Castaneda's books have been attacked by critics like Weston La Barre and Richard de Mille for containing fanciful and possibly concocted elements, it is likely that the early volumes in particular are based substantially on shamanic tradition – even if some of the material has been borrowed from elsewhere. For example, there are parallels between the shamanic figure don Genaro, a friend of don Juan, and the famous Huichol shaman Ramon Medina.

One of Castaneda's friends, the anthropologist Barbara Myerhoff, was studying the Huichol Indians at the same time that Castaneda was claiming to be studying Yaqui sorcery, and Myerhoff introduced Ramon Medina to Castaneda. It may be that Castaneda borrowed an incident in *A Separate Reality* – where don Genaro leaps across a precipitous waterfall clinging to it by magical 'tentacles of power' – from an actual Huichol occurrence.

Myerhoff and another noted anthropologist, Peter Furst, watched Ramon Medina leaping like a bird across a waterfall which cascaded three hundred metres below over slippery rocks. Medina was exhibiting the balance of the shaman in 'crossing the narrow bridge to the other world'. Myerhoff told Richard de Mille how pleased she felt, in terms of validation, when Castaneda related to her that the sorcerer don Genaro could also do similar things. It now seems, she feels, that Castaneda was like a mirror, his own accounts reflecting borrowed data from all sorts of sources, including her own. The rapid mystical running known as 'the gait of power', for example, was likely to have come from accounts of Tibetan mysticism, and there were definite parallels between don Juan's abilities and statements in other anthropological, psychedelic and occult sources.[20]

Even in death, Castaneda remains controversial. However, while Castaneda's brand of shamanic sorcery was always elusive – no one ever knew for sure whether don Juan really existed – another, more accessible approach to practical shamanism was being introduced to the personal-growth movement by an American anthropologist who really did have impeccable academic credentials: Dr Michael Harner.

A former visiting professor at Columbia, Yale and the University of California, Harner is now director of the Foundation for Shamanic Studies in Mill Valley, California. Born in Washington, DC, in 1929, Harner spent the early years of his childhood in South America. In 1956 he returned to do fieldwork among the Jivaro Indians of the Ecuadorian Andes and between 1960 and 1961 visited the Conibo Indians of the Upper Amazon in Peru. His first period of fieldwork was conducted as 'an outside observer of the world of the shaman', but his second endeavour – which included his psychedelic initiation among the Conibo – led him to pursue shamanism first-hand. In 1964 he returned to Ecuador to experience the supernatural world of the Jivaro in a more complete way.

After arriving at the former Spanish settlement of Macas, Harner made contact with his Jivaro guide, Akachu. Two days later he ventured with him northwards, crossing the Rio Upano and entering the forest. It was here that he told his Indian friend that he wished to acquire spirit-helpers, known to the Jivaro as *tsentsak*. Harner offered gifts to Akachu and was told that the first preparatory task was to bathe in the sacred waterfall. Later he was presented with a magical pole to ward off demons. Then, after an arduous journey to the waterfall, Harner was led into a dark recess behind the wall of spray – a cave known as 'the house of the Grandfathers' – and here he had to call out, attracting the attention of the ancestor spirits. He now had his first magical experiences: the wall of falling water became iridescent, a torrent of liquid prisms. 'As they went by,' says Harner, 'I had the continuous sensation of floating upward, as though they were stable and I was the one in motion . . . It was like flying inside a mountain.'

Deeper in the jungle, Akachu squeezed the juice of some psychedelic datura plants he had brought with him and asked Harner to drink it that night. Reassuring him, Akachu told him he was not to fear anything he might see, and if anything frightening did appear, he should run up and touch it.

That night was especially dramatic anyway, with intense rain, thunder and flashes of lightning. After a while the effects of the datura became apparent and it was clear that something quite specific was going to happen.

Suddenly Harner became aware of a luminous, multicoloured serpent writhing towards him. Remembering his advice from Akachu, Harner charged at the visionary serpent with a stick. Suddenly the forest was empty and silent and the monster had gone. Akachu later explained to Harner that this supernatural encounter was an important precursor to acquiring spirit-helpers. And his triumph over the serpent had confirmed that he was now an acceptable candidate for the path of the shaman.

Harner believes, as the Jivaro do, that the energising force within any human being can be represented by what the Indians call a 'power animal'. One of the most important tasks of the shaman is to summon the power animal while in trance, and undertake visionary journeys with the animal as an ally. It is in such a way that one is able to explore the 'upper' and 'lower' worlds of the magical universe. The shaman also learns techniques of healing which usually entail journeys to the spirit world to obtain sources of 'magical energy'. This energy can then be transferred to sick or dis-spirited people in a ceremonial healing rite.[21]

After living with the Conibo and Jivaro, Michael Harner undertook further fieldwork among the Wintun and Pomo Indians in California, the Lakota Sioux of South Dakota and the Coast Salish in Washington State. The techniques of applied shamanism which he now teaches in his workshops, and which are outlined in his important book *The Way of the Shaman*, are a synthesis from many cultures, but they are true to the core essence of the tradition. 'Shamanism,' says Harner, 'takes us into the realms of myth and the Dreamtime . . . and in these experiences we are able to contact sources of power and use them in daily life.'[22]

I first met Michael Harner at the International Transpersonal Conference in Melbourne, in 1980, and his lectures and workshops made an immediate impression. Harner is a large, friendly man with a dense grey-black beard and mischievous eyes, and he would chuckle when presenting the paradoxes of the shaman's universe. He told the assembled group about power animals and magical forces in Nature without at all attempting to present a logical rationale. He explained how, for the Jivaro Indians, an individual could reach maturity only if protected by special power allies that accompanied that person and provided vitality and purpose. He showed us how to meditate on the repetitive rhythm of a beaten drum and how to ride this rhythm into the inner world, journeying down the root system of the cosmic tree or through smoke tunnels into the sky. He asked us not to judge these events when they occurred to us but to consider them on their own terms. We were, he said, entering a shamanic mode of trance consciousness where anything could happen. But because we saw strange, surreal events unfolding before us, or mythic animals in unfamiliar locales, we should not recoil from this experience but should instead participate in the process of discovering a new visionary universe within ourselves.

Harner's workshop technique was remarkably simple. After blessing the group with his rattles, he would start pounding his large flat drum and encourage us to dance free-form around the room with our eyes half-closed, attuning ourselves to any form of spontaneous expression that would flow through us.

After only a short time, many people adopted animal postures and forms, and began to express these in very individual ways. Some people became bears and lumbered slowly around the room. Others became snakes or lizards. There were several wild cats, the occasional elephant and a variety of birds. I myself seemed to have an eagle-hawk ally as I winged around through the group.

Harner then asked us to lie down on the floor and close our eyes. He began drumming in a monotonous, steady rhythm, to allow us to ride down into the shamanic underworld. Harner had explained to us that this was not an 'evil' domain but simply the 'reverse' of our familiar, day-to-day world – a place where a different kind of reality prevailed. The technique was to imagine yourself entering the trunk of a large tree through a door at its base. Perhaps there were steps inside, but soon one would see the roots leading down at an angle of around forty-five degrees. Following the root tunnel you then journeyed still further – down, down, down – all the time propelled and supported by the constancy of the drumming. Finally you would see a speck of light at the end of the tunnel. Gradually drawing towards it, you would pass through into the light and look around at the new surroundings. Various animals would pass by, but we were asked to look for one that presented itself to us four times. That animal was possibly our own magical ally. Perhaps we would engage in conversation with this creature, be shown new magical vistas or landscapes, fly in the air, or be given gifts or special knowledge. Harner emphasised that any of these things could happen, but it was up to us to accept the visionary experience on its own terms. If elephants began flying through the air, then so be it. There was no question of the experience being dismissed as simple 'imagination'. Imagination, in Harner's view, was a different type of reality, not an illusory world to be rationalised away or belittled.

After a full day of drumming and magical journeying, the climax, for me, came in the evening. Harner told us that he had been experimenting with journeys up into the sky, as well as the more familiar ventures into the underworld. He asked us to imagine entering a smoke tunnel either by wafting upwards on smoke from a campfire or by entering a fireplace and soaring towards the sky through a chimney. As we entered the smoke tunnel, he explained, we would see it unfolding before us, taking us higher and higher into the sky.

At some time or other, Harner said, a water bird would present itself as an ally, to lift us still higher into the sky world. Why this should be a water bird was not explained. He was also keen to know whether any of us saw any 'geometric structures', although he didn't wish to elaborate on this in case his comments had the effect of programming us into a specific visionary experience. As it turned out, several people in the group had visions of geometric 'celestial' architecture.

The room was quite dark as Harner began to beat on his drum and I found it easy to visualise the fireplace in my living room at home. The following is a transcript of my magical journey, recorded soon afterwards:

> I enter the fireplace and quickly shoot up the chimney into a lightish grey whirling cloud tunnel. Soon I am aware of my guardian – a pelican with a pink beak.
>
> Mounting the pelican's back I ride higher with it into the smoke tunnel. In the distance I see a golden mountain rising in the mist . . .
>
> As we draw closer I see that, built on the top of the mountain, is a magnificent palace made of golden crystal, radiating lime-yellow light. I am told that this is the palace of the phoenix, and I then see that golden bird surmounting the edifice. It seems to be connected with my own power-hawk.
>
> I feel awed and amazed by the beauty of this place, but the regal bird bids me welcome. Then the hawk comes forward and places a piece of golden crystal in my chest. I hold my breath deeply as I receive it, for it is a special gift.
>
> The drum is still sounding but soon Michael indicates with a specific drum-beat that we should return. However, I am still high in the sky and find it very hard to re-enter the smoke tunnel. When I finally do begin to return the heavens remain golden, and as I travel down into the tunnel I look up to see saint-like figures rimming the tunnel, farewelling me . . .

This journey was a very awesome one for me. After returning to an awareness of the workshop location and the people around me, I initially found it very difficult to articulate my thoughts. I seemed lost for words but was anxious, nevertheless, to communicate a sense of the importance that the journey had had for me. I felt I had been in a very sacred space. My direct interaction with the hawk that had planted a crystal in my chest had been totally unexpected, but this seemed at the time to be a rare and special privilege.

I later discovered, as I conducted shamanic visualisation workshops like this myself, that mythic and symbolic journeys of this kind were not unusual. Indeed, the combination of the visualisation and the repetitive drumming made it comparatively easy for participants to enter a sense of magical or sacred space.

My next meeting with Michael Harner was in New York in November 1984, as an interviewer for a television documentary. This provided me with an opportunity to see Harner working with an experienced group of shamanic explorers, many of whom were regularly encountering archetypal imagery on their magical journeys.

On this occasion the workshop was being held in a large, open room in an old tenement building in Canal Street, lower Manhattan. Most of the participants were wearing casual, comfortable clothing and had brought cushions and blankets as well as hankerchiefs to drape over their eyes.

The session began as Harner shook his gourd rattle to the four quarters and then summoned the 'spirits' to participate in the shamanic working. He also encouraged the group to chant a Jivaro shaman song:

> *I have spirits,*
> *Spirits have I . . .*
> *I have spirits,*
> *Spirits have I . . .*
> *I, I, I . . .*

The group members formed themselves into the shape of a 'spirit-canoe' and each person present was asked to visualise themselves riding in it, sailing down to the 'lower world'.

A dis-spirited Yoruba woman named Regina was lying in the centre of the canoe, and it was for her that tonight's shamanising would be done. After the initial procedures had been performed, Harner explained, he would join the canoe, lie beside her, and endeavour to journey on her behalf to the magical world. There he would look for a healing spirit which he could bring back with him and transfer to her body, thus revitalising her and making her well again.

Harner completed his circle of the spirit-canoe, laid down his gourd rattle and rested beside Regina. A young man seated at the rear of the canoe now began to beat on the drum. It was a regular and monotonous drum beat, intended to simulate the gallop of a horse and the rhythm of the heart – the sort of regular rhythm on which one could 'ride' into the inner world. The shaman and his helpers in the spirit-canoe now visualised the vessel passing down into the earth through 'the crack between the worlds'.

The sonorous drumming continued, intensifying its rhythm. Harner had managed to locate a spirit in the lower world and was now clutching it symbolically to his chest. He rose to his knees, still clasping the 'creature' in his hands, and, as the drumming stopped, indicated that Regina should also sit up. Cupping his hands together above her head, Harner 'blew' the spirit into her body. Then, repeating the same action, he whispered to her: 'I have given you a deer.'

Regina knew that she was obliged to acknowledge this gift in a ceremonial context. Well versed in Yoruba ritual dance, she was familiar with the concept of propitiating the healing spirits. Gracefully, ever gracefully, she began dancing around inside the spirit-canoe, welcoming the presence of the magical creature who had restored health and vitality to her body. With lilting gestures and lyrical expressions of form, she danced her power animal – a dance that was completely free-flowing and unstructured.

When the work was done, Regina sat down to rest and Michael Harner announced to the group that the shamanic session was complete. Later Regina told me how special it was to receive this gift of healing. 'Michael is a very strong shaman . . . and when he gave me my power animal, I felt a surge of energy. The dancing is very spontaneous . . . I was letting go with all the energy he had breathed in . . .'

Other members of the group revealed that they, too, had made their own spirit journeys at the same time, but to other regions of the magical terrain. Some of these experiences revealed the extraordinary range of mythological images which become available through the shamanic process. One woman, for example, had ventured to the upper world:

I was flying. I went up into black sky – there were so many stars – and then I went into an area that was like a whirlwind. I could still see the stars and I was turning a lot, and my power animals were with me. Then I came up through a layer of clouds and met my teacher – she was a woman I'd seen before. She was dressed in a long, long gown and I wanted to ask her how I could continue with my shamanic work, how to make it more a part of my daily life. Then she took me into her, into her belly. I could feel her get pregnant with me and felt her belly stretching. I felt myself inside her. I also felt her put her hands on top of her belly and how large it was! She told me that I should stop breathing, that I should take my nourishment from her, and I could actually feel myself stop breathing. I felt a lot of warmth in my belly, as if it were coming into me, and then she stretched further and actually broke apart. Her belly broke apart and I came out of her, and I took it to mean that I needed to use less will in my work, and that I needed to trust her more and let that enter into my daily life. That was the end of my journey – the drum stopped and I came back at that point.[23]

Harner believes that mythic experiences of this sort are common during the shamanic journey and reveal a dimension of consciousness rarely accessed in daily life:

Simply by using the technique of drumming, people from time immemorial have been able to pass into these realms which are normally reserved for those approaching death, or for saints. These are the realms of the upper and lower world where one can get information to puzzling questions. This is the Dreamtime of the Australian Aboriginal, the 'mythic time' of the shaman. In this area, a person can obtain knowledge that rarely comes to other people.[24]

This of course begs the question of whether the shaman's journey is just imagination. Is the mythic experience really real? Harner's reply is persuasive:

Imagination is a modern western concept that is outside the realm of shamanism. 'Imagination' already pre-judges what is happening. I don't think it is imagination as we ordinarily understand it. I think we are entering something which, surprisingly, is universal – regardless of culture. Certainly people are influenced by their own history, their cultural and individual history. But we are beginning to discover a map of the upper and lower world, regardless of culture. For the shaman, what one sees – that's real. What one reads out of a book is secondhand information. But just like the scientist, the shaman depends upon first-hand observation to decide what's real. If you can't trust what you see yourself, then what can you trust?[25]

Harner is now deeply committed to shamanic research and is engaged in training tribal peoples in shamanic techniques which have disappeared from their own indigenous cultures. Several groups, including the Sami (formerly known as Lapps) and the Inuit (formerly known as Eskimo) have approached him to help restore sacred knowledge lost as a result of missionary activity or Western colonisation. Harner and his colleagues at the Foundation for Shamanic Studies have been able to help them with what he calls 'core shamanism' – general methods consistent with those once used by their ancestors. In this way, he believes, 'members of these tribal societies can elaborate and integrate the practices on their own terms in the context of their traditional cultures' – and shamanic knowledge can once again be restored to the indigenous traditions.

10

Archetypes and Cyberspace

From the perspective of the late 1990s, as we prepare to embrace the new millennium, it is fascinating to relate the ancient spiritual tradition of shamanism to the new developments in computer technology and cyberspace – a connection which in theory would seem to be all but impossible. However, for cyber-explorers like Terence McKenna a fusion of this sort presents no problems at all. McKenna is both a shamanic adventurer and an internationally recognised spokesperson for the metaphysics of the new technology. For him the shamanic tradition is essentially about 'externalising the soul' – making tangible both the human spirit and what he calls 'the Logos of the planet'. He also believes that computer innovations like the World Wide Web, which take us into a type of global collective consciousness, can help us achieve it. And although the shamanic model of the spiritual universe is undoubtedly archaic, in McKenna's opinion it is also the most accurate map of the 'soul' or 'psyche' that we have.

McKenna, born in 1946, graduated from the University of California in Berkeley with majors in ecology, resource conservation and shamanism. His original interest was specifically in Central Asian shamanism. During the late 1960s he went to Nepal to learn the Tibetan language and also to study indigenous Bon-Po shamanism. He then lived for a time in India and the Seychelles before deciding to visit those regions of the world where shamanism was still being practised as a living tradition. This took him to several islands in Indonesia – including Sumatra, Sumba, Flores, the Moluccas and Ceram – and later to South America, where he observed shamanic practices first-hand.

In the upper Amazon basin of Colombia, Peru and Ecuador shamans make extensive use of *ayahuasca*, a psychedelic beverage made from the tree-climbing forest vine known botanically as *Banisteriopsis caapi*. Taking this beverage allows the shaman to enter the supernatural realm, to have initiatory visions, and to make contact with ancestors and helper-spirits. McKenna was interested in the fact that from a biochemical view, *ayahuasca* appeared to resemble psilocybin, the active principle in the sacred psilocybe mushrooms used by shamans in the highlands of central Mexico. He also believes – and this is where he enters the realm of anthropological controversy – that the intake of psilocybin by primates living in the African grasslands before the last Ice Age may have led to the origins of human language itself.

Psilocybe mushrooms produce a mystical state of consciousness where the soul 'speaks' to the mind. These mushrooms also grow prolifically in cattle dung and McKenna argues that the entry of psilocybin into the food chain in Africa between 15,000 and 20,000 years ago, and the subsequent domestication of cattle, may have led to the establishment of the first Palaeolithic religion – that of the great horned goddess.[1] More specifically still, he maintains that psilocybin itself has a unique role to play in human culture because of its role as an inspirational guiding agent. It is, says McKenna, quite literally the Logos of the planet. During an interview I conducted with him, he explained the significance of this concept, both in relation to shamanism and with regard to the origins of the Western philosophical tradition:

Under the influence of psilocybin there is an experience of contacting a speaking entity – an interiorised voice that I call the *Logos*. If we don't go back to Hellenisic Greek terminology then we are left with only the vocabulary of psychopathology. In modern times to hear 'voices' is to be seriously deviant: there is no other way to deal with this. And yet if we go back to the Classical literature the whole goal of Hellenistic esotericism was to gain access to this thing called the *Logos*. The *Logos* spoke the Truth – an incontrovertible Truth. Socrates had what he called his *daimon* – his informing 'Other'. And the ease with which psilocybin induces this phenomenon makes it, from the viewpoint of a materialist or reductionist rooted in the scientific tradition, almost miraculous.[2]

For Terence McKenna the psilocybin experience is central to understanding the origins of spiritual awareness on our planet, and is also linked to the development of ancient religious structures:

> What I think happened is that in the world of prehistory all religion was experiential and it was based on the pursuit of ecstasy through plants. And at some time, very early, a group interposed itself between people and the direct experience of the 'Other'. This created hierarchies, priesthoods, theological systems, castes, rituals, taboos. Shamanism, on the other hand, is an experiential science which deals with an area where we know nothing . . . So the important part of the Human Potential Movement and the New Age, I believe, is the re-empowerment of ritual, the rediscovery of shamanism, the recognition of psychedelics and the importance of the Goddess.[3]

Extending this still further, McKenna, like those South American and Mexican shamans who use visionary sacraments respectfully, maintains that psychedelics like psilocybin put the individual in touch with the 'mind' of the planet:

> This is the Oversoul of all life on Earth. It's the real thing . . . I take very seriously the idea that the *Logos* is real, that there is a guiding Mind – an Oversoul – that inhabits the biome of the planet, and that human balance, dignity and religiosity depend on having direct contact with this realm. That's what shamanism is providing. It was available in the West until the fall of Eleusis and the Mystery traditions – to some people – but then was stamped out by barbarians who didn't realise what they had destroyed.[4]

Shifting our perspective now to the present-day, postindustrial era – and this does involve, admittedly, a very substantial leap in time – McKenna believes that there is a type of parallel between the Oversoul of the planet which has presented itself in shamanism and the ancient

Mystery traditions, and the emerging consciousness now permeating cyberspace via the medium of the Internet. Basically, McKenna says, the new cyberculture is forcing us to redefine our notions of linear thinking and our relationship to the cosmos at large. In a recent interview with the cultural critic Mark Dery, McKenna explained that in his view the future of humanity rests in its capacity to embrace a perspective that is really a type of technological or scientific shamanism:

> I expect to see the coming decades transform the planet into an art form; the new man, linked in a cosmic harmony that transcends time and space . . . I believe in what I call a forward escape, meaning that you can't go back and you can't stand still, so you've got to go forward, and technology is the way to do this. Technology is an extension of the human mental world, and it's certainly where our salvation is going to come from; we cannot return to the hunter-gatherer pastoralism of 15,000 years ago.[5]

Nevertheless, according to McKenna, these new techno-shamanic directions in society will be essentially metaphysical, because they will take us beyond notions of linear progress and development:

> My position is that all of history involves making the *Logos* more and more concrete. In the same way that McLuhan saw print culture as replacing an earlier eye-oriented manuscript culture, my hope is that the cyberdelic culture is going to overcome the linear, uniform bias of print and carry us into the realm of the visible *Logos*. . . what these new technologies are doing is dissolving boundaries . . .[6]

Techno-visionary 'Realities'

So how exactly does the shamanic perspective relate to the world of cyberspace? How does the world of cyberculture challenge our notions of rational and linear thinking? It is useful in this context to reflect on the increasing cultural impact of the Internet itself.

The word 'cyberspace' was coined by William Gibson, who used it in his 1984 novel *Neuromancer*. Gibson described a scenario where 'console cowboys' could put on their cyberspace helmets and project their awareness into three-dimensional 'virtual' environments. Here Gibson was anticipating that the human imagination would create its own perceptual 'realities' within a technological setting.

Now, just fifteen years after the publication of Gibson's novel, the realm of virtual reality has already established itself as a valuable tool in such fields as architecture and medicine. The Internet is rapidly becoming the preferred means of communication around the planet, and ventures into cyberspace are an everyday occurrence. And yet one would have to concede that the concept of cyberspace itself has interesting philosophical connotations.

In her recent book *The Pearly Gates of Cyberspace*, the science writer Margaret Wertheim argues that the Internet is providing us with a new concept of space that did not exist before – the interconnected 'space' of the global computer network.[7] And, as she points out, this is a very recent phenomenon indeed. During the early 1980s few people outside the military and academic field of computer science had network access, but now there are over 100,000 sites on the Internet. 'As of mid-1998,' writes Wertheim, 'there are 100 million people using the Internet regularly, and it is estimated that in the next decade, there will be close to one billion people online. In just over 25 years, this space has sprung into being from nothing, making it surely the fastest-growing territory in history.'

It is the unique nature of the cyberspace experience that Wertheim finds so fascinating. When one person communicates with another online there is no sense of physicality, for cyber-journeys cannot be measured in a literal sense. 'Unleashed into the Internet,' she says, 'my "location" can no longer be fixed purely in physical space. Just "where" I am when I enter cyberspace is a question yet to be answered, but clearly my position cannot be pinned down to a mathematical location.' So all we can really confirm about the nature of cyberspace itself is that it involves a form of digital communication where information is relayed back and forth from one computer site to another, and where people share the outpourings of each other's minds.

This is not simply a communication of literal information, however. As many Internet enthusiasts have discovered, the world of cyberspace is also a realm where fantasy personas can be created in virtual reality – where human beings can interact with each other in ways limited only by their imagination. Individuals can pose as members of the opposite sex, as fantasy beings – even as dark and evil gods – and this has become a central feature of the development of role-play on the Internet. So in a very specific way the Internet has become an extension of the human psyche, a forum for both its realities and its fantasies. From an esoteric or mystical perspective, though, what is so intriguing about this interplay between technology and the human imagination is that here we are dealing with the equation 'As I imagine, so I become' – and this is the very essence of magic. It comes as no surprise, then, that neopagans and occultists of all descriptions have been quick to embrace the Internet as a new means of communication and fantasy role-play. For many, the World Wide Web provides a pathway into the mythic conjurings of the world at large, an enticing and increasingly seductive means of engaging with the global imagination.

Techno-pagans and Digital Magic

The relationship between neopagans and technology appears to have its roots in the American counter-culture itself, for it is now widely acknowledged that the present-day computer ethos owes a substantial debt to the psychedelic consciousness movement. The conservative *Wall Street Journal* even ran a front-page article in January 1990 asking whether virtual reality was equivalent to 'electronic LSD'.[8]

It would seem that the somewhat unlikely fusion between pagans and cyberspace arose simply because techno-pagans are capable of being both technological and mystical at the same time. As the cyberpunk novelist Bruce Sterling has written:

> Today, for a surprising number of people all over America, the supposed dividing line between bohemian and technician simply no longer exists. People of this sort may have a set of windchimes and a dog with a knotted kerchief round its neck, but they're also quite likely to own a multimegabyte Macintosh running MIDI synthesizer software and trippy fractal simulations.[9]

The American psychedelic culture of the late 1960s and early 1970s was essentially about experiencing the psyche through mind-altering drugs

– the word 'psychedelic' itself literally means 'mind revealing' – and this type of consciousness exploration would have a direct impact on the rise of the new technology. According to Mark Dery, Timothy Leary regarded the rise of the personal computer as a clear vindication of the counter-culture, for he believed that without the psychedelic revolution the personal computer would not have burst onto the world scene so soon. 'It's well known,' he told Dery,

> that most of the creative impulse in the software industry, and indeed much of the hardware, particularly at Apple Macintosh, derived directly from the sixties consciousness movement. [The Apple co-founder] Steve Jobs went to India, took a lot of acid, studied Buddhism, and came back and said that Edison did more to influence the human race than the Buddha. And [Microsoft founder Bill] Gates was a big psychedelic person at Harvard. It makes perfect sense to me that if you activate your brain with psychedelic drugs, the only way you can describe it is electronically.[10]

What Mark Dery calls the 'cyberdelic wing' of the computer movement clearly has its roots in the 1960s counter-culture – indeed, Terence McKenna is a shining example of the fusion between technology and metaphysics. The Wiccan computer buff Sara Reeder also remembers the early years well:

> Silicon Valley and the modern Wiccan revival literally took root and grew up alongside each other in the rich black clay surrounding San Francisco Bay . . . both blossomed in the 1960s – the Valley through the miracle of the space program, the Pagan community by way of Haight Street's prominence as the worldwide Counterculture HQ.[11]

At this time, Timothy Leary, as patron saint of the hippie movement, was urging his followers to 'turn on, tune in and drop out' on LSD, a psychedelic synthesised from ergot in a Swiss laboratory. A generation later, he would switch his allegiance to the world of computers, announcing that 'the PC is the LSD of the 1990s'. For Leary, there was a clear relationship between the consciousness movement and the new technology:

What is so intriguing about our own era in history is that the human quest for knowledge and understanding in the last 25 years has seen an amazing blend of shamanic techniques, psychedelic drugs and the international global boom in resurrecting the pre-Christian, pagan, totemic and Hindu traditions. At the same time, with these computers . . . you have a situation where you can walk around in realities of your own construction. So we are very much on a threshold. I don't want to put any limits on what I'm saying, but here we have ancient techniques merging with the most modern. Computers give us the ways to communicate with the basic language of the universe – which is *quanta-electronic*. Matter and bodies are just electrons that have decided to come together, buzzing around with information.[12]

Meanwhile, Stewart Brand, a former Merry Prankster and the creator of the *Whole Earth Catalogue*, would also become an icon of the cyberdelic movement. He has been credited with creating the computer hacker subculture as the direct result of an article he published in *Rolling Stone* magazine in 1972.[13]

According to Dery, these psychedelic roots have left their mark, and the cyberdelic phenomenon as he understands it now has clearly identifiable characteristics, encompassing a cluster of subcultures:

among them Deadhead computer hackers, 'ravers' (habitués of all-night electronic dance parties known as 'raves'), techno-pagans, and New Age technophiles. Cyberdelia reconciles the transcendentalist impulses of sixties counterculture with the infomania of the nineties. As well, it nods in passing to the seventies, from which it borrows the millenarian mysticism of the New Age and the apolitical self-absorption of the human potential movement.[14]

Another cyberculture enthusiast, Erik Davis, has a similar perception, describing technopagans as 'a small but vital subculture of digital savants who keep one foot in the emerging technosphere and one foot in the wild and woolly world of Paganism'.[15] And for Douglas Rushkoff, author of *Cyberia: Life in the Trenches of Hyperspace*, 'the neopagan revival incorporates ancient and modern skills in free-for-all sampling of what-ever works, making no distinction between occult magic and high technology. In the words of one neopagan, "The magic of today is the technology of tomorrow. It's all magic. It's all technology." '[16]

Neopagans generally regard technology and magic as interchangeable. Ever pragmatic, they seem to be primarily concerned with what works. If technology is effective in producing something physically useful, and if rituals and magical incantations can produce a specific spiritual or psychological outcome, for many neopagans this means they are compatible. According to Erik Davis, 'it is this pragmatic hands–on instrumentality that allows some Pagans to powerfully reimagine "technology" as both a metaphor and a tool for spiritual work.'[17]

Many Wiccans openly affirm the relationship between magic and the computer culture. An urban neopagan witch named Green Fire told Douglas Rushkoff:

> High technology and high magic are the same thing. They both use tools from inner resources and outer resources. Magic from the ancient past and technology from the future are really both one. That is how we are creating the present; we're speeding up things, we are quickening our energies; time and space are not as rigid as they used to be . . . Those of us who know how to work through time and space are using our abilities to *bend* time and space into a reality that will benefit people the most . . . We humans are all shape-shifters. We just learn to access our DNA codes. It's very computer-oriented. We are computers; our minds are computers, our little cells are computers. We are bio–organic computers . . .[18]

Other neopagans regard the new technology as a type of freedom. For the Californian neopagan writer Tom Williams,

> Far from being seen as the tool of the oppressor, technology harnessed with the proper spiritual motivation can be a blast of liberation . . . Take up the athame, the wand and the light-sound machine, the cup and the pentacle and the oscilloscope and the computer. Dedicate them to the service of the Life Force, to the Unio Mystica and to the praise of the Great Mother and weave their power together into ritual, song and the sacred accomplishment of the Great Work![19]

Michael Hutchison, author of the intriguingly titled bestseller *Mega Brain Power: Transform Your Life with Mind Machines and Brain Nutrients*, feels much the same way. For him, what he calls 'consciousness technology' is coming to the aid of humanity in an unexpected way:

> To some it may seem odd and paradoxical that machines – the synthetic, hard, material devices of this electronic temporal reality – may serve as gateways to the spirit, tools of transcendence. But in fact this fusion of spirituality, or the 'inner quest', and science, 'the external quest', is the central force of the emerging new paradigm.[20]

Many neopagan groups use computer technology and the Internet to advise their friends and members about seasonal rites, celebrations, workshops and conferences, and they also provide information on pagan rites of passage, including handfastings (weddings), childblessings and funerals. For example, the London-based Pagan Federation, established in 1971, uses the Internet to promote neopaganism, Druid, Wiccan, Odinic, northern, Celtic, eco-magic and women's spirituality groups, and its American counterparts, like the Church of All Worlds, Circle Sanctuary and the Church of Wicca, do much the same thing for their equivalent memberships. Contemporary pagans also communicate with each other through newsgroups – discussion forums where they can chat about various topics like magical ceremonies, spells and the occult powers of herbs. Jem Dowse makes the point that new pagans who happen to live in the American Bible Belt make use of this new technology to access like-minded people without fear of repercussions.[21]

Some techno-pagans have sought to extend the scope of their digital magic still further by conducting rituals over the Internet and even establishing virtual shrines in cyberspace. The Wiccan practitioner Sara Reeder explains that 'while Christians and other mainstream religions ignored the Net for years – their members had an established network of churches and clergy to turn to – we became the first religious movement to depend heavily on it for growth and cohesion. And cyberspace, in turn, became the first mass Pagan gathering place since ancient times.'[22] For her, computer technology does not restrict the essential poetry of the ritual experience:

Our rituals have always taken place in the realm of the imagination, so we can make effective ritual anywhere we can exercise our love for poetry and storytelling. I've led online rituals for thirty in chat rooms that allowed us to talk to each other two lines at a time; some of them were as memorable and powerful as any I've attended in person . . . As VRML and other technologies open the sensual band-with, allowing us to share songs, images, and even virtual bodies to the mix, cyberspace ritual will allow us to open up our private dreamscapes, and share our internal visions with each other in much more intimate ways. The traditional Neo-Pagan focus on individual creativity, combined with our emphasis on poetry and fluid ritual forms, may well make us the first to pioneer online altars and sacred sites, once more setting the example for other religions to follow.[23]

Magical Role-Play

As neopagan rituals begin to extend their reach into cyberspace, it is also useful to consider the origins of magical role-play – for role-play can also involve the use of mythic archetypes and computer technology.

Fantasy and magical role-play practices developed initially from games like Dungeons and Dragons, which were popular in the late 1970s and early 1980s. Here participants explored underground vaults, tunnels and mazes, and encountered various monsters and alien entities – orcs, dwarfs, skeleton men and the wandering souls of the dead – en route to discovering fabulous gold and jewels. Games of this sort would usually be located in a fantasy world based in medieval Europe, on another planet or on an 'alternative Earth' where history had taken a different turn of events and magic now ruled the laws of the land. The overall pattern of the game would be determined by a gaming master and each of the principal characters would be 'designed' or created by the players themselves.[24]

For some players, though, many of these games soon proved unconvincing and unsatisfying, and some enthusiasts began creating more innovative games by drawing instead on the imagery of fantasy worlds described by writers like Michael Moorcock, Marion Zimmer Bradley, Andre Norton and H. P. Lovecraft. As Bruce Galloway observes, it soon became 'much more challenging and a great deal more fun, to design your own world'.[25]

In the more developed forms of role-play the gaming master – sometimes known as the 'keeper of arcane lore' – has to set the rules for the adventure, build up its legends and history, and establish the main characters and magical weapons. And there are hierarchies of power. For example, in some forms of magical role-play a 'cunning man' or 'wise woman' can develop with time into a witch or wizard or even into a high runic sorcerer, and the characters themselves may acquire a variety of occult skills, including the ability to shape-shift, communicate with animals, levitate or achieve invisibility. During these games, participants also learn magical spells of 'absolute command'. Spells, according to Galloway, 'are the building blocks of active magic' and can be used for either protection or assault.[26]

Ars Magica: The Storytelling Game of Mythic Magic is one of the most impressive role-playing systems in this genre. Now in its third edition, it offers a variety of enticing magical roles to its participants:

In this game you can play a Magus, with the full power of legendary wizards, or the companion of such a sorcerer, a talented ally with your own unique motivations and antipathies.

As a Magus, your life is devoted to the art of magic. Without it you are nought but a scholar and a keeper of old books, so you guard your mastery with every grain of will and fury. Your essence arises from conjury, and your dedication to it brings you immense power.

As a sorcerer's companion you have a life beyond the sphere of sorcery and are not a mere vassal of the wizards. Your ability to move through worlds both magical and mundane makes you invaluable to them. Whether you be a drunken mercenary, cunning street-urchin or itinerant friar, you must win your fortune through your wits and courage.

Together you journey forth to gather magical ingredients, delve into forgotten tombs, explore the bizarre realm of the faerie, travel to the great cities of the south and combat the infernal forces of the underworld. The world is yours for the taking.[27]

Ars Magica identifies three different types of character: Magi, Companions and Grogs. The Grogs are servants, stable-hands, guards and messengers. There are many individual characters within this threefold hierarchy and players have to conceptualise the character they wish to play, adding specific details of their own to make the figure into one they can readily identify with. All the characters have acknowledged 'virtues' and 'flaws', and in this game they are accorded point scores for different attributes – intelligence, perception, strength, stamina, presence, communication, dexterity and quickness.

The key challenge with magical role-play, however, was always to move fantasy worlds of this type online so that they could be accessed on the Internet. This was eventually done through the establishment of 'multi-user domains', or MUDs. Participants with a personal computer simply had to use a modem and network passwords to log on to a computer containing a MUD. Some MUDs were public, while others were restricted to a select group of role-players controlled by a 'wizard' or 'tinker' who was essentially in charge of its mythic content and terrain.

Nowadays the range of MUDs is extensive. There are MUDs based on *Star Trek* and Frank Herbert's science-fiction *Dune* series. As Margaret Wertheim notes:

> Today's MUDs have morphed into a huge range of virtual worlds . . . MUDers are involved in an ongoing process of world-making. To name is to create, and in MUD worlds, the simple act of naming and describing is all it takes to generate a new alter ego or 'cyber self' . . . The interlocking imaginative and social mesh of a MUD means that actions taken by one player may affect the virtual lives of hundreds of others. The very vitality and robustness of a MUD emerges from the collective will of the group. As in the physical world, relationships are built, trusts are established, bonds are created and responsibilities ensue.[28]

However, there is often a blurring between the worlds of 'everyday' reality and 'fantasy' reality. One MUDer told the online researcher Mizuko Ito, 'To me there is no real body. Online, it is how you describe yourself and how you act that makes up the real you.'

This may well be a characteristic response from a number of the new cyberspace explorers. According to Douglas Rushkoff, for some game players 'all of life is seen as a fantasy role-playing game in which the stakes are physically real but the lessons go beyond physical reality'. One of the role-players Rushkoff interviewed for his book *Cyberia* – Nick Walker, a game master and aikido instructor from New Jersey – believed he could pick and choose the traits of various role-play characters and incorporate them into his own personality: 'The object in role-playing games is playing with characters whose traits you want to bring into your own life. You can pick up their most useful traits, and discard their unuseful ones . . .' As Rushkoff observes, this is very much like consciously choosing one's own character traits in order to become a 'designer being'.[29]

Clearly, for many online role-players the appeal of activities like this can be explained simply by the fact that fantasy is so much more enticing and seductive than the routines of the everyday world. According to Dr Brenda Laurel, a specialist in the field of interactive computer systems,

> Reality has always been too small for the human imagination. The impulse to create an 'interactive fantasy machine' is only the most recent manifestation of the age-old desire to make our fantasies palpable – our insatiable need to exercise our imagination, judgment, and spirit in worlds, situations, and personae that are different from those in our everyday lives . . .[30]

However, there is also the possibility that for many participants fantasy role-play will lead to some form of increased spiritual self-awareness, and Brenda Laurel hopes for this too. 'Imagination,' she says, 'is the laboratory of the spirit.'

Dark Archetypes

Although many neopagan responses to cyberspace are innovative and essentially positive, there is also an occult underbelly – a darker realm which feeds on fear and powerlessness in a rapidly changing world. For me, the archetype that embodies these feelings most powerfully is that of the Alien – the space entity created by H. R. Giger, which featured in the Oscar-winning film of the same name and has since become an icon of the cyberculture in the 1990s. Giger now has an impressive website on the Internet, and an increasing sphere of influence. At least one PC game, Cyberdream's Darkseed, is based on Giger's artwork, and as Mark Dery has noted, 'cyberpunk bands such as Cyberaktif and Front Line Assembly routinely cite him as an inspiration. The highest tribute is paid by modern primitives who emblazon themselves with Giger's slavering, mace-tailed Alien – a cyberpunk rite of passage . . .'[31]

Selections of Giger's work are now on permanent display at his museum in Castle St Germain in Gruyères, Switzerland, which opened in June 1998, and the Limelight nightclub in Manhattan recently inaugurated its H. R. Giger room, featuring exhibits of several of his most surreal and visionary artworks. The paintings draw strongly on the left-hand path of Western magic as well as on fantasy and horror fictions like H. P. Lovecraft's *The Necronomicon*. There is an unquestionable potency, even a macabre beauty, in his biomechanoid creations, but his nightmare fusions of the human and the mechanical also evoke a sense of no escape – a sense that we are all trapped in a virtual hell of our own making. Perhaps this is a portent of our times.

A few years ago I met Giger at his home in Zürich, for I was interested to learn from him, first-hand, about his own creative process and how he regarded the haunting, nightmarish images now inhabiting his dark, visionary art. Visiting Giger's house, and seeing the large surreal panels which adorn its walls, was like experiencing an exorcism.

Giger told me that he did not understand the processes which underly his paintings, but that he makes use, essentially, of the mediumistic or 'automatic' style adopted by several surrealists, including Max Ernst, Oscar Dominguez and Wolfgang Paalen. Giger maintains that he opens the door to his unconscious mind by confronting a blank canvas and suspending conscious thought. Then, as the spontaneous images start to build before his eyes, he adds details and texture with his airbrush. Giger likes the airbrush because of its tremendous directness: 'It enables me to project my visions directly onto the pictorial surface, freezing them immediately.'

There is no doubt that, in terms of his art, Giger is a magician – conjuring dramatic visionary creations which propel us into the darker recesses of the imagination. And his paintings have an evil authenticity about them. They have been praised by distinguished visionary artists like Ernst Fuchs and Salvador Dalí and display a magical calibre rarely seen in modern art. One can also link him in spirit with earlier tortured masters of the visionary perspective, like Hieronymus Bosch and Lucas Cranach.

Giger lives in an unobtrusive double-storey terraced house, a few minutes' drive from Zürich's busy international airport. His living room downstairs is dominated by the remarkable paintings which first earned him international recognition, works which feature Medusa-like women with ghostly-pale skin and snakes in their hair, and strange shapes and forms writhing all around. Claws, needles, machine guns and barbs also feature strongly in these paintings. For most people the works are both disturbing and fascinating at the same time – they also have an extraordinary three-dimensional quality which lifts them beyond the plane of the wall so that they become part of the living ambience of the room.

In the centre of the long table which occupies Giger's living room is an engraved pentagram, and candlesticks whose flames cast an eerie light on the paintings nearby. A tall row of shelves in one corner of the room reveals a row of skulls and authentic shrunken heads from a cannibal tribe. It is here that Giger has placed the Oscar he received for the special effects in *Alien* – a tribute to his bizarre imagination.

Upstairs Giger has his studio. At one end it is total chaos – a litter of splattered paint, brushes and discarded works of art. Here he experiments with his airbrush techniques, spraying patterns through metal grids and exploring different textures of light and shade.

At the other end of the long, open room is a large black table with bulbous legs and an extraordinary mirror sheen on its pristine surface. Fashioned substantially from heavy moulded plastic, it is accompanied by several tall chairs surmounted with skulls and shaped to give the impression of distorted vertebrae. An ashen-grey version of these chairs – seemingly fashioned from bone – has pride of place at the head of the table. And gracing the long wall above is another large panel, this one depicting a horned devil, a silver pentagram and dark, hostile serpents.

Giger has little real explanation for these exotic images. 'I try to come close to my imagination,' he says in his broken English. 'I have something in my head and I try to work it out – like a kind of exorcism.'

Giger recognises the adverse effect his work has on many of the people who see it, but he is keen to point out that if his work seems dark, this is not necessarily the way he is himself. 'My childhood was very happy,' he says, almost apologetically, 'and my parents have been very nice to me.' He ponders a while and then adds,' I think that most of the images in my paintings are evil, but you can't say that I'm evil. It's just that evil is much, much more interesting than Paradise . . .'

Hans Ruedi Giger was born in 1940 in the small Swiss town of Chur, which he describes as an 'unbearable' place of 'high mountains and petty-bourgeois attitudes'. Growing up there, he had nightmares in his parents' house and would imagine 'gigantic bottomless shafts bathing in pale yellow light'. In his own *Necronomicon* – a visionary homage to Lovecraft – Giger writes that 'on the walls, steep and treacherous wooden stairways without bannisters led down into the yawning abyss' and the cellar in the house gave rise to the image of 'a monstrous labyrinth, where all kinds of dangers lay in wait for me'. This feeling is certainly conveyed in his paintings for, time and again, the figures seem trapped and tormented in gruesome, tortuous tunnels and there is no apparent path of escape.

As a child, Giger built skeletons of cardboard, wire and plaster, and he recalls that he had an 'overwhelming disgust of worms and snakes' – a loathing which still manifests itself in his paintings today. He also had a fascination with pistols and guns of all sorts, and during his military service was nearly shot on more than one occasion.

If Giger is haunted by images from his past, this is quite understand-able, for there have been many crises in his life. Probably the most traumatic involved the beautiful actress Li Tobler. Giger met Li in 1966 when she was eighteen and living with another man. Soon Giger moved into her attic apartment and they became lovers. Giger recalls that Li had 'enormous vitality and a great appetite for life'. She also wanted her life to be 'short but intense'.

Li is the prototype for the many ethereal women in Giger's paintings who peer forth from the torment of snakes, needles and stifling bone prisons – to a world beyond which is forever out of reach. Giger painted Li's body several times with an airbrush, and there are several photographs of her posing naked like a woman of mystery struggling to emerge from a nightmare that has possessed her soul.

Around the time the photographs of Li were taken, Giger inherited his present house as a legacy from his uncle, and Li moved in. But the idyll, says Giger, was all too short. Li had a hectic schedule for her theatrical performances around the country, was irresistibly drawn to numerous other lovers, and was beginning to wilt under the pressures of life in the fast lane. On Whit Monday 1975, she shot herself with a revolver.

It may be too simplistic to say that Li haunts Giger still, for his life is full of beautiful and exotic women who are fascinated by his art and by his glamorous and bohemian lifestyle. But there is no doubting that the simultaneous agony and joy of life with Li Tobler established the dynamic of fear and elusive transcendence which is present in many of his paintings.

Giger maintains that though he has studied the works of Aleister Crowley – like many other cyberspace enthusiasts – he is not a magician in the conventional sense. He says he does not perform rituals, engage in invocations or summon spirits. But one could hardly find a better temple of the black arts than Giger's main living room, for the beings which inhabit his paintings are themselves like a pantheon of demons. Giger, in a very real way, makes magic spontaneously. When the thin veil across his psyche is drawn aside just a little, tempestuous visions of evil and alienation come forth. It is as if the dark gods are emerging once again from the nightmares of the past.

And now Giger's presence has returned once again to New York – the home of dreams and aspirations. In 1981 he produced an impressive series of paintings of the New York infrastructure, employing machine templates as stencils to provide his compositions with an alien, mechanistic quality. His vision then was of a city of mazes where heavy machinery competed with oversized metallic cockroaches and burrowing subway cars. Giger returned to New York in 1984 for his exhibition 'The Dune You'll Never See' and came back again in 1993 for a special party held to honour his friend Timothy Leary. Giger now has his permanent magical shrine at Limelight on West 20th Street, and New York continues to fascinate him. 'There is no crazier place imaginable,' he says, 'and I paint what frightens me.'[32]

Stealing Fire from Heaven

So where does this leave us as we prepare to embrace the new millennium? Where are the magical undercurrents in contemporary Western culture taking us? Are we searching now for new mythologies to help us define our future?

It seems to me that a distinct polarity is now emerging – requiring us to make a choice which takes us potentially in one of two quite different directions. The first of these alternatives focuses primarily on the sacred dimensions of Nature, and engages us in a magic of the Earth and the cosmos. This is of course the option chosen by devotees of Wicca and Goddess worship, who venerate the gods and goddesses associated with the cycles of the Moon and Sun in the natural environment. Then there is another option, which takes us further into the archetypal realms of cyberspace and virtual reality as their myriad potentials unfold before us. And although techno-paganism seeks to embrace both of these dimensions, it seems to me that the main pathways within Western magic will begin increasingly to diverge. Increasingly, I believe, a choice will be made between Nature and the new technology.

As we have seen, magic in the twentieth century is essentially about the quest for personal transformation. Occultists of all persuasions invoke their gods and goddesses as archetypes of the divine potential they seek within themselves. This is the act of stealing fire from heaven. But clear choices now present themselves: can this fire of sacred inspiration be found both within the natural world and in the furthest reaches of cyberspace?

As the information superhighway runs ever further, I believe many magical devotees will feel powerfully drawn towards embracing the new technology in all its diversity. Sacred shrines and archetypal symbols will find a richer and more convincing graphic expression on the Internet so that they really do become magical doorways in their own right – the cyberspace equivalent of the Magic Theatre in Hermann Hesse's novel *Steppenwolf*. The explorers entering these doorways will then engage ever more completely in virtual worlds, blending technological motifs with mythic archetypes to produce fusions we can only begin to envisage at the present time. Perhaps this magic will produce the Gigers of the future – where elements of the mechanistic world merge with what is human, yielding ever more bizarre permutations of cyber-magical mythology. Furthermore, the cyber-shamans of the future will have to integrate these new sacred images within their own being in order to make sense of it all, for if they fail to do this their psyches will surely be engulfed by a whirlpool of virtual magical imagery.

Other magical practitioners, I believe, will turn more completely towards the esoteric traditions of former cultures and will choose instead to identify only with the mythic archetypes of the past – but those which have a sense of resonance and meaning for the present. Already this has begun to happen. The contemporary magical revival has seen not only a return to medieval esotericism and the mythic traditions of the Celts, as well as a revival of interest in the gods and goddesses of ancient Greece, Rome, Egypt and Mesopotamia, but there has also been a very specific resurgence, in certain quarters, of traditions like Odinism and Druidry, and the magic of the various shamanic cultures around the world. In many cases this return to an archaic past also brings with it a thirst for authentic simplicity – for rituals which embrace the Earth, Sun, Moon and sky as they are found in the real world, not in the virtual realms of cyberspace.

For this reason I believe that many magical devotees, in time, will take the decision to withdraw from the new technology, at least in part – using it peripherally perhaps as a means of information exchange, while channelling the quest for personal transformation into an engage-ment with completely natural processes. Andrew Siliar, a neopagan from Arizona, makes this point very effectively in a letter published recently in the Wiccan journal *Green Egg*:

> Paganism is a Nature religion, rooted deep in the Earth, honoring the Gods and Goddesses, feeling the heartbeat of the Mother Earth, loving and honoring all of Her creatures. And now we have this wonderful new technology, along with computer graphics. We can link up with other people on-line, and now we can be techno-witches, and cyber wizards . . . I'm sorry, but that doesn't sound like much of a Nature Religion to me anymore . . . I need no on-line link to let me feel the power of the Goddess, I just touch the Earth and connect.[33]

253

So we may well find ourselves engaging in the future with two main traditions — natural magic and techno-cybermagic — along with all the assorted mythologies they will bring in their wake. Meanwhile, the magical quest itself remains a journey of self-knowledge and transcendence, and magical devotees and practitioners will continue to find their sense of sacred meaning in their own way. As Stewart Brand wrote thirty years ago: 'We are as gods. And we might as well get good at it.'

Glossary of Terms

Adam Kadmon Judaic concept of the archetypal man, the primordial human being formed in the creation of the universe. Adam Kadmon is also, metaphorically, 'the body of God'.

adept An initiate or occult master: one who has gained profound magical powers or insights through initiation.

Ain Soph Aur Hebrew expression meaning 'the limitless light'. In the Kabbalah it represents the source from which all else comes forth.

alchemy The ancient science of transmuting base metals into gold and silver. The alchemists also sought an elixir that could prolong life indefinitely. In some degree at least, alchemy was also a metaphor for spiritual transformation, so one can regard it not only as a precursor of modern chemistry but also as a spiritual philosophy in its own right.

All Hallows' Eve or **Halloween** A major pagan festival representing the change of season from autumn to winter, celebrated on 31 October. Traditionally, it was also a time when the souls of the deceased revisited their former homes and once again enjoyed the company of their kinfolk and friends.

androgyne In alchemy the androgyne is a sacred symbol because male and female polarities are united within one being, which therefore represents totality, unity, oneness.

arcane Anything hidden or mysterious, especially those things requiring a 'key' to be understood.

archetype In the psychology of C. G. Jung, a primordial image found in the collective unconscious. Archetypes are often personifications of processes or events in Nature (e.g. the Sun-hero or the lunar goddess) or universal expressions of familial figures (e.g. the Great Father or the Great Mother).

archons In Gnosticism, planetary rulers who guarded the world collectively and who were assigned to certain 'spheres' within the cosmos.

astral plane Occult concept of a plane of existence and perception paralleling the physical dimension but one phase removed from it and also containing imagery from the unconscious mind.

athame In witchcraft, a double-edged ritual sword or dagger used in magical ceremonies to direct power. It has a black handle and magical symbols are sometimes engraved on its blade.

bewitchment The act of gaining power over another person by means of spells, incantations or sorcery.

black magic Magic performed with evil intent. The 'black magician' or sorcerer calls upon the supernatural powers of darkness – devils, demons and evil spirits – and performs ceremonies invoking bestial or malevolent forces, often with the intent of harming another person. See **magic**.

Black Mass Satanic practice, deliberately parodying the central ritual of Roman Catholicism, in which the Host (representing the body of Christ) is stolen from a church, consecrated by an unfrocked priest, and desecrated. The ceremony may also involve reciting the Lord's Prayer backwards.

body of light Occult term for the astral body. Magicians believe that the 'body of light' takes the form conjured in the imagination during a ritual visualisation and that occultists can transfer their consciousness to this form, bringing it to life on the astral plane.

Book of Shadows In contemporary Wicca, the personal book of spells, rituals and folklore that a witch compiles after being initiated into a coven. The Book of Shadows is kept secret and, traditionally, is destroyed when the witch dies.

cauldron Ancient magical symbol connoting transformation and germination. It is an image signifying new life, and has a strong association, like the cup, with the element water. Medieval witches were said to stir their magical concoctions in a cauldron.

celestial From the Latin *caelestis*, meaning 'heavenly' – anything divine or blessed. Sometimes the term is used to describe the 'higher spheres' of mystical consciousness.

ceremonial magic Magic that employs rituals, symbols and ceremony as a means of representing the mystical and transcendent forces linking the universe and humanity. See **magic**.

Choronzon In Western magic, the demon of chaos and guardian of the Abyss. Aleister Crowley described this entity as 'the first and deadliest of all the powers of evil'.

chthonian From the Greek *chthon*, 'earth', deities or spirits from the earth or underworld, often associated with the souls of the dead.

circle In mythology, a symbol of totality or wholeness, and in Western magic an important symbol of sacred space, used in ceremonial workings.

collective unconscious Concept developed by C. G. Jung, who believed that certain primordial images in the unconscious mind were not individual in origin, but 'collective' – symbolic expressions of the 'constantly repeated experiences of humanity'. In Jung's view these collective images were mostly religious, and were acknowledged almost universally as significant, regardless of cultural differences.

cone of power In witchcraft, the ritual act of visualising a 'cone of energy' and directing it towards whatever goal or task is at hand. Witches with psychic vision claim it is perceived as a silver-blue light that rises from the magic circle in a spiral.

conjuration The act of evoking spirits by means of ritual formulae or magical 'words of power'. The ceremonial magician seeks to manifest these spirits within a triangle inscribed upon the floor of the temple.

coven A group of witches, or Wiccans, who gather together to perform magical ceremonies and invocations. Traditionally there are thirteen members in a coven.

crystal Mystical symbol of the spirit. Its associations may derive from the fact that crystal, though solid and tangible, is also transparent. Among many shamanic groups, natural crystals are power objects.

cube Symbol of the four elements, associated with solidity and endurance. In some magical ceremonies, the altar consists of a double cube

and has ten exposed faces, reflective of the ten spheres of consciousness on the Tree of Life.

curse Invocation or oath made with evil intent. Curses are associated
with black magic or sorcery and are intended to harm or destroy
opponents or property.

death posture Term used by the English occultist and artist Austin
Osman Spare to describe a state of self-induced trance in which he
would 'open' himself psychically to the formulation of magical images
in his mind.

deity From the Greek *deus*, a god or supreme being.

demiurge From the Greek *demiurgos*, a 'fashioner' or 'architect', the
creator of the world. For the Gnostics the demiurge was not the
supreme reality, but a middle-ranking deity who proposed laws for
the world which the initiated could transcend.

demon From the Greek *daimon*, a devil or evil spirit.

deosil In witchcraft, the ritual act of moving to the right – the direction
of the sun – when facing a magic circle. This is said to produce
positive magic. Compare with **widdershins**.

Devil, the The personification of evil, called Lucifer or Satan in Christianity, Eblis in Islam and Ahriman in Zoroastrianism. Some occultists
regard the Devil as a negative archetype within the mind, personifying
adverse and destructive human characteristics.

Druids Celtic priests in pre-Christian Britain and Gaul. The Druids
were skilled in astronomy and medicine and worshipped the Sun,
making use of much earlier Neolithic cromlechs and stone
circles that had already been erected. The centre of Druidism was at
Anglesey, but the Druids also raised monoliths at Aldborough and
York in the northeast and made use of Stonehenge as an observatory-
temple.

ecstasy A state of rapture, joy or spiritual enlightenment in which a
person feels lifted up into a state of visionary transcendence.

elementals Spirit creatures said to personify the characteristics of the
four elements. These creatures are salamanders (fire), mermaids and
undines (water), sylphs (air) and gnomes and goblins (earth).

elements In some mystical traditions the manifested world is divided
into elements. In Pythagorean mysticism and medieval alchemy, for
example, all aspects of the physical world were said to consist of

varying amounts of fire, earth, air and water, while the fifth element – the quintessence – was spirit.

elixir of life In alchemy, a drink said to restore youth or bestow immortality. It was associated with the philosopher's stone, from which these life-giving properties derived. See **philosopher's stone**.

emanation A vibration that issues forth from a single source. In Gnostic mysticism the world was considered the most physical, dense or 'gross' emanation of the Godhead.

emerald tablet The tablet of emerald (*Tabula Smaragdina*) that was allegedly found clasped between the hands of the corpse of Hermes Trismegistus, mythic founder of the Hermetic tradition. The tablet included a text upon which the principles of medieval alchemy were based.

esbat In witchcraft, a meeting of members of a coven on the night of the full Moon. There are thirteen esbats during the year and tradition-ally the esbat lasts from midnight till cock-crow. See also **sabbats**.

esoteric Term applied to teachings reserved only for initiates of a group. The word also denotes something mysterious, occult or 'hidden'.

feminine principle In mystical cosmologies there is an interplay between masculine and feminine forces. The feminine principle is usually regarded as receptive (symbolising the womb from which the universe is born), lunar/negative (reflecting light rather than provid-ing it) and intuitive rather than intellectual.

fetish Symbolic object or talisman regarded by an individual as having the magical power to ward off evil. Some fetish objects are believed to house protective spirits.

Gnostic One who believes in gnosis, or 'higher spiritual knowledge'. The term is also used to describe esoteric sects which emerged in the early Christian centuries and were regarded by the orthodox Church Fathers as heretical.

God In monotheistic religions, the supreme being or ruler of the universe.

Godhead The essential nature of God.

gods and goddesses In polytheistic religions, higher beings personify-ing various idealised human attributes, or aspects of Nature and the cosmos.

Goetia Tradition of black magic, including incantations, ceremonies and techniques of sorcery associated with medieval grimoires.

gold Metal associated with the Sun. Gold also represents the 'inner light' of mystical illumination and to this extent is the supreme 'spiritual' metal.

Great Goddess The personification of fertility and the regenerative powers of Nature. The Great Goddess took many different forms in classical and ancient mythology. For example, she was Cybele in Phrygia, Astarte in Phoenicia, Isis in Egypt, Demeter in the Greek Mystery religion and Dana among the Celts.

grimoire Any medieval collection of magical spells, rituals and incantations. These often purported to originate in ancient Egypt or Israel. Grimoires include *The Sacred Magic of Abra-Melin the Mage*, *The Lesser and Greater Keys of Solomon* and *The Grimoire of Armadel*.

Hell Fire Club Eighteenth-century satanic club, founded by Sir Francis Dashwood, whose members gathered at Medmenham on the Thames. The group sang blasphemous hymns and conducted orgies in chambers excavated beneath a hill, and within the ruins of a disused abbey.

heresy A religious teaching regarded as contrary to, or deviating from, the established and orthodox form of a doctrine or belief.

Hermetica Collection of ancient mystical tracts and dialogues, primarily Greek in origin, which refer to Hermes Trismegistus – a prophet or spiritual figure thought to be a combination of Hermes and Thoth – and also to the healing gods Asklepios and Imhotep.

hierarchy of adepts In many mystical and occult groups the idea of a hierarchy of spiritual masters has been popular. In Western magic some occultists, among them MacGregor Mathers and Aleister Crowley, claimed privileged contact with 'Secret Chiefs' to bolster their magical authority. See also **Secret Chiefs**.

Holy Guardian Angel In Western magic, the spark of divine Godhead regarded as the essence of every man and woman. Knowledge of the Holy Guardian Angel is synonymous with the mystical concept of 'cosmic consciousness'.

horned god Symbol of male sexuality in witchcraft. The horned god is often identified with Cernunnos, a Celtic deity combining the attributes of a bull, a man, a serpent and a fish. His ancient Greek counterpart was Pan, god of Nature, who presided over the woods and forests and played his magical pipes.

Illuminati Term used by occultists from the late fifteenth century onwards to describe spiritual adepts who had received mystical insights or 'illumination' from a transcendental source. In recent times the idea of a secret brotherhood of the Illuminati has been popularised by the occult fantasy writer Robert Anton Wilson.

individuation In the psychology of C. G. Jung, the concept of 'making the self whole'. For Jung this process included harmonising the forces of one's external life with the events of both the personal unconscious and the collective unconscious.

initiate One who has successfully passed through a ritual of initiation. In many magical traditions an initiate is regarded as one who possesses superior esoteric knowledge.

initiation Magical ceremony involving a sense of transition or self-transformation. The subject may be granted access to new symbolic mysteries, given a secret name or 'words of power', or granted a higher ceremonial rank. Sometimes magical initiation may not be formally acknowledged unless the candidate has had a particular visionary experience that confirms his or her new magical status.

inner light In both the mystical and magical traditions, the light of the god or goddess within one's being. The experience of the 'inner light' is used to indicate that every person is potentially divine and contains the spark of Godhead within.

invocation In ceremonial magic, the act of summoning an angel, god or archetypal being by using sacred god names, or words of power. Magical invocations take place within the magical circle, which in a ritual context is regarded as a sacred space.

journey of the soul In shamanism, the trance journey undertaken by a medicine man or healer in order to recover the soul of a person who has been bewitched by the spirits of disease.

Kabbalah The esoteric or mystical branch of Judaism. The Kabbalah presents a symbolic explanation of the origin of the universe, the relationship of human beings to the Godhead, and an emanationist approach to Creation whereby the infinite light – Ain Soph Aur – manifests itself through the different spheres, or levels, on the Tree of Life.

Left-hand path From the Latin *sinister*, 'left' – the path of black magic and sorcery. Practitioners in this tradition seek to use magic to acquire personal power, rather than seeking spiritual transcendence.

Logos Greek term meaning 'word' or 'thought', used in Gnostic terminology to convey the idea that deities or archetypal beings are associated with sacred utterances or meanings in the manifest universe. In the Kabbalah the world comes into being when the sacred name of God is uttered.

LSD The psychedelic drug lysergic acid diethylamide, first synthesised by the Swiss pharmacologist Dr Albert Hofmann and derived from ergot fungus. One of the most potent psychedelics yet discovered, it is capable of producing profound, and at times terrifying, visionary states of consciousness.

lunar goddess Personification of the Moon. Traditionally in Western magic, the Sun has been regarded as a masculine force and the Moon as feminine. Ancient lunar goddesses include Isis and Hathor (Egypt), Astarte (Phoenicia), Ishtar (Babylonia), Artemis, Hecate and Selene (Greece) and Diana and Luna (Rome).

macrocosm and microcosm From the Greek *makros kosmos*, 'great world', and *mikros kosmos*, 'little world', the concept that the individual, and even the world itself, is a copy in miniature of God's universe. This view was advocated by the Christian theologian Origen and taken up by several Renaissance mystics and occultists, among them Paracelsus and Cornelius Agrippa. Similarly, in the medieval Kabbalah, the primordial or archetypal man, Adam Kadmon, is regarded as reflecting the image of God and thereby provides the necessary link between humanity and the creator of the universe.

Magi The legendary 'wise men of the East' from whom the term 'magic' is derived. The Magi were a priestly caste and were one of the six tribes of Medes described by Herodotus. Skilled in interpreting dreams and divining the future by the stars, the Magi were regarded with great awe. Their beliefs intermingled with the doctrines of Zoroastrianism, and may actually have preceded it.

magic The act of seeking to harness the secret powers of Nature and the cosmos, thereby influencing events for one's own purpose. If the purpose is beneficial, it is known as white magic, but if it is intended to bring harm to others or destroy property, it is regarded as black

magic. In contemporary magical practice, white magicians seek to
activate the spiritual archetypes of the unconscious mind by identifying with life-sustaining deities such as Osiris, Apollo, Ra and
Horus (male) and Isis, Aphrodite, Hathor and Demeter (female).
Black magicians invoke personifications or darkness or evil.

magical correspondences A system for comparing the gods and goddesses of different pantheons in terms of their symbolic roles and
attributes. In 1909 a list of correspondences developed by MacGregor
Mathers and supplemented by Aleister Crowley was published under
the title *777*.

magical name A special name taken by a ritual magician to confirm
membership in a particular magical order, or the attainment of a
specific grade of magical initiation. This name is usually kept secret
and is known only to other magicians of a comparable or higher
magical rank.

Major Arcana In the Tarot, the twenty-two 'mythological' cards, or
trumps, which are assigned by occultists to paths on the Kabbalistic
Tree of Life. See **Tarot**.

male principle In mystical cosmologies there is an interplay between
masculine and feminine forces. The male principle is usually regarded
as positive, outward going, dynamic and solar (as distinct from lunar).
It is also intellectual rather than intuitive.

materia prima In alchemy, the 'first substance' or universal first cause
from which all other substances derive. For base metals to be trans-
muted into silver or gold, they first had to be reduced to the *materia
prima* and then reconstituted as one of the 'noble' metals associated
more directly with God.

May Day Pagan festival of rebirth and renewal celebrated on the first
day of May. Associated with the Celtic festival of Beltane, May Day
includes among its ceremonies the election of a Queen of May, who
personifies the powers of fertility.

Merkabah Mystical tradition in the Kabbalah featuring the Merkabah,
or Throne Chariot of God, which could ascend or descend through
the different heavenly halls or palaces known as the Hekhaloth, the
last of which revealed the divine glory of God.

Middle Pillar In the Kabbalah, the central 'pillar' on the Tree of Life.
The Tree, which consists of ten *sephiroth*, or emanations of God, can

be viewed as being aligned in three vertical columns, beneath Kether, Chokmah and Binah respectively. The column beneath Kether is regarded by occultists as the magical equivalent of the mystical 'Middle Way'. The spheres which lead to Kether on the Middle Pillar are, in order of ascent, Malkuth, Yesod, Tiphareth and Daath.

Minor Arcana In the Tarot, the fifty-six minor cards. These fall into four suits: swords, wands, pentacles and cups. See **Major Arcana** and **Tarot**.

monism The mystical and religious belief that all is one, that a supreme and infinite being encompasses all aspects of Creation.

monotheism The belief in one God only. Monotheism may be contrasted with polytheism, in which a pantheon of gods is recognised and worshipped. Christianity and Islam are examples of monotheistic religions.

Mother Goddess The mother of the manifested universe: it is from her womb that Creation comes forth. The Mother Goddess appears in every religion in which fertility rites have played an important role, for she personifies the forces of Nature and the cycles of fertility.

mystic One who through contemplation, meditation or self-surrender seeks union with the Godhead and who believes in the attainment of universal wisdom, cosmic consciousness or spiritual transcendence.

myth A story or fable relating to a god or supernatural being. Myths may sometimes embody universal principles in Nature and the cosmos and often express the spiritual values of the culture in which they arise.

names of power Magical conjurations and ritual formulae which include sacred god names and are deemed to have a potent magical effect.

nature worship The worship of the life-sustaining forces in Nature, associated with the cycles of the seasons which inevitably result in the rebirth of spring and new life. Nature worship relates also to fertility and sexuality and is usually associated with deities of the Earth and Moon.

neophyte One who is a candidate for magical initiation.

Neoplatonism School of philosophy which blended the ideas of Plato and various Eastern religions. Neoplatonism was developed in the third century by Plotinus and his successors, Iamblichus, Porphyry and Proclus. Neoplatonism was condemned by the Emperor Justinian in 529 but was revived during the Renaissance by the Hermeticists Pico della Mirandola and Marsilio Ficino.

New Aeon Expression used by the magician Aleister Crowley and his followers to describe the two-thousand-year cycle that commenced in 1904, following his illumination through the entity Aiwaz. The New Aeon is sometimes referred to as the Aeon of Horus because Crowley considered himself to be the magical child of the gods.

occultism From the Latin *occulere*, 'to hide', a term used to suggest the secret and hidden tradition of esoteric knowledge. The word is sometimes used to describe the study of magic, Theosophy and spiritualism and may also be used with reference to secret societies.

old religion Expression used by some Wiccan devotees to describe witchcraft. The term acquired special significance following the publication in 1921 of Margaret Murray's influential book *The Witch-Cult in Western Europe*, which described witchcraft as an ancient fertility cult.

pagan One who is not a Christian, Jew or Muslim. The term has been used to describe the heathen or 'nonbeliever' but has now assumed a new currency among practitioners of magic and witchcraft. In this context it refers to a person who worships the sacred aspects of Nature.

pantheism The religious and mystical belief that the whole universe is God and that every part of the universe is an aspect or manifestation of God.

pantheon A group of gods and goddesses who are worshipped collectively.

pathworking A guided-imagery technique in Western magic where the subject is led along 'inner pathways' of conscious awareness in order to experience archetypal visions. Pathworkings are often based on imagery associated with the Tarot paths upon the Tree of Life.

pentagram A five-pointed star. The pentagram is an important symbol in Western magic and represents the four elements fire, earth, air and water surmounted by spirit. The pentagram is regarded as a symbol of human spiritual aspirations when the point faces upwards, but becomes a symbol of bestiality and retrograde spiritual evolution when inverted.

philosopher's stone In alchemy, the first substance from which all other metals derive. See *materia prima*.

Pleroma From a Greek word meaning 'fullness', a term used by the Gnostics to signify the world of light – the universal soul. It is also the abode of the heavenly aeons.

polytheism The belief in, and worship of, more than one god.

possession Emotional or mental state in which a person feels possessed by a spirit or discarnate entity, which takes over aspects of the personality totally or in part, and appears to operate independently of the person concerned.

power animal In shamanism, a creature which appears on the spirit journey of the soul while the shaman is in a state of trance. The power animal may become a spirit-ally, assisting the shaman in times of need.

psychedelic Any drug that helps to reveal the contents of the unconscious mind, such as LSD, mescaline and psilocybin. The term was coined by the English psychiatrist Dr Humphry Osmond.

psychic One who possesses paranormal powers or extrasensory perception. The term is sometimes used to describe someone who claims contact with the spirit world.

rebirth Mystical term which can refer either to reincarnation or to the act of spiritual awakening.

reincarnation The belief that one's core identity or self survives physical death and may be reborn in different physical bodies, in a succession of future lives. Belief in reincarnation is commonly associated with the concept of spiritual evolution.

right-hand path In Western magic, the path associated with spiritual illumination, transcendence and positive aspirations. Compare with **left-hand path**.

ritual A prescribed form of religious or magical ceremony, often designed to invoke or placate a deity.

runes From the German *Raunen*, meaning a 'secret' or 'mystery', occult symbols associated with northern Europe. According to one tradition, the Scandinavian god Odin hung for nine days and nights on the World Tree and paid with one of his eyes for his knowledge of the runes.

sabbats In Wicca, the major celebrations of the pagan calendar. The greater sabbats are Candlemas (2 February), May Eve (30 April), Lammas (1 August) and Halloween (31 October); the 'lesser sabbats' are those marked by the midsummer and midwinter solstices, and the equinoxes in spring and autumn.

sacred That which is holy or dedicated to a god or goddess.

scarab In ancient Egyptian mythology the symbol of Khepera, the Sun god, in his aspect as lord of rebirth and immortality. Members of the Temple of Set also maintain that Set, god of darkness, is personified by the scarab.

Secret Chiefs In the Hermetic Order of the Golden Dawn, high-ranking spiritual beings who were believed to provide guidance and inspiration to the leaders of the Inner Order.

secret tradition Occult concept of a line of mystical and magical adepts who have passed their esoteric knowledge from generation to generation since time immemorial. According to this perspective, this sacred knowledge has been jealously guarded by initiates, and withheld from the world at large.

self In mysticism and occult philosophy, the divine essence of one's being. It may be contrasted to the ego, which mystics regard as a transitory entity that disappears at death. The self, on the other hand, contains the spark of Godhead and is regarded as the source of pure consciousness.

sephiroth The ten spheres, or spiritual emanations, upon the Kabbalistic Tree of Life. See **Kabbalah**.

shape–shifting The supernatural ability to transform one's shape into that of an animal, bird or mythic creature.

shaman/shamaness A sorcerer, magician or spirit healer who is able to enter a trance state under will, and who serves as an intermediary between people and the realm of gods and spirits.

sigil A magical symbol that represents a specific supernatural being or entity. In medieval magic, sigils were used to summon spirits, angels and demons. In more recent times, the trance occultist Austin Osman Spare developed his own alphabet of magical sigils to release atavistic images from his unconscious mind.

soul The eternal, immaterial, spiritual dimension of an organism which animates its physical form and gives it life. In some indigenous magical traditions animals, plants and inanimate objects like rocks can have souls. The soul is usually considered to be a part of God or directly connected to the spiritual realm.

spell A magical incantation believed to have a tangible outcome – either for good or evil.

spirit The divine spark or 'essence' within each person which, according to mystical belief, unites that person with the Godhead. It is the vital ingredient in life.

subconscious In modern analytic psychology, that part of the mind which lies below the threshold of consciousness.

talisman A magical charm, worn to attract good fortune. The talisman is often inscribed with the god name or image of the supernatural power believed to bring luck and protection to the person wearing it.

Tarot A pack of seventy-eight cards of medieval origin, regarded as the precursor of modern playing cards and commonly used in divination. The Tarot pack is divided into the Major Arcana (twenty-two cards) and the Minor Arcana (fifty-six cards); the latter are divided in turn into four suits: wands, swords, cups and pentacles. The cards of the Major Arcana are considered by many to have archetypal significance and have been correlated in the Western occult tradition with the paths on the Kabbalistic Tree of Life.

Tetragrammaton In the Jewish mystical tradition, the sacred four-lettered name of God rendered variously as IHVH, JHVH or YHVH. The name has been transcribed as Jehovah or, more recently, as Yahweh, but was never written down by devout Jews because it was considered too sacred for general expression.

Theosophy From the Greek *theos*, 'a god', and *sophos*, 'wise', a term for divine wisdom. The Theosophical Society was founded in New York in 1875 by Madame Helena Blavatsky, Colonel HS Olcott and William Q. Judge and has been instrumental in influencing many contemporary esoteric and mystical beliefs.

theurgy From the Greek *theourgos*, 'a divine worker', the working of miracles through supernatural aid. Among the Neoplatonists, miraculous effects were sought through magical invocations to the gods and spirits, and the word is now associated with 'divine magic', 'high magic' and Gnostic magic – the magic of spiritual self-knowledge.

thought-form A mental image that forms on the astral plane as a result of willed intent. Occultists believe that it is possible to transfer consciousness to thought-forms and use them as 'magical bodies' on the inner planes. Thought-forms can also personify the collective will of a magical group.

Tree of Life In the Kabbalah, a multiple symbol consisting of ten spheres, or *sephiroth*, through which, according to mystical tradition, the Creation of the world came about. The Tree is surmounted by Ain Soph Aur ('the limitless light') and the different spheres upon the Tree itself represent different aspects of divine manifestation.

Void, the The supreme, transcendent reality which lies beyond form and manifestation. Often regarded as the First Cause and sometimes identified with the Godhead, the Void is also characterised in some cosmologies as a state of formlessness or chaos. In the Kabbalah the Void is known as **Ain Soph Aur**.

wheel of the year In Wicca, the cycle of the seasons – with special reference to the greater and lesser sabbats which mark the different celebrations of the pagan calendar.

Wicca An alternative name for contemporary witchcraft which may derive from the old English root *wit*, meaning 'wisdom', or the Indo-European root *wic*, meaning 'to bend'. According to the Wiccan priestess Margot Adler, the latter definition characterises the Wiccan as someone 'skilled in the craft of shaping, bending and changing reality'.

widdershins In witchcraft the ceremonial act of facing the magical circle and moving to the left. It is associated with negative magic and is the opposite of moving deosil, or with the Sun.

will In Western magic, the focusing of one's personal intent for a magical outcome. Acts of invocation and evocation are performed in such a way as to ensure that the magician retains control over the supernatural forces summoned in a ceremonial working.

witch A practitioner of witchcraft, or Wicca – one who has been initiated as a member of a coven. The term is more commonly used to describe female practitioners, but can be used for males as well. See **Wicca**.

Bibliography

Adler, M., *Drawing Down the Moon*, Beacon Press, Boston 1986

Alvarado, L., *Psychology, Astrology and Western Magic: Image and Myth in Self-Discovery*, Llewellyn, St Paul, Minnesota 1991

Aquino, M., *The Church of Satan*, Temple of Set, San Francisco 1983

—*The Crystal Tablet of Set*, Temple of Set, San Francisco 1983

Ashcroft-Nowicki, D., *Highways of the Mind: The Art and History of Pathworking*, Aquarian Press, Wellingborough 1987

—*The Shining Paths: An Experiential Journey through the Tree of Life*, Aquarian Press, Wellingborough 1983

Bardon, F., *The Practice of Magical Evocation*, Rudolf Pravica, Graz-Puntigam, Austria 1967

Barnstone, W. (ed), *The Other Bible*, Harper & Row, San Francisco 1984

Barton, B., *The Secret Life of a Satanist*, Feral House, Los Angeles 1990

Beskin, G., and Bonner, J., *Austin Osman Spare 1886–1956: The Divine Draughtsman*, catalogue, Morley Gallery, London 1987

Blair-Ewart, A. (ed.), *Mindfire: Dialogues in the Other Future*, Somerville House, Toronto 1995

Bolen, J. S., *Goddesses in Everywoman*, Harper & Row, New York 1985

—*Gods in Everyman*, HarperCollins, New York 1989

Bracelin, J. L., *Gerald Gardner: Witch*, Octagon Press, London 1960

Budapest, Z, *The Holy Book of Women's Mysteries*, Parts One and Two, Susan B. Anthony #1 Coven, Los Angeles, 1979–80

Budge, E. A. (ed.), *Lefefa Sedek: The Bandlet of Righteousness*, Luzac, London 1929

Burckhardt, T., *Alchemy*, Penguin Books, Baltimore 1971
Butler, W. E., *Apprenticed to Magic*, Aquarian Press, London 1962
—*Magic and the Qabalah*, Aquarian Press, London 1964
—*The Magician: His Training and Work*, Aquarian Press, London 1959
—*Magic: Its Ritual, Power and Purpose*, Aquarian Press, London 1952
Campbell. J., *The Hero with a Thousand Faces*, Pantheon, New York 1949
—*The Inner Reaches of Outer Space: Metaphor as Myth and as Religion*, Harper & Row, New York 1988
—*Myths to Live By*, Viking Press, New York 1972; Souvenir Press, London 1973
Case, P. F., *The Tarot*, Macoy Publishing Co., New York 1947
Castaneda, C., *The Art of Dreaming*, HarperCollins, New York 1993
—*Journey to Ixtlan*, Simon & Schuster, New York 1972
—*A Separate Reality*, Simon & Schuster, New York 1971
—*Tales of Power*, Simon & Schuster, New York 1974
—*The Teachings of Don Juan*, University of California Press, Berkeley 1968
Christ, C. P., and Plaskow, J. (ed.) *Womanspirit Rising*, Harper & Row, San Francisco 1979
Churton, T., *The Gnostics*, Weidenfeld & Nicolson, London 1987
Colquhoun, I., *Sword of Wisdom*, Spearman, London 1975
Couliano, I. P., *The Tree of Gnosis*, HarperCollins, San Francisco 1992
Crawford, A., and Edgar, R. (ed.), *Transit Lounge: Wake-up Calls and Travelers' Tales from the Future*, Craftsman House, Sydney 1997
Crowley, A., *Book Four*, Sangreal Foundation, Dallas 1972
—*The Book of Lies*, Haydn Press, Devon 1962
—*The Book of Thoth*, Weiser, New York 1969
—*Magick in Theory and Practice*, privately published, Paris 1929 (republished by Dover and Castle Books, New York, various editions)
—*The Qabalah of Aleister Crowley*, Weiser, New York 1973
—*The Vision and the Voice*, Sangreal Foundation, Dallas 1972
Crowley, V., *Wicca: The Old Religion in the New Millennium*, Thorsons, London 1996
Crowther, P., *Lid off the Cauldron*, Muller, London 1981
Daab, R., 'An Interview with Jean Houston', *Magical Blend* issues 18, 19 and 20, Berkeley 1988
Daly, M., *Gyn/Ecology*, Beacon Press, Boston 1978
Davis, E., 'TechnoPagans: The Roots of Digital Magick', *Green Egg*, vol. 29, no. 129, August–September 1997
—'Technopagans: May the Astral Plane be Reborn in Cyberspace', *Wired*, July 1995

de Mille, R., *Castaneda's Journey*, Capra Press, Santa Barbara 1976
—*The Don Juan Papers*, Ross-Erikson, Santa Barbara 1980
Dery, M., *Escape Velocity: Cyberculture at the End of the Century*, Hodder & Stoughton, London 1996
Dowse, J., 'Cyberpagans!', *Pagan Dawn*, no. 119, London, Beltane 1996
Drury, N., *Echoes from the Void: Writings on Magic, Visionary Art and the New Consciousness*, Prism Press, Dorset, 1994
—*The Elements of Shamanism*, Element, Dorset 1989
—*Exploring the Labyrinth: Making Sense of the New Spirituality*, Allen & Unwin, Sydney 1999; Continuum, New York 1999
—*The Occult Experience*, Hale, London 1987
—*Pan's Daughter*, Mandrake, Oxford 1993
—*The Path of the Chameleon*, Spearman, London 1973
Edinger, E., *Ego and Archetype*, Penguin, London 1973
Eliade, M., *Cosmos and History*, Harper & Row, New York 1959
—*The Sacred and the Profane*, Harper & Row, New York 1961
—*Shamanism*, Princeton University Press, New Jersey 1972
Farrar, J. and S., *Eight Sabbats for Witches*, Hale, London 1981
—*The Witches' Bible*, Magickal Childe, New York 1985
—*The Witches' Goddess*, Hale, London 1987
—*The Witches' Way*, Hale, London 1984
Farrar, S., *What Witches Do*, Phoenix, Custer, Washington 1983
Feinstein, D., and Krippner, S., *Personal Mythology*, Tarcher, Los Angeles 1988
Ferguson, J., *An Illustrated Encyclopaedia of Mysticism and the Mystery Religions*, Thames & Hudson, London 1976
Fortune, D., *Applied Magic*, Aquarian Press, London 1962
—*Psychic Self-Defence*, Rider, London 1930
Fuller, J. O., *The Magical Dilemma of Victor Neuburg*, W. H. Allen, London 1965
Furst, P. T. (ed.), *Flesh of the Gods*, Allen & Unwin, London 1972
Galloway, B. (ed.), *Fantasy and Wargaming*, Patrick Stephens, Cambridge 1981
Gardner, G. B., *High Magic's Aid*, Michael Houghton, London 1949
—*The Meaning of Witchcraft*, Aquarian Press, London 1959
—*Witchcraft Today*, Rider, London 1954
Giger, H. R., *Necronomicon*, Big O Publishing, London 1978 (republished by Morpheus International)
  N.Y.City, Ugly Publishing, Zürich 1981
  Retrospektive 1964–1984, ABC Verlag, Zürich 1984
Gilbert, R. A., *Revelations of the Golden Dawn*, Quantum/Foulsham, London 1997

Ginsburg, C., *The Kabbalah: Its Doctrines, Development and Literature*, Routledge & Kegan Paul, London 1956

Goldenberg, N., *Changing of the Gods*, Beacon Press, Boston 1979

Gottlieb, R. S. (ed.), *A New Creation: America's Contemporary Spiritual Voices*, Crossroad, New York 1990

Grant, K. *Cults of the Shadow*, Muller, London 1975

—*Hecate's Fountain*, Skoob, London 1992

—*Images and Oracles of Austin Osman Spare*, Muller, London 1975

—*The Magical Revival*, Muller, London 1972

Grant, R. (ed.), *Gnosticism: An Anthology*, Collins, London 1961

Gray, W. G., *Inner Traditions of Magic*, Weiser, Maine 1984

Greer, M. K., *Women of the Golden Dawn*, Park Street Press, Rochester, Vermont 1995

Guiley, R. E., *The Encyclopedia of Witches and Witchcraft*, Facts on File, New York 1989

Halifax, J., (ed.), *Shamanic Voices*, Arkana, New York 1991

Harner, M., *The Jivaro*, University of California Press, Berkeley 1984

—*The Way of the Shaman*, Harper & Row, San Francisco 1980

Harper, G. M., *Yeats's Golden Dawn*, Macmillan, London 1974

Harvey, G., *Listening People, Speaking Earth*, Hurst, London 1997

Harvey, G., and Hardman, C. (ed.), *Paganism Today*, Thorsons, London 1996

Heckethorn, C. W., *The Secret Societies of All Ages and Countries*, University Books, New York 1966

Houston, J., *The Hero and the Goddess*, Ballantine, New York 1992

—*The Search for the Beloved: Journeys in Sacred Psychology*, Crucible, Wellingborough 1990

—'Myth and Pathos in Sacred Psychology', *Dromenon*, vol. 3, no. 2, Spring 1981

Howe, E., *The Magicians of the Golden Dawn*, Routledge & Kegan Paul, London 1972

Hume, L., *Witchcraft and Paganism in Australia*, Melbourne University Press, Melbourne 1997

Hutchison, M., *Mega Brain Power*, Hyperion, New York 1994

Jamal, M., *Shape Shifters*, Arkana, New York and London 1987

Johns, J., *King of the Witches: The World of Alex Sanders*, Coward-McCann, New York 1969

Jonas, H., *The Gnostic Religion*, 2nd edn, Beacon Press, Boston 1963

Jones, P., and Matthews, C. (ed.), *Voices from the Circle*, Aquarian Press, London 1990

Jordan, M., *Witches: An Encyclopedia of Paganism and Magic*, Kyle Cathie, London 1996

Jung, C. G. *Man and His Symbols*, Dell, New York 1968

—*Memories, Dreams, Reflections*, Random House, New York 1961

—*Symbols of Transformation*, Bollingen Foundation, New Jersey 1956

—*Two Essays in Analytical Psychology*, Routledge & Kegan Paul, London 1953

Kalweit, H., *Dreamtime and Inner Space*, Shambhala, Boston 1988

Kaplan, A., *Meditation and Kabbalah*, Weiser, New York 1982

Kelly, A., *Crafting the Art of Magic*, Llewellyn, St Paul, Minnesota 1991

Kerr, H., and Crow, C. L. (ed.), *The Occult in America: New Historical Perspectives*, University of Illinois Press, Urbana and Chicago 1983

King, F. *Ritual Magic in England*, Spearman, London 1970 (republished as *Modern Ritual Magic*, Prism Press, Dorset 1989)

—*Sexuality, Magic and Perversion*, New English Library, London 1972

—(ed.), *Astral Projection, Magic and Alchemy*, Spearman, London 1971

—(ed.), *The Secret Rituals of the O.T.O.*, C. W. Daniel, London 1973

King, F., and Skinner, S., *Techniques of High Magic: A Manual of Self-Initiation*, C. W. Daniel, London 1976

King, F., and Sutherland, I., *The Rebirth of Magic*, Corgi, London 1982

Knaster, M., 'The Goddesses in Jean Shinoda Bolen', *East West*, March 1989

Knight, G., *A History of White Magic*, Mowbray, London and Oxford 1978

Larsen, S., *The Shaman's Doorway*, Harper & Row, New York 1976

Larsen, S. and R., *A Fire in the Mind: The Life of Joseph Campbell*, Doubleday, New York 1991

LaVey, A., *The Satanic Bible*, Avon, New York 1969

—*The Satanic Rituals*, Avon, New York 1972

Leary, T., *Chaos and Cyberculture*, Ronin, Berkeley, California 1994

—*Flashbacks*, Tarcher, Los Angeles 1983

Lesh, C., 'Goddess Worship: The Subversive Religion', *Twelve Together*, Los Angeles, May 1975

Letchford, F. W., *From the Inferno to Zos*, First Impressions, Thame, Oxford 1995

Levenda, P., *Unholy Alliance: A History of Nazi Involvement with the Occult*, Avon, New York, 1995

Levi, E., *The Key of the Mysteries*, Rider, London 1959

Lewis, J. R. (ed.), *Magical Religion and Modern Witchcraft*, State University of New York Press, Albany 1996

Luhrmann, T. M., *Persuasions of the Witch's Craft*, Harvard University Press, Cambridge, Massachusetts 1989

Lyons, A., *The Second Coming: Satanism in America*, Dodd Mead, New York 1970

McKenna, T., *The Archaic Revival*, HarperCollins, San Francisco 1991
—*True Hallucinations*, HarperCollins, San Francisco 1993
Majidi, A., 'H. R. Giger: Night Visionary', *Manhattan's Entertainment Magazine*, vol. 1, issue 7, New York, September 1998
Mathers, S. L., *The Book of the Sacred Magic of Abramelin the Mage*, De Laurence, Chicago 1932
—*The Greater Key of Solomon*, De Laurence, Chicago 1914
—*The Grimoire of Armadel*, Routledge & Kegan Paul, London 1980
—*The Lesser Key of Solomon*, De Laurence, Chicago 1916
Matt, D. C., *The Essential Kabbalah*, HarperCollins, New York 1995
Matthews, C. and J., *The Western Way*, Arkana, London 1994
Murray, M., *The Witch-Cult in Western Europe*, Oxford University Press, New York 1971
Newton, J. F., *The Builders*, Allen & Unwin, London 1924
Norton, R., *The Art of Rosaleen Norton*, 2nd edition, Walter Glover, Sydney 1982
O'Hare, G., *Pagan Ways*, Llewellyn, St Paul, Minnesota 1997
Osbon, D. K. (ed.), *Reflections on the Art of Living: A Joseph Campbell Companion*, HarperCollins, New York 1991
Pagels, E., *The Gnostic Gospels*, Weidenfeld & Nicolson, London 1979
Peters, T., *The Cosmic Self*, HarperCollins, San Francisco 1991
Redgrove, H. S., *Alchemy: Ancient and Modern*, Rider, London 1922
Reeder, S., 'Children of the Digital Gods', *Green Egg*, vol. 29, no. 129, August–September 1997
Regardie, I., *The Eye in the Triangle: An Interpretation of Aleister Crowley*, Falcon Press, Phoenix, Arizona 1982
—(ed.), *The Golden Dawn*, vols. 1–4, Aries Press, Chicago 1937–40
—*The Middle Pillar*, Aries Press, Chicago 1945
—*The Tree of Life: A Study in Magic*, Rider, London 1932
Rheingold, H., *Virtual Reality*, Mandarin, London 1992
Richardson, A., *Dancers to the Gods*, Aquarian Press, Wellingborough 1985
—*Priestess: The Life and Magic of Dion Fortune*, Aquarian Press, Wellingborough 1987
Robertson, L. D., *God the Mother*, Cesara, Clonegal 1984
—*The Religion of the Goddess*, Cesara, Clonegal 1984
Robertson, O., *Dea: Rites and Mysteries of the Goddess*, Cesara, Clonegal, n.d.
Robertson, S., *The Aleister Crowley Scrapbook*, Foulsham, London 1988
Robinson, J. M. (ed.), *The Nag Hammadi Library in English*, Harper & Row, San Francisco 1977
Roszak, T., *Unfinished Animal*, Harper & Row, New York 1975

—*The Voice of the Earth*, Simon & Schuster, New York 1992

Rushkoff, D., *Cyberia: Life in the Trenches of Hyperspace*, HarperCollins, San Francisco 1994

Russell, J. B., *A History of Witchcraft: Sorcerers, Heretics and Pagans*, Thames & Hudson, London and New York 1980

Scholem, G., *Major Trends in Jewish Mysticism*, Schocken, New York 1961

—*On the Mystical Shape of the Godhead*, Schocken, New York 1997

—*Origins of the Kabbalah*, Princeton University Press, New Jersey 1990

Seligmann, K., *Magic, Supernaturalism and Religion*, Pantheon, New York 1971

Semple, G. W., *Zos Kia*, Fulgur, London 1995

Shumaker, W., *The Occult Sciences in the Renaissance*, University of California Press, Berkeley 1979

Spare, A. O., *The Book of Pleasure*, privately published, London 1913 (republished 93 Publishing, Montreal 1975)

Starhawk, *Dreaming the Dark*, Beacon Press, Boston 1982

—*The Spiral Dance*, Harper & Row, New York 1979

Sterling, B., *The Hacker Crackdown*, Bantam, New York 1992

Stevens, J., *Storming Heaven: LSD and the American Dream*, Atlantic Monthly Press, New York 1987

Suster, G., *The Legacy of the Beast*, Weiser, Maine 1989

Symonds, J., *The Great Beast*, Mayflower, London 1973

—*The Magic of Aleister Crowley*, Muller, London 1958

Symonds, J., and Grant, K. (ed.), *The Confessions of Aleister Crowley*, Hill and Wang, New York 1969

—(ed.), *The Magical Record of the Beast 666*, Duckworth, London 1972

Valiente, D. *An ABC of Witchcraft, Past and Present*, Hale, London 1973, revised 1984

—*Witchcraft for Tomorrow*, Hale, London 1978

Waite, A. E., *The Holy Kabbalah*, University Books, New York 1960

Walker, B., *Gnosticism: Its History and Influence*, Aquarian Press, Wellingborough 1983

Wertheim, M., *The Pearly Gates of Cyberspace*, Norton, New York 1998

Widengren, G., *Mani and Manichaeism*, Holt, Rinehart and Winston, New York 1965

Wilby, B. (ed.), *The New Dimensions Red Book*, Helios, Cheltenham 1968

Wild, L. (ed.), *The Ninth Night*, vol. 1, nos. 1 and 2, Sydney 1998, published on the Internet

Williams, T., 'Navigation Systems for the Spirit', *Green Egg*, vol. 29, no. 120, August–September 1997

Wilson, C., *Aleister Crowley: The Nature of the Beast*, Aquarian Press, Wellingborough 1987

Yates, F., *The Rosicrucian Enlightenment*, Shambhala, Boulder, Colorado 1987

Notes

Chapter One

1. see Gareth Knight, *A History of White Magic*, Mowbray, London and Oxford 1978, p. 15
2. see Ioan P. Couliano, *The Tree of Gnosis*, HarperCollins, San Francisco 1992
3. ibid, p. 33
4. see James M. Robinson, Introduction to *The Nag Hammadi Library in English* Harper & Row, San Francisco 1977, p. 4
5. see Wallis Barnstone (ed.), *The Other Bible*, Harper & Row, San Francisco 1984, p. 627
6. according to Robert M. Grant, Ptolemaeus was head of the Valentinian school in Italy and succeeded Valentinus around the year 160
7. Robert M. Grant (ed.), *Gnosticism: An Anthology*, Collins, London 1961, p. 163
8. ibid, p. 163
9. see Wallis Barnstone, op. cit., p. 669
10. quoted in Geo Widengren, *Mani and Manichaeism*, Holt, Rinehart and Winston, New York 1965, p. 26
11. ibid., p. 53
12. from Plotinus, 'The Ascent to Union with the One' in A. H. Armstrong (ed.), *Plotinus*, Allen & Unwin, London 1953, p. 137

13. admittedly, not all scholars agree on this point. The late Ioan P. Couliano believed that Scholem overstated the connection between Kabbalah and Gnosticism (see Couliano's *The Tree of Gnosis*, HarperCollins, San Francisco 1992, p. 42 et seq.). However, Scholem believed quite emphatically that the Kabbalistic text *Bahir*, which predates the *Zohar*, makes it clear that the 'thirteenth century Kabbalists became the heirs of Gnostical symbolism' (*Major Trends in Jewish Mysticism*, Schocken, New York 1961, p. 214).

14. see Gerschom G. Scholem, *Major Trends in Jewish Mysticism*, Schocken, New York 1961, p. 209

15. ibid, pp. 215–16

16. ibid, pp. 218–19

17. Christian Ginsburg, *The Kabbalah: Its Doctrines, Development and Literature*, Routledge & Kegan Paul, London 1956, p. 102

18. see A. E. Waite, *The Holy Kabbalah*, University Books, New York 1960, p. 201

19. see John Ferguson, *An Illustrated Encyclopaedia of Mysticism and the Mystery Religions*, Thames & Hudson, London 1976, p. 99

20. quoted in Wayne Shumaker, *The Occult Sciences in the Renaissance*, University of California Press, Berkeley, California 1979, p. 202

21. ibid, p. 203

22. Tobias Churton, *The Gnostics*, Weidenfeld & Nicolson, London 1987, p. 104

23. from W. Scott (trans.), *Hermetica* vol. 1, quoted in Caitlin and John Matthews, *The Western Way*, Arkana, London 1994, p. 216

24. quoted in Tobias Churton, *The Gnostics*, op. cit., p. 113

25. ibid, p. 115

26. ibid, p. 112

27. John and Caitlin Matthews, *The Western Way*, op. cit., p. 218

28. see Kurt Seligmann, *Magic, Supernaturalism and Religion*, Pantheon, New York 1971, pp. 82–83 (first published under the title *The History of Magic* in 1948)

29. quoted in H. Stanley Redgrove, *Alchemy: Ancient and Modern*, Rider, London 1922, pp. 10–11

30. quoted in M. Berthelot, *La Chimie au Moyen Age*, vol. 2, Paris 1893, p. 262

31. Redgrove, op. cit., p. 14

32. see Titus Burckhardt, *Alchemy*, Penguin Books, Baltimore 1971, p. 97

33. ibid, pp. 73 and 75

34. Joseph Fort Newton, *The Builders*, Allen & Unwin, London 1924, pp. 17–18

35. see Charles W. Heckethorn, *The Secret Societies of All Ages and Countries*, vol. 2, University Books, New York 1966, pp. 16–17
36. Newton, op. cit., p. 192
37. ibid, p. 211
38. quoted in J. F. Newton, op. cit., p. 130
39. text quoted in Francis King, *Modern Ritual Magic*, Prism Press, Dorset 1989, pp. 15–16
40. see Frances A. Yates, *The Rosicrucian Enlightenment*, Shambhala, Boulder, Colorado 1987, p. 45
41. Kurt Seligmann, op. cit., p. 291
42. see F. A. Yates, op. cit., pp. 52–53
43. see Joseph Fort Newton, op. cit., pp. 51–52
44. ibid, p. 53
45. ibid, p. 58

Chapter Two

1. quoted in Ellic Howe, *The Magicians of the Golden Dawn*, Routledge & Kegan Paul, London 1972, p. 12
2. some members of the Golden Dawn itself also had their doubts about the authenticity of Anna Sprengel. See R. A. Gilbert, *Revelations of the Golden Dawn*, 1997, p. 30
3. for detailed histories of the Golden Dawn, readers are referred to the excellent studies by Ellic Howe, Ithell Colquhuon, R. A. Gilbert and Mary K. Greer, listed in the Bibliography
4. see Ellic Howe, op. cit., p. 127
5. ibid
6. see Francis King, *Modern Ritual Magic*, Prism Press, Dorset 1989, p. 97
7. see George Mills Harper, *Yeats's Golden Dawn*, Macmillan, London 1974, p. 77 The full text of Yeats's essay is provided as an appendix in this book.
8. Yeats was initiated into the grade of Adeptus Minor on 10 July 1912, eleven years after he had written his essay
9. Francis King, op. cit, p. 57
10. see Israel Regardie (ed.), *The Golden Dawn*, vol. 1, Aries Press, Chicago 1937, pp. 35–36
11. specifically, these were the rituals of the Stella Matutina, a late form of the Golden Dawn
12. there are ten *sephiroth* and twenty-two interconnecting paths upon the

Tree of Life, so the thirty-second path is both the culmination of all of these (10 + 22) and the initial point of departure if one remembers that here the mystic is retracing the path to Unity Consciousness

13. Daath is sometime referred to as the 'eleventh' *sephirah* on the Tree of Life. It is not a true *sephirah* but represents the Abyss – the gulf between the three *sephiroth* of the Trinity and the seven lower *sephiroth* which are the seven days of Creation.

14. Nevill Drury, *The Path of the Chameleon*, Spearman, London 1973, p. 142

Chapter Three

1. Mathers's manuscript *The Book of Correspondences* was circulated among senior Golden Dawn students in the 1890s. Ithell Colquhoun, author of a biography of Samuel Mathers, *Sword of Wisdom*, believes that Crowley and another Golden Dawn member, Allan Bennett, borrowed a substantial portion of the material in 777 from their teacher. The Tarot listings in 777, for example, are conventional, whereas Crowley derived his own symbolic meanings and rearranged the correspondences to fit in with his own magical philosophy after leaving the Golden Dawn in 1900. Had the material in 777 belonged entirely to Crowley, this would not have been the case. Nevertheless the inclusion of Harpocrates in this list as a deity linked to Kether reflects his own personal cosmology (see Chapter Four).

2. see Israel Regardie, *The Tree of Life: A Study in Magic*, Rider, London 1932, p. 106

3. see Franz Bardon, *The Practice of Magical Evocation*, Rudolf Pravica, Graz-Puntigam, Austria 1967, p. 20

4. see Eliphas Levi, *The Key of the Mysteries*, Rider, London 1959, p. 174

5. see E. A. Wallis Budge (ed.), *Lefefa Sedek: The Bandlet of Righteousness*, Luzac, London 1929, p. 3

6. ibid, p. 4

7. ibid, p. 5

8. see Aleister Crowley, *Book Four*, Sangreal Foundation, Dallas 1972, p. 42 (first published in 1913)

9. Crowley believed that vision of the Higher Self would help supersede the more limited scope of the ego, thus assisting the process of spiritual transformation. 'Ultimately,' wrote Crowley, 'the Magical Will so identifies itself with [the individual's] whole being that it becomes unconscious.' (*Book Four*, p. 46)

10. see Dion Fortune, *Applied Magic*, Aquarian Press, London 1962, pp. 56–57

11. ceremonial magicians assume that these magical entities are resident in the astral planes and may be evoked through ritual – sometimes to visible appearance. Interested readers are referred to the practical writings and magical diaries of Aleister Crowley and also Franz Bardon's seminal work *The Practice of Magical Evocation*.

12. Samuel Mathers translated *The Greater Key of Solomon* and *Goetia: The Book of Evil Spirits*, as well as *The Grimoire of Armadel*, and these are available in various editions – see Bibliography

13. see Aleister Crowley, *Book Four*, op. cit., p. 23

14. ibid, p. 112

15. the magicians of the Golden Dawn utilised a visualisation technique known as the Middle Pillar exercise to activate their inner awareness. The Middle Pillar exercise involved visualising different spheres upon the central axis of the Tree of Life, starting with Kether and culminating in Malkuth. These visualisations also included meditations on specific symbolic colours and the intoning of appropriate god names. See Israel Regardie, *The Middle Pillar*, Aries Press, Chicago 1945 (reprinted in various editions).

16. quoted in Francis King (ed.), *Astral Projection, Magic and Alchemy*, Neville Spearman, London 1971, pp. 73–74

17. ibid, p. 69

18. quoted in Israel Regardie (ed.), *The Golden Dawn*, vol. 4, Aries Press, Chicago 1940, p. 43 *n*. The god name HCOMA is not Kabbalistic but derives from an 'angelic language' called Enochian, transcribed by the Elizabethan occultists Dr John Dee and Edward Kelley and utilised in Golden Dawn rituals and visualisations.

19. quoted in King, op. cit., p. 66

20. see Paul Foster Case, *The Tarot*, Macoy Publishing Company, New York 1947, p. 123. Case was a member of the Golden Dawn Thoth-Hermes Temple in New York and later established the Builders of the Adytum, an occult organisation which offered a correspondence course based on Golden Dawn teachings.

21. see Aleister Crowley, *The Book of Thoth*, Weiser, New York 1969, p. 86

22. see Paul Foster Case, op. cit., p. 59

23. see Francis King, op. cit., p. 67

24. a specific allusion to Golden Dawn inner Order levels of ritual attainment

25. quoted in Francis King, op. cit., pp. 58–59

Chapter Four

1. Aleister Crowley, *Magick in Theory and Practice*, privately published, Paris 1929, (republished in 1973 by Routledge & Kegan Paul, London), p. xv
2. ibid, p. xvi
3. ibid, p. xvii
4. ibid, p. 4
5. ibid, p. 4
6. see John Symonds, *The Great Beast*, Mayflower Books, London 1973, p. 43
7. the text of *The Book of the Law* is included as an appendix in *The Magical Record of the Beast 666*, edited by John Symonds and Kenneth Grant, Duckworth, London 1972
8. see Aleister Crowley, *Magick in Theory and Practice*, op. cit., p. 12
9. see Kenneth Grant, *The Magical Revival*, Muller, London 1972, p. 20
10. see Aleister Crowley, *Magick in Theory and Practice*, op. cit., p. 11
11. see Kenneth Grant, op. cit., p. 45
12. ibid, p. 144
13. interested readers are referred to Colin Wilson's highly accessible account of Crowley's insatiable search for sexual partners in *Aleister Crowley: The Nature of the Beast*, Aquarian Press, Wellingborough 1987
14. see Kenneth Grant, op. cit., p. 145
15. see John Symonds and Kenneth Grant (ed.), *The Confessions of Aleister Crowley*, Hill and Wang, New York 1969, p. 395. The A ∴ A ∴ is the Argenteum Astrum (or Silver Star), the magical order which Crowley established in 1907.
16. ibid, p. 396
17. ibid, pp. 399–400
18. ibid, p. 397
19. ibid, p. 403
20. quoted in Gerald Suster, *The Legacy of the Beast*, Samuel Weiser, Maine 1989, p. 44
21. see John Symonds, *The Great Beast*, op. cit., p. 122
22. quoted in John Symonds, *The Magic of Aleister Crowley*, Muller, London 1958, p. 35
23. see Colin Wilson, *Aleister Crowley: The Nature of the Beast*, op. cit., p. 90
24. ibid, p. 91. Colin Wilson makes reference to an entry in Neuburg's magical diary which describes how Crowley on one occasion rebuked him by giving him thirty-two strokes of a gorse switch, drawing blood. 'He is

apparently a homosexual sadist,' wrote Neuburg, 'for . . . he performed the ceremony with obvious satisfaction.'

25. see Aleister Crowley, *The Vision and the Voice*, Sangreal Foundation, Dallas, Texas 1972, pp. 57–58

26. see John Symonds, *The Great Beast*, op. cit., p. 138

27 ibid, p. 161

28. ibid, p. 163

29. quoted in John Symonds, *The Great Beast*, op. cit., p. 144

30. see Francis King, *Sexuality, Magic and Perversion*, New English Library, London 1972, p. 100

31. see John Symonds, *The Great Beast*, op. cit., p. 277

32. ibid, p. 337 – a quote from Loveday's personal account

33. see Francis King (ed.), *The Secret Rituals of the OTO*, C. W. Daniel, London 1973, p. 29

34. John Symonds was fascinated by Crowley's phallic signature and notes in *The Great Beast*: 'Crowley had long identified himself with the penis, just as he identified his mistress – any mistress – with the vagina. He did not consider a woman as a person in her own right. Thus Leah Hirsig was "pure Yoni decorated by the rest of her" . . .' (from Crowley's Magical Record, 17 August 1920). See Symonds, op. cit., p. 415. Elsewhere, Crowley expands on this a little. In *777*, in a note about the 'will of women', he identifies their key roles as the mother, the wife and the whore.

35. see Sandy Robertson's fascinating collection of Crowleyian memorabilia, *The Aleister Crowley Scrapbook*, Foulsham, London 1988, p. 125

36. see Gerald Suster, *The Legacy of the Beast*, op. cit., p. 204

Chapter Five

1. see Alan Richardson, *Dancers to the Gods*, Aquarian Press, Wellingborough 1985, p. 16

2. quoted in Alan Richardson, *Priestess: The Life and Magic of Dion Fortune*, Aquarian Press, Wellingborough 1987, p. 112

3. see Alan Richardson, *Dancers to the Gods*, op. cit., p. 34

4. see Dion Fortune, *Applied Magic*, Aquarian Press, London 1962, p. 91

5. a Gnostic sect, the Melchizedekians, maintained that there was a spiritual power greater than Jesus Christ. This was Melchizedek, 'the light gatherer', who is said to have performed a comparable role in the heavens to that of Jesus on Earth. In Gnostic thought the archons, as intermediary cosmic powers associated with the Earth, were regarded as basically evil. But

Melchizedek is said to have gathered particles of light in their midst and returned them to the 'Treasure-house' or Pleroma, in the transcendent realms of the cosmos. Melchizedek is thus regarded as a greater figure of light in the Gnostic tradition.

6. see Alan Richardson, *Priestess: The Life and Magic of Dion Fortune*, op. cit., p. 117

7. quoted in R. A. Gilbert, *Revelations of the Golden Dawn*, Quantum/Foulsham, Slough 1997, p. 124

8. see Dion Fortune, *Psychic Self-Defence*, Rider, London, and Samuel Weiser, New York 1930, pp. 152–56

9. published in the *Occult Review*, January 1933

10. see Kenneth Grant, *The Magical Revival*, Muller, London 1972, p. 177

11. it has been suggested in a recent article in *Gnosis* magazine (No. 43, Spring 1997) that there may have been a secret sexual dimension to the rituals of the Golden Dawn, but the arguments put forward by the authors, John Michael Greer and Carl Hood, seem to me to be very unconvincing. Sexual magic was more the domain of occultists like Austin Osman Spare, who was never a member of the Golden Dawn, and Aleister Crowley, who developed his interest in sex magic after leaving this magical order.

12. see chapter by 'FPD' entitled 'The Old Religion' in Basil Wilby (ed.), *The New Dimensions Red Book*, Helios, Cheltenham 1968

13. see Dion Fortune, *Applied Magic*, op. cit., p. 4

14. see 'FPD', 'The Old Religion', op. cit., p. 47

15. ibid, p. 49

16. ibid, p. 78

17. Butler's books on the Western esoteric tradition include *Magic: Its Ritual Power and Purpose* (1952), *The Magician: His Training and Work* (1959), *Apprenticed to Magic* (1962) and *Magic and the Qabalah* (1964) – see Bibliography

18. for further information on Spare's life, readers are referred to F. W. Letchford, *From the Inferno to Zos*, First Impressions, Thame, Oxford 1995, Gavin W. Semple, *Zos Kia*, Fulgur, London 1995 and Geraldine Beskin and John Bonner, *Austin Osman Spare 1886–1956: The Divine Draughtsman*, Morley Gallery catalogue, London, September 1987

19. Spare was very familiar with the writings of Freud, Krafft-Ebing and Havelock Ellis

20. see Austin Osman Spare, *The Book of Pleasure*, privately published, London 1913, pp. 52–53 (reissued in facsimile edition by 93 Publishing, Montreal 1975)

21. see Gavin W. Semple, op. cit., p. 7

22. see Kenneth Grant, *Images and Oracles of Austin Osman Spare*, Muller, London 1975, p. 33

23. This had been preceded by *A Book of Satyrs* (c. 1911) which contained 'satires' on the church, politics, officialdom and other 'follies'. It is not a major work.

24. Spare became a member of the Argenteum Astrum in 1910 after contributing some drawings to Crowley's occult journal *The Equinox*

25. see *The Book of Pleasure*, p. 50

26. Spare believed that the self lived 'in millions of forms', and that it was obliged to experience 'every conceivable thing', all the infinite possibilities inherent in the manifested universe. Any incomplete existence or situation required a reincarnation to finalise it or make it whole: 'I have incarnated that which I need to rationalise.' Spare also thought that by exploring the recesses of the mind one would undoubtedly uncover past incarnations, 'for whatever is attained is but a re-awakening of an earlier experience of the body'.

27. in his autobiography *Memories, Dreams, Reflections*, Carl Jung warned against the possibility of allowing the symbolic contents of dreams and visions to be indulged in, rather than checked. Jung believed that the perception of dual, but intermingled, levels of awareness – in Spare's case, atavism and everyday reality – could lead to schizophrenia. One wonders whether Spare would agree.

28. for a full account of Rosaleen Norton's trance explorations, see Nevill Drury, *Pan's Daughter: The Magical World of Rosaleen Norton*, Collins, Sydney 1988 (republished by Mandrake, Oxford 1993)

29. a facsimile of this edition, *The Art of Rosaleen Norton*, was published by Walter Glover in Sydney in 1982

30. see *The Art of Rosaleen Norton*, op. cit., p. 38

31. There is also a degree of resemblance here, in my opinion, to the Tarot image of Temperance, which similarly reflects a state of spiritual unity or balance. Rosaleen Norton denied a direct influence from the Tarot, though, regarding it more as an intuitive than a specific source of imagery.

Chapter Six

1. see Doreen Valiente, *An ABC of Witchcraft, Past and Present*, Robert Hale, London 1973, p. 155, and Rosemary Ellen Guiley, *The Encyclopedia of Witches and Witchcraft*, Facts on File, New York and Oxford, 1989, p. 69

2. see Doreen Valiente, 'The Search for Old Dorothy' in Janet and Stewart

Farrar, *The Witches' Way*, Robert Hale, London 1984, p. 283 et seq.

3. see Doreen Valiente, *An ABC of Witchcraft*, op. cit., p. 156

4. see Francis King, *Ritual Magic in England*, Neville Spearman, London 1970, p. 180

5. see Rosemary Ellen Guiley, *op. cit.*, p. 134

6. for a full description of these initiations, see Janet and Stewart Farrar, *The Witches' Way*, Robert Hale, London 1984

7. see Doreen Valiente, *An ABC of Witchcraft*, op. cit., p. 203

8. see *Man, Myth and Magic*, issue 40, London 1970

9. it must be noted, though, that Patricia and Arnold Crowther were not averse to a certain measure of media publicity themselves. They produced the first radio series in Britain dealing with witchcraft – *A Spell of Witchcraft* – for Radio Sheffield in 1971, and also wrote two books together: *The Witches Speak* (1965) and *The Secrets of Ancient Witchcraft* (1974). After her husband's death in 1974, Patricia Crowther continued her appearances on both radio and television and also published several other books, including her autobiography, *Witch Blood!* (1974) and *Lid off the Cauldron* (1981).

10. Janet Owen (Farrar) was initiated by Alex Sanders, and Stewart Farrar by Sanders's wife Maxine, in 1970

11. personal interview with Janet and Stewart Farrar, Drogheda, Ireland, December 1984

12. see N. Goldberg, *Changing of the Gods: Feminism and the End of Traditional Religions*, Beacon Press, Boston 1979, p. 90

13. see Mary Daly, *Gyn/Ecology: The Metaethics of Radical Feminism*, Beacon Press, Boston 1978, p. 190

14. see Mary Farrell Bednarowski, 'Women in Occult America' in Howard Kerr and Charles L. Crow (ed.), *The Occult in America: New Historical Perspectives*, University of Illinois Press, Urbana and Chicago 1983, p. 190

15. see Judy Davis and Juanita Weaver, 'Dimensions of Spirituality', *Quest*, 1, 1975, p. 2

16. see Carol P. Christ and Judith Plaskow (ed.), *Womanspirit Rising: A Feminist Reader in Religion*, Harper and Row, San Francisco 1979, p. 272

17. personal communication to the author, December 1984

18. see Cheri Lesh, 'Goddess Worship: the Subversive Religion', *Twelve Together*, Los Angeles, May 1975

19. interview for the documentary *The Occult Experience*, produced for Channel 10, Sydney, in 1985, and released in the United States on Sony home video

20. following his association with Starhawk, Matthew Fox came to the view

that there was a connection between the Nature spirituality in Wicca and the sense of wholeness-in-Christ expressed in his own Creation spirituality. However, he was heavily criticised by the Roman Catholic authorities for this perception, Cardinal Joseph Ratzinger referring to Fox's book *Original Blessing* as 'dangerous and deviant'. See Ted Peters, *The Cosmic Self*, HarperCollins, San Francisco 1991, pp. 126–27

21. see Alexander Blair-Ewart, *Mindfire: Dialogues in the Other Future*, Somerville House, Toronto 1995, p. 128

22. see Starhawk, 'The Goddess' in Roger S. Gottlieb (ed.), *A New Creation: America's Contemporary Spiritual Voices*, Crossroad, New York 1990, p. 213

23. personal communication to the author

24. personal communication to the author

25. personal communication to the author

Chapter Seven

1. quoted from the Pagan Federation, *The Pagan Federation Information Pack*, second edition, London 1992, p. 14

2. see Starhawk, *Dreaming the Dark*, Beacon Press, Boston 1982, pp. 8–9

3. see Starhawk, 'The Goddess', in Roger S. Gottlieb (ed.), *A New Creation: America's Contemporary Spiritual Voices*, Crossroad, New York 1990, pp. 213–14

4. see Margot Adler, *Drawing Down the Moon*, revised edition, Beacon Press, Boston 1986, p. 35

5. quoted in Dennis D. Carpenter, 'Emergent Nature Spirituality' in James R. Lewis (ed.), *Magical Religion and Modern Witchcraft*, State University of New York Press, Albany 1996, p. 57

6. see Starhawk, 'The Goddess', op. cit., p. 221

7. quoted in Lynne Hume, *Witchcraft and Paganism in Australia*, Melbourne University Press, Melbourne 1997, p. 70

8. see Starhawk, *The Spiral Dance*, revised edition, HarperCollins, San Francisco 1989, p. 72

9. see Lynne Hume, op. cit., pp. 28–29. 'Today's witch, however,' Hume also notes, 'is more likely to be handed a computer disc, or a printout of a computerised version of the coven's Book of Shadows, when the time is appropriate, usually after initiation.'

10. quoted in James R. Lewis (ed.), *Magical Religion and Modern Witchcraft*, op. cit., p. 100

11. see Aidan Kelly, *Crafting the Art of Magic*, Llewellyn, St Paul, Minnesota

1991, p. 52, and also Janet and Stewart Farrar, *Eight Sabbats for Witches*, Robert Hale, London 1981

12. see Graham Harvey, *Listening People, Speaking Earth*, Hurst, London 1997, p. 40

13. see V. Crowley, 'The Initiation', in Prudence Jones and Caitlin Matthews (ed.), *Voices from the Circle: The Heritage of Western Paganism*, Aquarian Press, London 1990, pp. 77–79

14. quoted in Janet and Stewart Farrar, op. cit, pp. 42–43

15. quoted in James R. Lewis (ed.), op. cit., p. 62

16. see Doreen Valiente, *An ABC of Witchcraft*, Robert Hale, London, 2nd revised edn 1984, p. 108

17. see Gwydion O'Hare, *Pagan Ways*, Llewellyn, St Paul, Minnesota 1997, p. 66

18. I am indebted to Gwydion O'Hare for much of this information – see *Pagan Ways*, op. cit., pp. 64–67

19. see Doreen Valiente, op. cit., p. 108

20. James W. Baker, in his essay 'White Witches: Historic Fact and Romantic Fantasy', points out that the Wiccan 'Wheel of the Year' is by no means purely Celtic. The major sabbats, Samhain, Imbolc, Beltane and Lughnassadh, were Celtic festivals, but Yule was an Anglo-Saxon celebration. Midsummer did not feature in Celtic celebrations and the vernal equinox was not considered important either. For this reason Baker refers to the eight-fold cycle of the Wheel of the Year as a modern invention – an 'invented tradition'. See James R. Lewis (ed.), op. cit., p. 178 and p. 187

21. see Janet and Stewart Farrar, op. cit., p. 61

22. ibid, p. 82.

23. see Lynne Hume, op. cit., p. 123

24. see Vivianne Crowley, 'Wicca as Modern-Day Mystery Religion' in Graham Harvey and Charlotte Hardman (ed.), *Paganism Today*, Thorsons, London 1996, p. 88

25. single-gender Wiccan groups develop their own rules and responses in relation to this issue

26. see Vivianne Crowley, 'Wicca as Modern-Day Mystery Religion', op. cit., p. 90

27. see Janet and Stewart Farrar, *The Witches' Way*, Robert Hale, London 1984, p. 30

28. see Vivianne Crowley, op. cit., p. 91

29. see Vivianne Crowley, *Wicca: The Old Religion in the New Millennium*, Thorsons, London 1996, pp. 227–28

30. see Lynne Hume, op. cit., p. 135

31. see Janet and Stewart Farrar, *The Witches' Way*, op. cit., p. 38

Chapter Eight

1. personal communication to the author
2. see Blanche Barton, *The Secret Life of a Satanist: The Authorized Biography of Anton LaVey*, Feral House, Los Angeles 1990, pp. 39–40
3. see Arthur Lyons, *The Second Coming: Satanism in America*, Dodd Mead, New York 1970, p. 173
4. see Blanche Barton, op. cit, p. 78
5. see Arthur Lyons, op. cit., pp. 183–84
6. ibid, pp. 184–85
7. quoted in Blanche Barton, op. cit., p. 243
8. ibid, p. 244
9. see Michael Aquino, *The Crystal Tablet of Set*, Temple of Set, San Francisco 1983, p. 23
10. personal communication to the author
11. Michael Aquino has since received a doctorate in political science from this university
12. see Michael Aquino, *The Crystal Tablet of Set*, op. cit., p. 27
13. personal communication to the author
14. see Don Webb, '*Xeper*: The Eternal Word of Set', Internet statement from the Temple of Set, 8 January 1999
15. personal communication to the author
16. see Michael Aquino, *The Church of Satan*, Temple of Set, San Francisco 1983, p. 68
17. see Don Webb, 'The Pylon System', Internet statement from the Temple of Set, 25 November 1998, p. 3
18. see Don Webb, 'The Black Beyond Black: The Temple of Set', undated statement on the Internet, p. 5
19. Membership of the Temple of Set is likely to number in the hundreds rather than the thousands, nevertheless. Although there were claims that the Church of Satan had 50,000 card-carrying members, the initial San Francisco membership was only around 50, climbing to a nationwide peak of 300 by 1975 – and the Temple of Set began as a splinter group from the Church of Satan.
20. see Don Webb, 'The Pylon System', op. cit., p. 2
21. ibid, p. 3
22. ibid, p. 4
23. personal communication to the author
24. personal communication to the author

25. readers interested in the history and development of the transpersonal movement may find my recent book worth consulting: *Exploring the Labyrinth: Making Sense of the New Spirituality* (see Bibliography)
26. see Don Webb, 'Seven of the Many Gateways' in Leon D. Wild (ed.), *The Ninth Night* vol. 1, no. 2., Sydney, June 1998, published on the Internet
27. see Michael Aquino, *Runes*, Vol. II:6, San Francisco 1984
28. ibid
29. see Michael Aquino, *Runes*, Vol. I:2, San Francisco 1983
30. personal communication to the author
31. see Anton LaVey, *The Satanic Bible*, Avon Books, New York 1969, p. 94
32. see Blanche Barton, op. cit., p. 46 et seq.
33. see Michael Aquino, *The Church of Satan*, op. cit., p. 193
34. see Leon D. Wild, 'An Introduction to the Left Hand Path', *The Ninth Night*, vol. 1, no. 1, Sydney, June 1998, published on the Internet
35. ibid
36. see Don Webb, 'The Black Beyond Black', op. cit., pp. 1, 4 and 10
37. see Don Webb, '*Xeper*: The Eternal Word of Set', ibid., p. 2

Chapter Nine

1. quoted in *Starfire: A Magazine of the New Aeon*, vol. 1, no. 3, London 1989, p. 89
2. interview with the author for the television documentary *The Occult Experience*, New York, December 1984 (released in the United States on Sony home video)
3. see C. G. Jung, *Man and His Symbols*, Dell, New York 1968, pp. 41–42
4. see C. G. Jung, *Two Essays in Analytical Psychology*, Routledge & Kegan Paul, London 1953, p. 68
5. ibid, pp. 65–66
6. ibid, p. 70
7. see C. G. Jung, 'The Relations Between the Ego and the Unconscious' (1928) in *Two Essays on Analytical Psychology*, op. cit.
8. quoted in Diane K. Osbon, *Reflections on the Art of Living: A Joseph Campbell Companion*, HarperCollins, New York 1991, p. 40
9. ibid, p. 123
10. see Mirka Knaster, 'The Goddesses in Jean Shinoda Bolen', *East West*, March 1989, p. 45. An interesting interview with Bolen is also included

in Alexander Blair-Ewart, *Mindfire: Dialogues in the Other Future*, Somerville House, Toronto 1995

11. ibid, p. 44
12. ibid, p. 73
13. see Richard Daab and Silma Smith, 'Midwife of the Possible: An Interview with Jean Houston', Part Three, *Magical Blend*, Fall 1988, p. 22
14. see Alexander Blair-Ewart, interview with Jean Houston in *Mindfire*, op. cit., p. 111
15. see Jean Houston, *The Hero and the Goddess*, Ballantine, New York 1992, p. 10
16. see Jean Houston, *The Search for the Beloved: Journeys in Sacred Psychology*, Crucible, Wellingborough, UK 1990, p. 13
17. see Jean Houston, 'Myth and Pathos in Sacred Psychology', *Dromenon*, vol. 3, no. 2, Spring 1981, p. 33
18. for a more detailed discussion of the debate surrounding Carlos Castaneda and Lynn Andrews, readers are referred to the chapter 'Two Controversies' in my book *The Elements of Shamanism*, Element Books, Dorset 1989
19. Castaneda's first four books have been his most influential: *The Teachings of Don Juan, A Separate Reality, Journey to Ixtlan* and *Tales of Power* (see Bibliography)
20. see Richard de Mille's interview with Barbara Myerhoff in his fascinating book *The Don Juan Papers: Further Castaneda Controversies*, Ross-Erikson, Santa Barbara 1980, p. 336 et seq.
21. when a person is 'dis-spirited', their animating force, or spirit, has departed. The shaman's role is to retrieve it.
22. personal communication to the author
23. personal communication recorded during the shamanic workshop
24. see Nevill Drury, *The Occult Experience*, Robert Hale, London 1987, p. 145
25. ibid

Chapter Ten

1. see 'Magic Plants and the Logos: Terence McKenna in conversation with Alexander Blair-Ewart' in Alexander Blair-Ewart, *Mindfire: Dialogues in the Other Future*. Somerville House, Toronto 1995, p. 60 et seq.
2. see 'Sacred Plants and Mystic Realities: An Interview with Terence McKenna' in my book *Echoes from the Void: Writings on Magic, Visionary Art and the New Consciousness*, Prism Press, Dorset 1994, p. 158. This

interview also appeared in Terence McKenna's anthology *The Archaic Revival*, HarperCollins, San Francisco 1991.

3. ibid, pp. 159–60 and p. 166

4. ibid, p. 166

5. see Mark Dery, 'The Inner Elf', in Ashley Crawford and Ray Edgar (ed.), *Transit Lounge; Wake-up Calls and Travelers' Tales from the Future*, Craftsman House, Sydney 1997, pp. 94–95.

6. ibid, p. 95

7. see Margaret Wertheim, *The Pearly Gates of Cyberspace: A History of Space from Dante to the Internet*, Norton, New York 1998

8. see Howard Rheingold, *Virtual Reality*, Mandarin/Reed International, London 1992, p. 354

9. see Bruce Sterling, *The Hacker Crackdown: Law and Disorder on the Electronic Frontier*, Bantam, New York 1992, p. 235

10. see Mark Dery, *Escape Velocity: Cyberculture at the End of the Century*, Hodder & Stoughton, London 1996, p. 28

11. see Sara Reeder, 'Children of the Digital Gods' in *Green Egg*, vol. 29, no. 129, August–September 1997, p. 15

12. see 'Computers, Consciousness and Creativity: An Interview with Dr Timothy Leary' in Nevill Drury, *Echoes from the Void*, op. cit., p. 172

13. 'Frantic Life and Symbolic Death among the Computer Bums', quoted in Mark Dery, *Escape Velocity*, op. cit., p. 27

14. see Mark Dery, *Escape Velocity*, op. cit., p. 22

15. see Erik Davis, 'Technopagans: May the Astral Plane Be Reborn in Cyberspace', *Wired*, July 1995, p. 128

16. see Douglas Rushkoff, *Cyberia: Life in the Trenches of Hyperspace*, HarperCollins, San Francisco 1994, p. 143

17. see Erik Davis, 'TechnoPagans: The Roots of Digital Magick' in *Green Egg*, vol. 29, no. 129, August–September 1997, p. 41

18. see Douglas Rushkoff, op. cit., pp. 145–46

19. see Tom Williams, 'Navigation Systems for the Spirit 'in *Green Egg*, vol. 29, no. 120, August–September 1997, p. 39

20. see Michael Hutchison, *Mega Brain Power: Transform Your Life with Mind Machines and Brain Nutrients*, Hyperion, New York 1994, p. 431

21. see Jem Dowse, 'Cyberpagans!' in *Pagan Dawn*, no. 119, Beltane 1996, p. 11

22. see Sara Reeder, 'Children of the Digital Gods', op. cit., p. 16

23. ibid, p. 17. VRML stands for 'virtual reality markup language' and is used to create three-dimensional imagery in cyberspace, whereas two-dimensional text-based websites are created with HTML (hypertext markup language).

Some readers may be interested to visit a virtual shrine on the Internet. Renée Rosen has her shrine to Lilith at the following website: http://www.lilitu.com/lilith/

24. see Bruce Galloway (ed.), *Fantasy and Wargaming*, Patrick Stephens, Cambridge 1981, pp. 6–7
25. ibid, p. 7
26. ibid, p. 152
27. published by White Wolf, Stone Mountain, Georgia, 3rd edition, 1992
28. see Margaret Wertheim, op. cit.
29. see Douglas Rushkoff, op. cit., p. 198
30. see Brenda Laurel, 'Toward the Design of a Computer-Based Interactive Fantasy System,' doctoral dissertation, Ohio State University, 1986, p. 1
31. see Mark Dery, *Escape Velocity*, op. cit., p. 280
32. see Afarin Majidi, 'H. R. Giger: Night Visionary', *Manhattan's Entertainment Magazine*, vol. 1, issue 7, September 1998
33. see Andrew Siliar, 'Cyber-Space Cadets' in *Green Egg*, vol. 29, no. 120, August–September 1997, p. 65

Index

Index